CERTAIN DIFFICULTIES

FELT BY ANGLICANS

IN CATHOLIC TEACHING

CONSIDERED

1. *In Twelve Lectures addressed in* 1850 *to the Party of the Religious Movement of* 1833.

BY

JOHN HENRY CARDINAL NEWMAN

VOL. I.

NEW EDITION

LONGMANS, GREEN, AND CO.

39 PATERNOSTER ROW, LONDON

NEW YORK AND BOMBAY

1897

TO THE RIGHT REVEREND

WILLIAM BERNARD ULLATHORNE,

D.D., O.S.B.,

BISHOP OF HETALONA,

AND VICAR-APOSTOLIC OF THE CENTRAL DISTRICT.

My Dear Lord,

In gaining your Lordship's leave to place the
following Volume under your patronage, I fear I may
seem to the world to have asked what is more gracious
in you to grant, than becoming or reasonable in me
to have contemplated.   For what assignable connection
is there between your Lordship's name, and a work,
not didactic, not pastoral, not ascetical, not devotional,
but for the most part simply controversial, directed,
moreover, against a mere transitory phase in an accidental school of opinion, and for that reason, both in
its matter and its argument, only of local interest and
ephemeral importance?

Such a question may obviously be put to me; nor
can I answer it, except by referring to the well-known
interest which your Lordship has so long taken in
the religious party to which I have alluded, and the

joy and thankfulness with which you have welcomed
the manifestations of God's grace, as often as first one
and then another of their number has in his turn
emerged from the mists of error into the light and
peace of Catholic truth.

Whatever, then, your Lordship's sentiments may be
of the character of the Work itself, I persuade myself
that I may be able suitably to present it to you, in consideration of the object it has in view; and that you,
on your part, will not repent of countenancing an
Author, who, in the selection of his materials, would
fain put the claims of charity above the praise of
critics, and feels it is a better deed to write for the
present moment than for posterity.

Begging your Lordship's blessing,

I am, my dear Lord,

Your Lordship's faithful and grateful Servant,

JOHN H. NEWMAN,

OF THE ORATORY.

July 14, 1850.

PREFACE.

———◇———

IT may happen to some persons to feel surprise, that
the Author of the following Lectures, instead of occupying himself on the direct proof of Catholicism, should
have professed no more than to remove difficulties from
the path of those who have already admitted the arguments in its favour. But, in the first place, he really
does not think that there is any call just now for an
Apology in behalf of the divine origin of the Catholic
Church. She bears her unearthly character on her
brow, as her enemies confess, by imputing her miracles
to Beelzebub. There is an instinctive feeling of
curiosity, interest, anxiety, and awe, mingled together
in various proportions, according to the tempers and
opinions of individuals, when she makes her appearance in any neighbourhood, rich or poor, in the person
of her missioners or her religious communities. Do
what they will, denounce her as they may, her enemies
cannot quench this emotion in the breasts of others, or
in their own. It is their involuntary homage to the
Notes of the Church; it is their spontaneous recognition of her royal descent and her imperial claim; it
is a specific feeling, which no other religion tends to
excite. Judaism, Mahometanism, Anglicanism, Method-

ism, old religions and young, romantic and common-place, have not this spell. The presence of the Church creates a discomposure and restlessness, or a thrill of exultation, wherever she comes. Meetings are held, denunciations launched, calumnies spread abroad, and hearts beat secretly the while. The babe leaps in Elizabeth's womb, at the voice of her in whom is enshrined and lives the Incarnate Word. Her priests appeal freely to the consciences of all who encounter them, to say whether they have not a superhuman gift, and that multitude by silence gives consent. They look like other men; they may have the failings of other men; they may have as little worldly advantages as the preachers of dissent; they may lack the popular talents, the oratorical power, the imposing presence, which are found elsewhere; but they inspire confidence, or at least reverence, by their very word. Those who come to jeer and scoff, remain to pray.

There needs no treatise, then, on the Notes of the Church, till this her mysterious influence is accounted for and destroyed; still less is it necessary just at this time, when the writings and the proceedings of a school of divines in the Establishment have, against their will and intention, done this very work for her as regards a multitude of our countrymen. What treatise indeed can be so conclusive in this day as the history, carried out before their eyes, of the religious teaching of the school in question, a teaching simple and intelligible in its principles, persuasive in its views, gradually developed, adjusted, and enlarged, gradually imbibed and mastered, in a course of years; and now converging in many minds at once to one issue, and in some of them already reaching it, and that issue the divinity of the Catholic Religion ? Feeling, then, that an exhibition of the direct Evidences in favour of Catholicism is not the want of the moment, the Author has had no thoughts of addressing himself to a work, which could not be executed by any one who undertook it, except at leisure and with great deliberation. At present the thinking portion of society is either very near the Catholic Church, or very far from her. The first duty of Catholics is to house those in, who are near their doors ; it will be time afterwards, when this has been done, to ascertain how things lie on the extended field of philosophy and religion, and into what new position the controversy has fallen : as yet the old arguments suffice. To attempt a formal dissertation on the Notes of the Church at this moment, would be running the risk of constructing what none would need to-day, and none could use to-morrow.

Those surely who are advancing towards the Church would not have advanced so far as they have, had they not had sufficient arguments to bring them still further. What retards their progress is not any weakness in those arguments, but the force of opposite considerations, speculative or practical, which are urged, sometimes against the Church, sometimes against their own submitting to her authority. They would have no doubt about their duty, but for the charges brought against her, or the remonstrances addressed to themselves ; charges and remonstrances which, whatever their logical cogency, are abundantly sufficient for their purpose, in a case where there are so many inducements, whether from wrong feeling, or infirmity, or even error of conscience, to listen to them. Such persons, then, have a claim on us to be fortified in their right perceptions

and their good resolutions, against the calumnies, prejudices, mistakes, and ignorance of their friends and of
the world, against the undue influence exerted on their
minds by the real difficulties which unavoidably surround a religion so deep and manifold in philosophy,
and occupying so vast a place in the history of nations
It would be wonderful, indeed, if a teaching which
embraces all spiritual and moral truth, from the highest
to the least important, should present no mysteries or
apparent inconsistencies ; wonderful if, in the lapse of
eighteen hundred years, and in the range of three-
fourths of the globe, and in the profession of thousands
of millions of souls, it had not afforded innumerable
points of plausible attack ; wonderful, if it could assail
the pride and sensuality which are common to our
whole race, without rousing the hatred, malice, jealousy,
and obstinate opposition, of the natural man ; wonderful, if it could be the object of the jealous and unwearied scrutiny of ten thousand adversaries, of the
coalition of wit and wisdom, of minds acute, far-seeing,
comprehensive, original, and possessed of the deepest
and most varied knowledge, yet without some sort of
case being made out against it ; and wonderful, moreover, if the vast multitude of objections, great and
small, resulting from its exposure to circumstances
such as these, acting on the timidity, scrupulousness,
inexperience, intellectual fastidiousness, love of the
world, or self-dependence of individuals, had not been
sufficient to keep many a one from the Church, who
had, in spite of them, good and satisfactory reasons for
joining her communion. Here is the plain reason why
so many are brought near to the Church, and then go
back, or are so slow in submitting to her.

Now, as has been implied above, where there is detachment from the world, a keen apprehension of the Unseen, and a simple determination to do the Divine Will, such difficulties will not commonly avail, if men have had sufficient opportunity of acquainting themselves with the Notes or Evidences of the Church. In matter of fact, as we see daily, they do not avail to deter those whose hearts are right, or whose minds are incapable of extended investigations, from recognizing the Church's Notes and acting upon them. They do not avail with the poor, the uneducated, the simple-minded, the resolute, and the fervent; but they are formidable, when there are motives in the background, amiable or unworthy, to bias the will. Every one is obliged, by the law of his nature, to act by reason; yet no one likes to make a great sacrifice unnecessarily; such difficulties, then, just avail to turn the scale, and to detain men in Protestantism, who are open to the influence of tenderness towards friends, reliance on superiors, regard for their position, dread of present inconvenience, indolence, love of independence, fear of the future, regard to reputation, desire of consistency, attachment to cherished notions, pride of reason, or reluctance to go to school again. No one likes to take an awful step, all by himself, without feeling sure he is right; no one likes to remain long in doubt whether he should take it or not; he wishes to be settled, and he readily catches at objections, or listens to dissuasives, which allow of his giving over the inquiry, or postponing it *sine die*. Yet those very same persons who would willingly hide the truth from their eyes by objections and difficulties, nevertheless, if actually forced to look it in the face, and brought under the direct power of the Catholic arguments, would often have strength and courage enough to take the dreaded step, and would find themselves, almost before they knew what they had done, in the haven of peace.

These were some of the reasons for the particular line of argument which the Author has selected; and in what he has been saying in explanation, he must not be supposed to forget that faith depends upon the will, not really on any process of reasoning, and that conversion is a simple work of divine grace. He aims at nothing more than to give free play to the conscience, by removing those perplexities in the proof of Catholicity, which keep the intellect from being touched by its cogency, and give the heart an excuse for trifling with it. The absence of temptation or of other moral disadvantage, though not the direct cause of virtuous conduct, still is a great help towards it; and, in like manner, to clear away from the path of an inquirer objections to Catholic truth, is to subserve his conversion by giving room for the due and efficacious operation of divine grace. Religious persons, indeed, do what is right in spite of temptation; persons of sensitive and fervent minds go on to believe in spite of difficulty; but where the desire of truth is languid, and the religious purpose weak, such impediments suffice to prevent conviction, and faith will not be created in the mind, though there are abundant reasons for its creation. In these circumstances, it is quite as much an act of charity to attempt the removal of objections to the truth, which, without excusing, are made the excuse for unbelief, as to remove the occasion of sin in any other department of duty.

It is plain that the Author is rather describing what his Lectures were intended to be, than what they have turned out. He found it impossible to fulfil what he contemplated within the limits imposed upon him by the circumstances under which they were written. The very first objection which he took on starting, the alleged connection of the Movement of 1833 with the National Church, has afforded matter for the greater part of the course; and, before he had well finished the discussion of it, it was getting time to think of concluding, and that, in any such way as would give a character of completeness to the whole. Else, after the seventh Lecture, it had been his intention to proceed to the consideration of the alleged claim of the National Church on the allegiance of its members; of the alleged duty of our remaining in the communion in which we were born; of the alleged danger of trusting to reason; of the alleged right of the National Church to forbid doubt about its own claims; of the alleged uncertainty which necessarily attends the claims of any religion whatever; of the tests of certainty; of the relation of faith to reason; of the legitimate force of objections; and of the matter of Catholic evidence. He is ashamed to continue the list much further, lest he should seem to have been contemplating what was evidently impracticable; all he can say in extenuation is, that he never aimed at going more fully into any of the subjects of which he was to treat, than he has done in the sketches which now he presents to the reader. Lastly, he had proposed to end his course with a notice of the objections made by Protestants to particular doctrines, as Purgatory, Intercession of the Saints, and the like.

Incomplete, however, as the Lectures may be with reference to the idea with which they were commenced, or compared with what might be said upon each subject which is successively treated, of course he makes no apology for the actual matter of them; else he should not have delivered or published them. It has not been his practice to engage in controversy with those who have felt it their duty to criticise what at any time he has written; but that will not preclude him, under present circumstances, from elucidating what is deficient in them by further observations, should questions be asked, which, either from the quarter whence they proceed, or from their intrinsic weight, have, according to his judgment, a claim upon his attention.

BIRMINGHAM, *July* 14, 1850.

CONTENTS.

—o—

PART I.

COMMUNION WITH THE ROMAN SEE THE LEGITIMATE ISSUE OF THE RELIGIOUS MOVEMENT OF 1833.

PART II.

DIFFICULTIES IN ACCEPTING THE COMMUNION OF ROME AS ONE, HOLY, CATHOLIC, AND APOSTOLIC.

PART I.

LECTURE I.

ON THE RELATION OF THE NATIONAL CHURCH TO THE NATION.

THERE are those, my brethren, who may think it
strange, and even shocking, that, at this moment,
when the liberalism of the age, after many previous
attempts, is apparently at length about to get possession of the Church and Universities of the nation, any
one like myself, who is a zealous upholder of the dogmatic principle in all its bearings, should be doing what
little in him lies to weaken, even indirectly, Institutions
which, with whatever shortcomings or errors, are the
only political bulwarks of that principle left to us by
the changes of the sixteenth century. For to help
forward members of the Established Church towards
the Catholic Religion, as I propose to do in these
Lectures, what is this but, so far, to co-operate with a
levelling party, who are the enemies of God, and truth,

A

and virtue? The Institutions in question, it may be
said, uphold what is right and what is holy as far as
they go, and, moreover, the duty of upholding it: they
do not in their genuine workings harm the Church;
they do but oppose themselves to sectarianism, free-
thinking, infidelity, and lawlessness. They are her
natural, though they may be her covert, allies; they
are the faithful nurses and conservators of her spirit;
they are glad, and proud, as far as they are allowed to
do so, to throw her mantle over themselves, and they
do her homage by attempting a mimic Catholicism.
They have preserved through bad times our old
churches, our forms, our rites, our customs, in a
measure, our Creed; they are taunted by our enemies
for their Catholic or Papistical tendency; and many of
those who are submitted to their teaching, look wist-
fully to us, in their forlorn struggle with those enemies
of ours, for encouragement and sympathy. Certainly,
reviewing the history of the last three centuries, we
cannot deny that those Institutions have uniformly
repressed the extravagance, and diluted the virulence,
of Protestantism. To the divines, to whom they have
given birth, our country is indebted for Apologies in
behalf of various of the great doctrines of the faith: to
Bull for a defence of the Creed of Nicæa, nay, in a
measure, of the true doctrine of justification, which the
most accomplished Catholic theologians of this day, as
well as of his own, treat with great consideration: to

Pearson for a powerful argument in behalf of the
Apostolical origin of Episcopacy; to Wall for a proof
of the primitive use of Infant Baptism; to Hooker for
a vindication of the great principle of religious order
and worship; to Butler for a profound investigation
into the connection of natural with revealed religion;
to Paley and others for a series of elaborate evidences
of the divinity of Christianity. It is cruel, it is impolitic, to cast off, if not altogether friends, yet at least
those who are not our worst foes; nor can we afford to
do so. If they usurp our name, yet they proclaim it in
the ears of heretics all about; they have kept much
error out of the country, if they have let much in; and
if Neo-Platonism, though false, is more honourable than
the philosophy of the academy or of the garden, by the
same rule, surely, we ought, in comparison with other
sects, to give our countenance to the Anglican Church
to compassionate her in her hour of peril, "and spare
the meek usurper's hoary head."

Well, and I do not know what natural inducement
there is to urge me to be harsh with her in this her
hour: I have only pleasant associations of those many
years when I was within her pale; I have no theory to
put forward, nor position to maintain; and I am come
to a time of life, when men desire to be quiet and at
peace;—moreover, I am in a communion which satis-
fies its members, and draws them into itself, and, by
the objects which it presents to faith, and the influences

which it exerts over the heart, leads them to forget the
external world, and look forward more steadily to the
future. No, my dear brethren, there is but one thing
that forces me to speak,—and it is my intimate sense
that the Catholic Church is the one ark of salvation,
and my love for your souls; it is my fear lest you ought
to submit yourselves to her, and do not; my fear lest I
may perchance be able to persuade you, and not use
my talent. It will be a miserable thing for you and
for me, if I had been instrumental in bringing you but
half-way, if I have co-operated in removing your invincible ignorance, but am able to do no more. It is this
keen feeling that my life is wearing away, which overcomes the lassitude which possesses me, and scatters
the excuses which I might plausibly urge to myself for
not meddling with what I have left for ever, which
subdues the recollection of past times, and which
makes me do my best, with whatever success, to bring
you to land from off your wreck, who have thrown
yourselves from it upon the waves, or are clinging to
its rigging, or are sitting in heaviness and despair upon
its side. For this is the truth: the Establishment,
whatever it be in the eyes of men, whatever its temporal greatness and its secular prospects, in the eyes
of faith is a mere wreck. We must not indulge our
imagination, we must not dream: we must look at
things as they are; we must not confound the past
with the present, or what is substantive with what is

the accident of a period. Ridding our minds of these illusions, we shall see that the Established Church has no claims whatever on us, whether in memory or in hope; that they only have claims upon our commiseration and our charity whom she holds in bondage, separated from that faith and that Church in which alone is salvation. If I can do aught towards breaking their chains, and bringing them into the Truth, it will be an act of love towards their souls, and of piety towards God.

I.

I have said, we must not indulge our imagination in the view we take of the National Establishment. If, indeed, we dress it up in an ideal form, as if it were something real, with an independent and a continuous existence, and a proper history, as if it were in deed and not only in name a Church, then indeed we may feel interest in it, and reverence towards it, and affection for it, as men have fallen in love with pictures, or knights in romance do battle for high dames whom they have never seen. Thus it is that students of the Fathers, antiquaries, and poets, begin by assuming that the body to which they belong is that of which they read in times past, and then proceed to decorate it with that majesty and beauty of which history tells, or which their genius creates. Nor is it by an easy process or a light effort that their minds are disabused of this error. It is an error for many reasons too dear to

them to be readily relinquished. But at length, either
the force of circumstances or some unexpected accident
dissipates it; and, as in fairy tales, the magic castle
vanishes when the spell is broken, and nothing is seen
but the wild heath, the barren rock, and the forlorn
sheep-walk, so is it with us as regards the Church of
England, when we look in amazement on that we
thought so unearthly, and find so commonplace or
worthless. Then we perceive, that aforetime we have
not been guided by reason, but biassed by education
and swayed by affection. We see in the English
Church, I will not merely say no descent from the first
ages, and no relationship to the Church in other lands,
but we see no body politic of any kind; we see nothing
more or less than an Establishment, a department of
Government, or a function or operation of the State,
—without a substance,—a mere collection of officials,
depending on and living in the supreme civil power.
Its unity and personality are gone, and with them its
power of exciting feelings of any kind. It is easier to
love or hate an abstraction, than so commonplace a
framework or mechanism. We regard it neither with
anger, nor with aversion, nor with contempt, any more
than with respect or interest. It is but one aspect of
the State, or mode of civil governance; it is responsible
for nothing; it can appropriate neither praise nor
blame; but, whatever feeling it raises is to be referred
on, by the nature of the case, to the Supreme Power

whom it represents, and whose will is its breath. And hence it has no real identity of existence in distinct periods, unless the present Legislature or the present Court can affect to be the offspring and disciple of its predecessor. Nor can it in consequence be said to have any antecedents, or any future; or to live, except in the passing moment. As a thing without a soul, it does not contemplate itself, define its intrinsic constitution, or ascertain its position. It has no traditions; it cannot be said to think; it does not know what it holds, and what it does not;[1] it is not even conscious of its own existence. It has no love for its members, or what are sometimes called its children, nor any instinct whatever, unless attachment to its master, or love of its place, may be so called. Its fruits, as far as they are good, are to be made much of, as long as they last, for they are transient, and without succession; its former champions of orthodoxy are no earnest of orthodoxy now; they died, and there was no reason why they should be reproduced. Bishop is not like bishop,

---

[1] This fact is strikingly brought out in Archbishop Sumner's correspondence with Mr. Maskell. "You ask me," he says, "whether you are to conclude that you ought not to teach, and have not *authority* of the Church to teach any of the doctrines spoken of in your five former questions, in the *dogmatical* terms there stated? To which I reply, *Are* they contained in the word of God? St. Paul says, 'Preach the word.' . . . Now, whether the doctrines concerning which you inquire are contained in the Word of God, and can be proved thereby, you have the same means of discovering as myself, and I have no special authority to declare." The Archbishop at least would quite allow what I have said in the text, even though he might express himself differently.

more than king is like king, or ministry like ministry; its Prayer-Book is an Act of Parliament of two centuries ago, and its cathedrals and its chapter-houses are the spoils of Catholicism.

I have said all this, my brethren, not in declamation, but to bring out clearly to you, why I cannot feel interest of any kind in the National Church, nor put any trust in it at all from its past history, as if it were, in however narrow a sense, a guardian of orthodoxy. It is as little bound by what it said or did formerly, as this morning's newspaper by its former numbers, except as it is bound by the Law; and while it is upheld by the Law, it will not be weakened by the subtraction of individuals, nor fortified by their continuance. Its life is an Act of Parliament. It will not be able to resist the Arian, Sabellian, or Unitarian heresies now, because Bull or Waterland resisted them a century or two before; nor on the other hand would it be unable to resist them, though its more orthodox theologians were presently to leave it. It will be able to resist them while the State gives the word; it would be unable, when the State forbids it. Elizabeth boasted that she "tuned her pulpits;" Charles forbade discussions on predestination; George on the Holy Trinity; Victoria allows differences on Holy Baptism. While the nation wishes an Establishment, it will remain, whatever individuals are for it or against it; and that which determines its existence will determine its voice. Of course the presence or departure of individuals will be one out of various disturbing causes, which may delay or accelerate by a certain number of years a change in its teaching: but, after all, the change itself depends on events broader and deeper than these; it depends on changes in the nation. As the nation changes its political, so may it change its religious views; the causes which carried the Reform Bill and Free Trade may make short work with orthodoxy.

2.

The most simple proof of the truth of this assertion will be found in considering what and how much has been hitherto done by the ecclesiastical movement of 1833, towards heightening the tone of the Established Church—by a movement extending over seventeen years and more, and carried on with great energy, and (as far as concerns its influence over individuals) with surprising success. Opinions which, twenty years ago, were not held by any but Catholics, or at most only in fragmentary portions by isolated persons, are now the profession of thousands. Such success ought to have acted on the Establishment itself; has it done so? or rather, is not that success simply and only in expectation and in hope, like the conversion of heathen nations by the various Evangelical societies? The Fathers have catholicised the Protestant Church at home, pretty much as the Bible has evangelised the Mahome-

tan or Hindoo religions abroad. There have been
recurring vaticinations and promises of good; but
little or no actual fulfilment. Look back year after
year, count up the exploits of the movement party, and
consider whether it has had any effect at all on the
religious judgment of the nation, as represented by the
Establishment. The more certain and formidable is
the growth of its adherents and well-wishers, so much
the more pregnant a fact is it, that the Establishment
has steadily gone on its own way, eating, drinking,
sleeping, and working, fulfilling its nature and its destiny, as if that movement had not been; or at least
with no greater consciousness of its presence, than any
internal disarrangement or disorder creates in a man
who has a work to do, and is busy at it.

The movement, I say, has formed but a party after
all, and the Church of the nation has pursued the
nation's objects, and executed the nation's will, in spite
of it. The movement could not prevent the Ecclesiastical Commission, nor the Episcopal mismanagement
of it. Its zeal, principle, and clearness of view, backed
by a union of parties, did not prevent the royal appoint-
ment of a theological Professor, whose sentiments were
the expression of the national idea of religion. Nor
did its protest even succeed in preventing his subsequent elevation to the Episcopal bench. Nor did
it succeed in preventing the establishment of a sort
of Anglo-Prussian, half-Episcopal, half-Lutheran See at

Jerusalem; nor the selection of two individuals of
heretical opinions to fill it in succession. Nor did it
prevent the intrusion of the Establishment on the
Maltese territory; nor has it prevented the systematic
promotion at home of men heterodox, or fiercely
latitudinarian, in their religious views, or professedly
ignorant of theology, and glorying in their ignorance.
Nor did the movement prevent the promotion of
Bishops and others who deny or explain away the
grace of Baptism. Nor has it hindered the two Archbishops of England from concurring in the royal decision, that within the national communion baptismal
regeneration is an open question. It has not heightened the theology of the Universities or of the Christian Knowledge Society, nor afforded any defence in its
hour of need to the National Society for Education.
What has it done for the cause it undertook? It has
preserved the Universities to the Established Church
for fifteen years; perhaps it prevented certain alterations in the Prayer-Book; it has secured at Oxford
the continuance of the Oath of Supremacy against
Catholics for a like period; it has hindered the promotion of high-minded liberals, like the late Dr. Arnold,
at the price of the advancement of second-rate men
who have shared his opinions. It has built Churches
and Colleges, and endowed Sees, of which its enemies
in the Establishment have gladly taken or are taking
possession; it has founded sisterhoods or enforced

confessions, the fruits of which are yet to be seen. On
the other hand, it has given a hundred educated men
to the Catholic Church; yet the huge creature, from
which they went forth, showed no consciousness of its
loss, but shook itself, and went about its work as of
old time—as all parties, even the associates they had
left, united, and even glorified, in testifying. And
lastly, the present momentous event, to which I have
already alluded, bearing upon the doctrine of Baptism,
which is creating such disturbance in the country, has
happened altogether independent of the movement, and
is unaffected by it. Those persons who went forward
to Catholicism have not caused it; those who have
stayed neither could prevent it, nor can remedy it. It
relates to a question previous to any of those doctrines
which it has been the main object of the movement
to maintain. It is caused, rather it is willed, by the
national mind; and, till the grace of God touches and
converts that mind, it will remain a fact done and over,
a precedent and a principle in the Establishment.

3.

This is the true explanation of what is going on
before our eyes, as seen whether in the decision of the
Privy Council, or in the respective conduct of the two
parties in the Establishment with relation to it. It
may seem strange, at first sight, that the Evangelical
section should presume so boldly to contravene the

distinct and categorical teaching of the national formularies on the subject of Baptism; strange, till it is
understood that the interpreter of their sense is the
Nation itself, and that that section in the Establishment
speaks with the confidence of men who know that they
have the Nation on their side. Let me here refer to the
just and manly admissions on this subject, of a high-
principled writer, which have lately been given to the
public :—

"There is" a "consideration," he says, "which, for
some time, has pressed heavily and painfully upon me.
As a fact, the Evangelical party plainly, openly, and
fully declare their opinions upon the doctrines which
they contend the Church of England holds; they tell
their people continually, what they ought, as a matter
of duty towards God and towards themselves, both to
believe and practise. Can it be pretended that we, as
a party, anxious to teach the truth, are equally open,
plain, and unreserved ? . . . And it is not to be alleged,
that only the less important duties and doctrines are so
reserved : as if it would be an easy thing to distinguish
and draw a line of division between them. . . . We do
reserve vital and essential truths; we often hesitate and
fear to teach our people many duties, not all necessary,
perhaps, in every case or to every person, but eminently
practical, and sure to increase the growth of the inner,
spiritual life we differ, in short, as widely from the
Evangelical party in the manner and openness, as in the

matter and details of our doctrine. . . . All this seems
to me to be, day by day and hour by hour, more and
more hard to be reconciled with the real spirit, mind,
and purpose of the English Reformation, and of the
modern English Church, shown by the experience of
three hundred years. . . . People often say it is wrong
to use such terms as 'the spirit of the Reformed English
Church;' or 'its intention,' 'purpose,' and the like.
And is it really so? was the Reformation nothing?
did it effect nothing, change nothing, remove nothing?
. . . . No doubt the Reformed Church of England
claims to be a portion of the Holy Catholic Church;
and it has been common for many of our own opinions,
to add also the assertion, that she rejects and condemns,
as being out of the Church Catholic, the Reformed
Churches abroad, Lutheran, Genevan, and others, together with the Kirk of Scotland, or the Dissenters at
home. Upon our principles, nay, on any consistent
Church principle at all, such a corollary must follow.
But there is a strangeness in it; it commends itself
perhaps to our intellect, but not to the eye or ear; nor,
it may be, to the heart or conscience."[1]

These remarks are as true as they are candid; and it
is, I hope, no disrespect to the Author, if, taking them
from their context, I use them for my own argument,
which is not indeed divergent, though distinct from his
own. Whether, then, they prove that the Evangelical

---

[1] Maskell's Second Letter, pp. 57-69.

party is as much at home in the *National Prayer-Book*
as the Anglican, I will not pronounce; but at least
they prove that that party is far more at home in the
National Establishment; that it is in cordial and intimate sympathy with the sovereign Lord and Master
of the Prayer-Book, its composer and interpreter, the
Nation itself,—on the best terms with Queen and
statesmen, and practical men, and country gentlemen,
and respectable tradesmen, fathers and mothers, school-
masters, churchwardens, vestries, public societies, newspapers, and their readers in the lower classes. The
Evangelical ministers of the Establishment have, in
comparison with their Anglican rivals, the spirit of the
age with them; they are congenial with the age; they
glide forward rapidly and proudly down the stream;
and it is this fact, and their consciousness of it, which
carries them over all difficulties. Jewell was triumphant over Harding, and Wake over Atterbury or Leslie,
with the terrors or the bribes of a sovereign to back them;
and their successors in this day have, in like manner,
the strength of public opinion on their side. The letter
of enactments, pristine customs, ancient rights, is no
match for the momentum with which they rush along
upon the flood of public opinion, which rules that every
conclusion is absurd, and every argument sophistical,
and every maxim untrue, except such as it recognises
itself.

4.

How different has it been with the opposite party?
Confident, indeed, and with reason, of the truth of its
great principles, having a perception and certainty of
its main tenets, which is like the evidence of sense
compared with the feeble, flitting, and unreal views of
doctrine held by the Evangelical body, still, as to their
application, their adaptation, their combination, their
development, it has been miserably conscious that it
has had nothing to guide it but its own private and
unaided judgment. Dreading its own interpretation of
Scripture and the Fathers, feeling its need of an infallible guide, yet having none; looking up to its own
Mother, as it called her, and finding her silent, ambiguous, unsympathetic, sullen, and even hostile to it; with
ritual mutilated, sacraments defective, precedents inconsistent, articles equivocal, canons obsolete, courts Protestant, and synods suspended; scouted by the laity,
scorned by men of the world, hated and blackened by
its opponents; and moreover at variance with itself,
hardly two of its members taking up the same position,
nay, all of them, one by one, shifting their own ground
as time went on, and obliged to confess that they were
in progress; is it wonderful, in the words of the
Pamphlet already referred to, that these men have exhibited "a conduct and a rule of a religious life," "full
of shifts, and compromises, and evasions, a rule of life,
based upon the acceptance of half one doctrine, all the

next, and none of the third, upon the belief entirely of
another, but not daring to say so ?" After all, they have
not been nearly so guilty " of shifts, and compromises,
and evasions," as the national formularies themselves;
but they have had none to support them, or, if I may
use a familiar word, to act the bully for them, under the
imputation. There was no one, with confident air and
loud voice, to retort upon their opponents the charges
urged against them, and no public to applaud though
there had been. Whether they looked above or below,
behind or before, they found nothing, indeed, to shake
or blunt their faith in Christ, in His establishment of
a Church, in its visibility, continuance, catholicity, and
gifts, and in the necessity of belonging to it : they
despised the hollowness of their opponents, the incon-
sequence of their arguments, the shallowness of their
views, their disrelish of principle, and their carelessness
about truth, but their heart sunk within them, under
the impossibility, on the one hand, of their carrying
out their faith into practice, *there*, where they found
themselves, and of realising their ideas in fact,—and the
duty on the other, as they were taught it, of making the
best of the circumstances in which they were placed
Such were they; I trust they are so still : I will not
allow myself to fancy that secret doubts on the one hand,
that self-will, disregard of authority, an unmanly, dis-
ingenuous bearing, and the spirit of party on the other,
have deformed a body of persons whom I have loved,

B

revered, and sympathised with. I speak of those many
persons whom I admired; who, like the hero in the
epic, did not want courage, but encouragement; who
looked out in vain for the approbation of authority;
who felt their own power, but shrank from the omen of
evil, the hateful raven, which flapped its wings over
them; who seemed to say with the poet—

> ——— Non me tua fervida terrent
> Dicta, ferox; Dii me terrent, et Jupiter hostis.

But their very desire of realities, and their fear of
deceiving themselves with dreams, was their insurmountable difficulty here. They could not make the
Establishment what it was not, and this was forced on
them day after day. It is a principle, in some sense
acknowledged by Catholic theologians, that the spirit
of an age modifies its inherited professions. Moralists
lay down, that a law loses its authority which the
lawgiver knowingly allows to be infringed and put
aside; whatever, then, be the abstract claims of the
Anglican cause, the fact is that the living community
to which they belong has for centuries ignored and
annulled them. It was a principle parallel to this
which furnished one of the reasons on which the judges
of the Queen's Bench the other day acted, when they
refused to prohibit the execution of the Royal decision,
in the appeal made from the Bishop of Exeter. His
counsel urged certain provisions in statutes of the reign

of Henry VIII., which had not been discussed in the
pleadings. "Were the language of 25 Henry VIII. c.
9, obscure instead of clear," observed the Chief Justice,
"we should not be justified in differing from the con-
struction put upon it by contemporaneous and long-
continued usage. There would be no safety for property
or liberty if it could be successfully contended, that all
lawyers and statesmen have been mistaken for centuries as to the true meaning of the Act of Parliament."
Whatever becomes of the general question, this was
at least the language of reason and common sense;
as physical life assimilates to itself, or casts off, whatever it encounters, allowing no interference with the
supremacy of its own proper principles, so is it with
life social and civil. When a body politic grows, takes
definite shape, and matures, it slights, though it may
endure, the vestiges and tokens of its rude beginnings.
It may cherish them as curiosities, but it abjures them
as precedents. They may hang about it, as the
shrivelled blossom about the formed fruit; but they
are dead, and will be sure to disappear as soon as they
are felt to be troublesome. Common sense tells us
these appendages do not apply to things as they are;
and, if individuals attempt to insist on them, they will
but bring on themselves the just imputation of vexa-
tiousness and extravagance. So it is with the Anglican
formularies; they are but the expression of the national
sentiment, and therefore are necessarily modified by it.

Did the nation grow into Catholicity, they might easily
be made to assume a Catholic demeanour; but as it
has matured in its Protestantism, they must take, day
by day, a more Evangelical and liberal aspect. Of
course I am not saying this by way of justifying
individuals in professing and using doctrinal and
devotional forms from which they dissent; nor am I
denying that words have, or at least ought to have, a
definite meaning which must not be explained away; I
am merely stating what takes place in matter of fact,
allowably in some cases, wrongly in others, according
to the strength, on the one hand, of the wording of
the formulary, and of the diverging opinion on the
other.

I say, that a nation's laws are a nation's property,
and have their life in the nation's life, and their interpretation in the nation's sentiment: and where that
living intelligence does not shine through them, they
become worthless and are put aside, whether formally or
on an understanding. Now Protestantism is, as it has
been for centuries, the Religion of England ; and since
the semi-patristical Church, which was set up for the
nation at the Reformation, is the organ of that religion,
it must live for the nation ; it must hide its Catholic
aspirations in folios, or in college cloisters ; it must call
itself Protestant, when it gets into the pulpit; it must
abjure Antiquity; for woe to it, if it attempt to thrust
the wording of its own documents in its master's path,

if it rely on a passage in its Visitation for the Sick, or on an Article of the Creed, or on the tone of its Collects, or on a catena of its divines, when the age has determined on a theology more in keeping with the progress of knowledge! The antiquary, the reader of history, the theologian, the philosopher, the Biblical student may make his protest; he may quote St. Austin, or appeal to the canons, or argue from the nature of the case; but *la Reine le veut;* the English people is sufficient for itself; it wills to be Protestant and progressive; and Fathers, Councils, Schoolmen, Scriptures, Saints, Angels, and what is above them, must give way. What are they to it? It thinks, argues, and acts according to its own practical, intelligible, shallow religion; and of that religion its Bishops and divines, will they or will they not, must be exponents.[1]

5.

In this way, I say, we are to explain, but in this way most naturally and satisfactorily, what otherwise would

---

[1] "It is not the practice for Judges to take up points of their own, and, *without argument*, to decide a case upon them. Lord Eldon used to say, that oftentimes hearing an argument in support of an opinion he had so taken up, convinced him he had been wrong—a great authority in favour of the good sense of the practice, which the Queen's Bench has disregarded in this case. In the Hampden case, the whole practice of the Court for two hundred and fifty years was set at naught by Lord Denman. In this case a course has been taken which has never hitherto been followed in questions of a mandamus to a railway, or a criminal information against a newspaper. *And both are Church cases."—Guardian,* May 1, 1850.

be startling, the late Royal decision to which I have
several times referred. The great legal authorities, on
whose report it was made, have not only pronounced,
that, as a matter of fact, persons who have denied the
grace of Baptism had held the highest preferments in
the National Church, but they felt themselves autho-
rised actually to interpret its ritual and its doctrine, and
to report to her Majesty that the dogma of baptismal
regeneration is not part and parcel of the national
religion. They felt themselves strong enough, in their
position, to pronounce " that the doctrine held by " the
Protestant clergyman, who brought the matter before
them, "was not contrary or repugnant to the declared
doctrine of the Church of England, as by law established." The question was not whether it was true
or not,—as they most justly remarked,—whether from
heaven or from hell; they were too sober to meddle
with what they had no means of determining; they
" abstained from expressing any opinion of their own
upon the theological correctness or error of the doctrine "
propounded: the question was, not what God had said,
but what the English nation had willed and allowed;
and, though it must be granted that they aimed at a
critical examination of the letter of the documents, yet
it must be granted on the other hand too, that their
criticism was of a very national cast, and that the
national sentiment was of great use to them in helping
them to their conclusions. What was it to the nation

or its lawyers whether Hooker used the word "charity" or "piety" in the extract which they adduced from his works, and that "piety" gave one sense to the passage, and "charity" another? Hooker must speak as the existing nation speaks, if he is to be a national authority. What though the ritual categorically deposes to the regeneration of the infant baptized? The Evangelical party, who, in former years, had had the nerve to fix the charge of dishonesty on the explanations of the Thirty-nine Articles, put forth by their opponents, could all the while be cherishing in their own breasts an interpretation of the Baptismal Service, simply contradictory to its most luminous declarations. Inexplicable proceeding, if they were professing to handle the document in its letter; but not dishonourable, not dishonest, not hypocritical, but natural and obvious, on the condition or understanding that the Nation, which imposes the document, imposes its sense,—that by the breath of its mouth it had, as a god, made Establishment, Articles, Prayer-Book, and all that is therein, and could by the breath of its mouth as easily and absolutely unmake them again, whenever it was disposed.

Counsel, then, and pamphleteers may put forth unanswerable arguments in behalf of the Catholic interpretation of the Baptismal service; a long succession of Bishops, an unbroken tradition of writers, may have faithfully and anxiously guarded it. In vain has the Caroline school honoured it by ritual observance; in vain has the Restoration illustrated it by varied learning; in vain did the Revolution retain it as the price for other concessions; in vain did the eighteenth century use it as a sort of watchword against Wesley; in vain has it been persuasively developed and fearlessly proclaimed by the movement of 1833; all this is foreign to the matter before us. We have not to enquire what is the dogma of a collegiate, antiquarian religion, but what, in the words of the Prime Minister, will give "general satisfaction;" what is the religion of Britons. May not the free-born, self-dependent, animal mind of the Englishman, choose his religion for himself? and have lawyers any more to do than to state, as a matter of fact and history, what that religion is, and for three centuries has been? are we to obtrude the mysteries of an objective, of a dogmatic, of a revealed system, upon a nation which intimately feels and has established, that each individual is to be his own judge in truth and falsehood in matters of the unseen world? How is it possible that the National Church, forsooth, should be allowed to dogmatize on a point which so immediately affects the Nation itself? Why, half the country is unbaptized; it is difficult to say for certain who are baptized; shall the country unchristianize itself? it has not yet advanced to indifference on such a matter. Shall it, by a suicidal act, use its own Church against itself, as its instrument whereby to cut itself off from the hope of another life? Shall it

confine the Christian promise within limits, and put
restrictions upon grace, when it has thrown open trade,
removed disabilities, abolished monopolies, taken off
agricultural protection, and enlarged the franchise?—
Such is the thought, such the language of the England
of to-day. What a day for the defenders of the dogma
in bygone times, if those times had anything to do with
the present! What a day for Bishop Lavington, who,
gazing on Wesley preaching the new birth at Exeter,
pronounced Methodism as bad as "Popery"! What
a portentous day for Bampton Lecturers and divinity
Professors! What a day for Bishop Mant and Archbishop Lawrence, and Bishop Van Mildert, and Archbishop Sutton, and, as we may trust, what a day had
it been for Archbishop Howley, taken away on its very
dawning! The giant ocean has suddenly swelled and
heaved, and majestically yet masterfully snaps the
cables of the smaller craft which lie upon its bosom,
and strands them upon the beach. Hooker, Taylor,
Bull, Pearson, Barrow, Tillotson, Warburton, and Horne,
names mighty in their generation, are broken and
wrecked before the power of a nation's will. One
vessel alone can ride those waves; it is the boat of
Peter, the ark of God.

6.

And now, my brethren, it is plain that this doctrine
does not stand by itself:—if the grace of Baptism is
not to be taught dogmatically in the National Church,

if it be not a heresy to deny it, if to hold it and not to
hold it be but matters of opinion, what other doctrine
which that Church professes stands on a firmer or more
secure foundation ?   The same popular voice which has
explained away the wording of the Office for Baptism,
may of course in a moment dispense with the Athanasian Creed altogether.   Who can doubt, that if that
symbol be not similarly dealt with in course of law in
years to come, it is because the present judgment will
practically destroy its force as efficaciously, and with
less trouble to the lawyers ?   No individual will dare
to act on views which he knows to a certainty would
be overruled as soon as they are brought before a legal
tribunal.   As to the document itself, it will be obvious
to allege that the details of the Athanasian Creed were
never intended for reception by national believers; that
all that was intended (as has before now been avowed)
was to uphold *a* doctrine of a Trinity, and that, provided
we hold this " scriptural fact," it matters not whether
we be Athanasians, Sabellians, Tritheists, or Socinians,
or rather we shall be neither one nor the other of them.
Precedents on the other hand are easily adducible of
Arian, Sabellian, and Unitarian Bishops and dignitaries, and of divines who professed that Trinitarianism
was a mere matter of opinion, both in former times
and now.   Indeed it might with much reason be maintained, were the question before a court, that, looking
at the matter historically, Locke gave the death-blow

to the Catholic phraseology on that fundamental doctrine among the Anglican clergy; and it is surely undeniable, that such points as the Eternal Generation of the Son, the Homoüsion, and the Hypostatic Union, have been silently discarded by the many, and but anxiously and apologetically put forward by the few. With this existing disposition in the minds of English Churchmen towards a denial of the Catholic doctrine of the Trinity, I surely am not rash in saying, that the recent judgment has virtually removed it from their authoritative teaching altogether.

Nor can eternal punishment be received as an Anglican dogma, against the strong feeling of the age, with so little in its favour in the national formularies; nor original sin, considering that the national suspicion of it is countenanced and defended by no less an authority of past times than Bishop Jeremy Taylor. And much less the inspiration of Scripture, and the existence of the evil spirit, doctrines which are not mentioned in the Thirty-nine Articles at all. Yet, plain though this be, at this moment the Evangelical members of the Establishment are extolling the recent judgment, and are transported at the triumph it gives them, as if it might not, or would not, in time to come, be turned against themselves; as if, while it directly affected the doctrine of baptismal grace, it had no bearing upon those of predestination, election, satisfaction, justification, and others, of which they consider them-

selves so especially the champions. Poor victims! do
you dream that the spirit of the age is working for you,
or are you indeed secretly prepared to go further than
you avow? At least some of you are honest enough to
be praising the recent judgment on its own account,
and blind enough not to see what it involves; and so
you contentedly and trustfully throw yourselves into
the arms of the age. But it is "to-day for me, to-
morrow for thee!" Do you really think the age is
stripping Laud or Bull of his authority, in order to set
up Whittaker or Baxter? or with what expedient are
you to elude a power, whose aid you have already
invoked against your enemies?[1]

7.

For us, Catholics, my brethren, while we clearly
recognise how things are going with our countrymen

---

[1] The Oxford tutors are more sharp-sighted; understanding the mental
state of the junior portion of the University, they see that a decision
like that of the Privy Council is fitted to destroy at once what little
hold the old Anglican system has on them, and to give entrance among
them to a scepticism on all points of religion. In a strong and spirited
protest, they quote against the Archbishop the very words he used on
another occasion, eight or nine years since. Yet his evasive interpretation of the Baptismal service is not the fault of the Archbishop, but of
the Reformers. No member of the Establishment can believe in a *system*
of theology of any kind, without doing violence to the formularies.
Those only go easily along Articles and Prayer-book, who do not *think*.
It is remarkable, the Archbishop's book on apostolical Preaching first
brought the present writer to a belief in baptismal regeneration in 1824.
He has the copy still, with his objections marked on the side, given him
for the purpose of convincing him by a dignitary whom he has ever loved
amid the gravest differences, Dr. Hawkins.

and while we would not accelerate the march of infidelity
if we could help it, yet we are more desirous that you
should leave a false church for the true, than that a
false church should hold its ground. For if we are
blessed in converting any of you, we are effecting a
direct, unequivocal, and substantial benefit, which outweighs all points of expedience—the salvation of your
souls. I do not undervalue at all the advantage of
institutions which, though not Catholic, keep out evils
worse than themselves. Some restraint is better than
none; systems which do not simply inculcate divine
truth, yet serve to keep men from being utterly hardened
against it, when at length it addresses them; they preserve a certain number of revealed doctrines in the
popular mind; they familiarize it to Christian ideas;
they create religious associations; and thus, remotely
and negatively, they may even be said to prepare and
dispose the soul in a certain sense for those inspirations
of grace, which, through the merits of Christ, are freely
given to all men for their salvation, all over the earth.
It is a plain duty, then, not to be forward in destroying
religious institutions, even though not Catholic, if we
cannot replace them with what is better; but, from fear
of injuring them, to shrink from saving the souls of the
individuals who live under them, would be worldly
wisdom, treachery to Christ, and uncharitableness to
His redeemed.

As to the Catholic Church herself, no vicissitude of

circumstances can hurt her which allows her fair play.
If, indeed, from the ultimate resolution of all heresies
and errors into some one form of infidelity or scepticism,
the nation was strong enough to turn upon her in persecution, then indeed she might be expelled from our
land, as she has been expelled before now. Then persecution would do its work, as it did three centuries ago.
But this is an extreme case, which is not to be anticipated. Till the nation becomes thus unanimous in
unbelief, Catholics are secured by the collision and
balance of religious parties, and are sheltered under
that claim of toleration which each sect prefers for itself.
But give us as much as this, an open field, and we ask
no favour; every form of Protestantism turns to our
advantage. Its establishments of religion remind the
world of that archetypal Church of which it is a copyist;
its Creeds contain portions of our teaching; its quarrels
and divisions serve to break up its traditions, and rid
its professors of their prejudices; its scepticism makes
them turn in admiration and in hope to her, who alone
is clear in her teaching and consistent in its transmission; its very abuse of her makes them inquire about
her. She fears nothing from political parties; she
shrinks from none of them; she can coalesce with any.
She is not jealous of progress nor impatient with con-
servatism, if either be the national will. Nor is there
anything for us to fear (except for the moment and for
the sake of individuals) in that movement towards

Pantheism, in the Protestant world,[1] which excites the special anxiety of many; for, in truth, there is something so repugnant to the feelings of man, in systems which deprive God of His perfections, and reduce Him to a name, which remove the Creator to an indefinite distance from His creatures, under the pretence of bringing them near to Him, and refuse Him the liberty of sending mediators and ordaining instruments to connect them with Him, which deny the existence of sin, the need of pardon, and the fact of punishment, which maintain that man is happy here and sufficient for himself, when he feels so keenly his own ignorance and desolateness,—and on the other hand, the sects and parties round about us are so utterly helpless to remedy his evils, and to supply his need,—that the preachers of these new ideas from Germany and America are really, however much against their will, like Caiphas, prophesying for us. Surely they will find no resting-place anywhere for their feet, and the feet of their disciples, but will be tumbled down from one depth of blasphemy to another, till they arrive at sheer and naked atheism, the *reductio ad absurdum* of their initial principles. Logic is a stern master; they feel it, they protest against it; they profess to hate it, and would fain dispense with it; but it is the law of their intellectual

---

[1] I am aware that the name of Pantheism is repudiated by several writers of the school I allude to, but I think it will be found to be the ultimate resolution of its principles.

nature. Struggling and shrieking, but in vain, will they make the inevitable descent into that pit from which there is no return, except through the almost miraculous grace of God, the grant of which in this life is never hopeless. And Israel, without a fight, will see their enemies dead upon the sea-shore.

I will but observe in conclusion, that, in thus explaining the feeling under which I address myself to members of the Anglican communion in these Lectures, I have advanced one step towards fulfilling the object with which I have undertaken them. For it is a very common difficulty which troubles men, when they contemplate submission to the Catholic Church, that perhaps they shall thus be weakening the communion they leave, which, with whatever defects, they see in matter of fact to be a defence of Christianity against its enemies. No, my brethren, you will not be harming it; if the National Church falls, it falls because it *is* national; because it left the centre of unity in the sixteenth century, not because you leave it in the nineteenth. Cranmer, Parker, Jewell, will complete their own work; they who made it, will be its destruction.

LECTURE II.

THE MOVEMENT OF 1833 FOREIGN TO THE NATIONAL CHURCH.

I.

MY object in these Lectures, my brethren, is not to construct any argument in favour of Catholicism, for there is no need. Arguments exist in abundance, and of the highest cogency, and of the most wonderful variety, provided severally by the merciful wisdom of its Divine Author, for distinct casts of mind and character;—so much so, that it is often a mistake in controversy to cumulate reasons for what is on many considerations so plain already, and the evidence of which is only weakened to the individual inquirer, when he is distracted by fresh proofs, consistent indeed with those which have brought conviction to him, but to him less convincing than his own, and at least strange and unfamiliar. Every inquirer may have enough of positive proof to convince him that the Catholic Religion is divine: it is owing to the force of counter-objections that his conviction remains in fact either defective or inoperative. I consider, then, that I shall

C

be ministering in my measure to the cause of truth, if I
do ever so little towards removing the difficulties, or
any of them, which beset the mind, when it is urged
to accept Catholicism as true.   It is with this view that
I have insisted on the real character of the Established
Church, and its relation to the nation; for, if it be
mainly as I have represented it, a department of government under the temporal sovereign, one at least
is struck off from the catalogue of your objections
You fear to leave it lest you should, by your secession
throw it into the hands of a latitudinarian party; but
it never has been in your hands, nor ever under your
influence.   It is in the hands of the nation; it is mainly
what the nation is: such is it, while you are in it; such
would it be, if you left it.   I do not deny you may by
your presence somewhat retard its downward career,
but you are not of the real importance to it, which
you fancy.

Now, in the course of the argument I made a remark,
which I shall to-day pursue.   I spoke of the movement
which began in the Establishment in 1833, or shortly
before; and I dwelt on the remarkable fact, that in
nearly twenty years that movement, though certainly it
exerted great influence over the views of individuals
nevertheless has created a mere party in the National
Church, having had the least possible influence over the
National Church itself; and no wonder, if that Church
be simply an organ or department of the State, for in

that case, all ecclesiastical acts really proceeding from the supreme civil government, to influence the Establishment, is nothing else than to influence the State, or even the Constitution.

Now I shall pursue the argument. I shall, by means of one or two suggestions, try to bring home to you the extreme want of congeniality which has existed between the movement of 1833 and the nation at large; and then assuming that you, my brethren, owe your principles to that movement, and that your first duty is to your principles, I shall infer your own want of congeniality with the national religion, however you may wish it otherwise; I shall infer that you have no concern with that national religion, have no place in it, have no reason for belonging to it, and have no responsibilities towards it.

I am then to point out to you, that, what is sometimes called, or rather what calls itself, the Anglo-Catholic teaching, is not only a novelty in this age (for to prove a thing new to the age, is not enough in order to prove it uncongenial), but that, while it is a system adventitious and superadded to the national religion, it is, moreover, not supplemental, or complemental, or collateral, or correlative to it,—not implicitly involved in it, not developed from it,—nor combining with it,—nor capable of absorption into it; but, on the contrary, most uncongenial and heterogeneous, floating upon it, a foreign substance, like oil upon the water. And my

proof shall consist, first, of what was augured of it
when it commenced; secondly, what has been fulfilled
concerning it during its course.

2.

As to the auguries with which it started, we need not
go beyond the first agents of the movement, in order to
have a tolerably sufficient proof that it had no lot, nor
portion, nor parentage in the Established Church; for
when those who first recommended to her its principles
and doctrines are found themselves to have doubted how
far these were congenial with her, when the very physi-
cians were anxious as to what would come of their own
medicines, who shall feel confidence in them? Such,
however, was the case: its originators confessed that
they were forcing upon the Establishment doctrines
from which it revolted, doctrines with which it never
had given signs of coalescing, doctrines which tended
they knew not whither. This is what they felt, this is
what with no uncertain sound they publicly proclaimed.

For instance, one, who, if any, is the author of the
movement altogether, and whose writings were published
after his death, says in one of his letters, "It seems
agreed among the wise, that we must begin by laying
a foundation." Again he writes to a friend, "I am
getting more and more to feel, what you tell me, about
the impracticability of making sensible people," that is,
the High Church party of the day, "enter into not

ecclesiastical views; and, what is most discouraging, I hardly see how to set about leading them to us." Elsewhere he asks, " How is it we are so much in advance of our generation?" And again, "The age is out of joint." And again, " I shall write nothing on the subject of Church grievances, till I have a tide to work with." Further he calls the Establishment "an incubus upon the country," and, "a upas tree:" and, lastly, within three or four months of his death, his theological views still expanding and diverging from the existing state of things, he exclaims, "How mistaken we may ourselves be on many points, that are only gradually opening on us!"[1]

Avowals of a like character are made with the utmost frankness in the very work which in 1837 professed formally to lay down and defend the new doctrines. The writer (that is, myself) begins by allowing that he is "discussing rather than teaching, what was *meant* to be simply an article of faith," viz., belief in "the Catholic Church," alleging in excuse that "the teaching of the Apostles concerning it is, in a good measure, withdrawn," and that, "we are, so far, left to make the best of our way to the promised land by our natural resources."[2] The preaching of the doctrines of the movement is compared, in its strangeness, to the original preaching of Christianity, and this

[1] Froude's Remains, vol. i.
[2] Prophetical Office of the Church. Vid. Via Media, vol. i., ed. 1877.

only alleviation is suggested, if it be any, that they who are startled at those doctrines, could not be *more* startled than "the outcasts to whom the Apostles preached in the beginning." Nay, it is categorically stated, that "these doctrines are in one sense as entirely new as Christianity when first preached." He continues, "Protestantism and Popery" (by Popery he means the popular Catholic system) "are real religions; no one can doubt about them; they have furnished the mould in which nations have been cast; but the Via Media, viewed as an integral system, has scarcely had existence except on paper." Presently he continues "It still remains to be tried, whether what is called Anglo-Catholicism, the religion of Andrewes, Laud, Hammond, Butler, and Wilson, is capable of being professed, acted on, and maintained in a large sphere of action, and through a sufficient period; or whether it be a mere modification or transition state, either of Romanism or of popular Protestantism, according as we view it." "It may be argued," he adds, and, as he does not deny, argued with plausibility, "that the Church of England, as established by law, and existing in fact, has never represented a certain doctrine, or been the development of a principle; that it has been but a name, or a department of the State, or a political party in which religious opinion was an accident, and therefore has been various." And this prospectus, as it may be called, of a new system, ends by stating that, "it

is proposed to offer helps towards the formation of a
recognised Anglican theology in one of its departments."
. . . . "We require a recognised theology," he insists,
"and, if the present work, instead of being what it is
meant to be, a first approximation to the required solution, in one department of a complicated problem,
contains, after all, but a series of illustrations demon-
strating our need, and supplying hints for its removal;
such a result, it is evident, will be quite a sufficient
return for whatever anxiety it has cost the writer to
have employed his own judgment on so serious a
subject."

I must add, in justice to this writer, and it is not
much to say for him, that he did not entertain the
presumptuous thought of creating, at this time of day,
a new theology himself; he considered that a theology
true in itself, and necessary for the position of the
Anglican Church, was to be found in the writings of
Andrewes, Laud, Bramhall, Stillingfleet, Butler, and
other of its divines, but had never been put together,
—as he expressly declares. Nor, in spite of his misgivings, was he without a persuasion that the theological
system contained in those writers, and derived, as he
believed, from the primitive Fathers, not only ought to
be, but might be, and, as he hoped, would be, acknow
ledged and acted upon by the Establishment. On the
other hand, I allow, of course, and am not loth to allow,
that, had he seen clearly that Antiquity and the Estab-

lishment were incompatible with each other, he would promptly have given up the Establishment, rather than have rejected Antiquity. Moreover, let it be observed, in evidence of his misgivings on the point, that, when he gets to the end of his volume, instead of their being removed, they return in a more definite form, and he confesses that " the thought, with which we entered upon the subject, is apt to recur, when the excitement of the inquiry has subsided, and weariness has succeeded, that what has been said is but a dream, the wanton exercise, rather than the practical conclusions, of the intellect."

3.

These auguries speedily met with a response, though in a less tranquil tone, in every part of the Establishment, and by each of the schools of opinion within it, —the High Church section, the Evangelical, and the Latitudinarian. They condemned, not only the attempt, but the authors of it. The late Dr Arnold, a man who always spoke his mind, avowed that his feelings towards a Roman Catholic were quite different from his feelings to the author of the above work. " I think the one," he continued, " a fair enemy, the other a treacherous one. The one is the Frenchman in his own uniform, the other is the Frenchman disguised in a red coat. I should honour the first and hang the second." For the Evangelical party, it is scarcely necessary to make the following extracts from the work of even a cautious and careful writer:—"If," says the writer of "Essays on the Church," "the grievances and warfare of Dissenters against it have greatly diminished in interest, a new and gigantic evil has arisen up in their room. . . Popery, not indeed of the days of Hildebrand or Leo the Tenth, but Popery as it first established itself in the seventh and eighth centuries, is already among us. . . . Popery has anew arisen up among us, in youthful vigour and in her youthful attractions. Such is the chief, the greatly preponderating peril, which besets the Church of England at the present day. It has in it all the essential features of Popery; but, apart from this, and were it never to proceed beyond the perils to which it has now reached, it is fraught with the fearful evil of a withering, parching, blighting operation, drying-up and banishing all spiritual life and influence from the Church."[1]

Lastly, a theological professor of the High Church section, in an attack which he delivered from the pulpit, viewed the movement from another point of view, yet in perfect accordance of judgment with the two writers who have been already cited : "Instead of quietly acquiescing," he says, "in what they cannot change, submitting in silence to their imagined privations, and patiently enduring this 'meagreness of Protestantism,' by a species of 'ecclesiastical agitation,' unexampled

[1] Essays on the Church, by a Layman, 1838, pp. 270, 299, 300. Ditto, 1840, p. 401.

in obtrusiveness and perseverance, they are unsettling
the faith of the weak, blinding the judgment of the
sober-minded, raising the hopes of the most inveterate
advocates of our Reformed and Protestant Church, and,
as far as a small knot of malcontents can well be supposed capable, they are compromising her character and
disturbing her peace." [1]

Yet even at this date, in spite of the success which
for five years had attended him, the author whom I
have already quoted felt no greater confidence than
before in his own congeniality with the National
Church; and, on occasion of the last-mentioned attack
upon him, scrupled not to avow the fact. "Sure I
am," said he, "that the more stir is made about those
opinions which you censure, the wider they will spread.
Whatever be the faults or mistakes of their advocates,
they have that root of truth in them, which, as I do
firmly believe, has a blessing with it. *I do not pretend
to say they will ever become widely popular*, that is
another matter: truth is never, or at least never long,
popular; nor do I say they will ever gain that powerful
external influence over the many which truth, vested
in the few, cherished, throned, energising in the few,
often has possessed; nor that they are not destined,
as truth has often been destined, to be cast away, and
at length *trodden under foot as an odious thing:* but of
this I am sure, that, at this juncture, in proportion as

---

[1] Faussett's Sermon, 1838, Preface to Third Edition.

they are known, they will make their way through the community, *picking out their own*, seeking and obtaining refuge in the hearts of Christians, high and low, here and there, with this man and that, as the case may be ; doing their work in their day, and raising a memorial and a witness to this *fallen generation* of what once has been, of what God would ever have, of what one day shall be in perfection; and that, not from what they are in themselves, because, viewed in the concrete, they are mingled, as everything human must be, with error and infirmity, but by reason of the spirit, the truth, the old Catholic life and power which is in them." [1]

4.

What was it, then, which the originators of the movement of 1833 demanded or desiderated in its behalf, in the communion for whose benefit it was intended? How came they to dread lest the principles of St. Athanasius and of St. Ambrose should fail to take root in the minds of their brethren, and to spread through the laity? In truth, when they feared that the good seed would fall, not on a congenial soil, but on hard, or stony, or occupied ground, they were fearing that the National Church, though they did not use the word, had no *life*. Life consists or manifests itself in activity of principle. There are various kinds of life, and each kind is the influence or operation in a

[1] The author's " Letter to Dr. Faussett."   Vid. Via Media. vol. ii.

body of those principles upon which the body is constituted. Each kind of life is to be referred, and is
congenial, to its own principle. Principles, distinct
from each other, will not take root and flourish in
bodies to which respectively they are foreign. One
principle has not the life of another. The life of a
plant is not the same as the life of an animated being,
and the life of the body is not the same as the life of
the intellect; nor is the life of the intellect the same
in kind as the life of grace; nor is the life of the
Church the same as the life of the State. When, then,
these writers doubted whether Apostolical principles,
as they called them, would spread through the laity of
England, they were doubting whether that laity lived,
breathed, energised, in Apostolical principles; whether
Apostolical principles were the just expression and the
constituent element of the national sentiment; whether
the intellectual and moral life of the nation was not
distinct from the life of the Apostolical age; and, if
the Establishment professed to be built upon the
principles and to partake of the life of the Apostolical
age, as they knew ought to be the case, then they
were doubting whether it really had those principles
and that life, in spite of its professions.

There was no doubt at all, there is no doubt at all,
that the Establishment has *some* kind of life. No one
ever doubted it; and one of its dignitaries triumphantly proves it in a passage which I will quote:—

Surely, my dear friend," says this accomplished writer,[1] with a reference to the present controversy, "it requires an inordinate faith in one's own logical dreams, an idolising worship of one's own opinions, to believe that the Church of England, blest as she has been by God for so many generations, raised as she has been by Him to be the mother of so many Churches, with such a promise shining upon her, and brightening every year, that her daughters should spread round the earth, that she, who has been chosen by God to be the instrument of so many blessings, and the presence of the Lord and His Spirit with whom was never more manifest than at this day, should forfeit her office and authority, as a witness of the truth, should be cut off from the body of Christ's Church, and should no longer be able to dispense the grace of the sacraments, because her highest law court has not condemned a proposition asserted by one of her ministers, concerning a very obscure and perplexing question of dogmatical theology. Surely this would be an extraordinary delusion; . . . for, whatever the dogmatical value of the opinion" in question "may be, the error is not one which indicates any want of personal faith and holiness, or any decay of Christian life in the Church."

No, I grant it would be very difficult to the imagination to receive it as a dogma, that there was no "life"

---

[1] Archdeacon Hare, in *Record* Newspaper.

in the National Church, or indeed no "faith." The
simple question is, What is meant by "life" and
"faith"? Will the Archdeacon tell us whether he
does not mean by faith a something very vague and
comprehensive? Does he mean, as he might say, the
faith of Marcus Antoninus, St. Austin, and Peter the
Hermit, of Luther, Rousseau, Washington, and Napo-
leon Bonaparte? Faith has one meaning to a Catholic,
another to a Protestant. And life,—is it the religious
"life" of England, or of Prussia, that he means, or is it
Catholic life, that is, the life which belongs to Catholic
principles? Else he will be arguing in a circle, if he
is to prove that Protestants have that life, which manifests "the presence of the Spirit," on the ground of
their having, as they are sure to have, a life congenial
and in conformity to Protestant principles. If then
"life" means strength, activity, energy, and well-being
of any kind whatever, in that case doubtless the national
religion is alive. It is a great power in the midst of
us; it wields an enormous influence; it represses a
hundred foes; it conducts a hundred undertakings.
It attracts men to it, uses them, rewards them; it
has thousands of beautiful homes up and down the
country, where quiet men may do its work and
benefit its people; it collects vast sums in the shape
of voluntary offerings, and with them it builds
churches, prints and distributes innumerable Bibles,
books, and tracts and sustains missionaries in all

parts of the earth. In all parts of the earth it opposes
the Catholic Church, denounces her as antichristian,
bribes the world against her, obstructs her influence,
apes her authority, and confuses her evidence. In all
parts of the world it is the religion of gentlemen, of
scholars, of men of substance, and men of no personal
faith at all. If this be life,—if it be life to impart
a tone to the court and houses of parliament, to
ministers of state, to law and literature, to universities
and schools, and to society,—if it be life to be a principle of order in the population, and an organ of
benevolence and almsgiving towards the poor,—if it be
life to make men decent, respectable, and sensible, to
embellish and refine the family circle, to deprive vice
of its grossness, and to shed a gloss over avarice and
ambition,—if indeed it is the life of religion to be the
first jewel in the Queen's crown, and the highest step
of her throne, then doubtless the National Church is
replete, it overflows with life; but the question has
still to be answered, Life of what kind? Heresy has
its life, worldliness has its life. Is the Establishment's
life merely national life, or is it something more? Is
it Catholic life as well? Is it a supernatural life? Is
it congenial with, does it proceed from, does it belong
to, the principles of Apostles, Martyrs, Evangelists,
and Doctors, the principles which the movement of 1833
thought to impose or to graft upon it, or does it revolt
from them? If it be Catholic and Apostolic, it will en-

dure Catholic and Apostolic principles; no one doubts
it can endure Erastian; no one doubts it can be patient
of Protestant; this is the problem which was started by
the movement in question, the problem for which, surely,
there has been an abundance of tests in the course of
twenty years.

5.

But the passage I have quoted suggests a second
observation. I have spoken of the *tests,* which the
last twenty years have furnished, of the real character
of the Establishment; for I must not be supposed to
be inquiring whether the Establishment has been
unchurched during that period, but whether it has been
proved to have been no Church from the first. The
want of congeniality which now exists between the
sentiments and ways, the moral life of the Anglican
communion, and the principles, doctrines, traditions of
Catholicism—this uncongeniality I am speaking of in
order to prove something done and over long ago before
the movement, in order to show that that movement of
1833 was from its very beginning engaged in propagating an unreality. The eloquent writer just quoted,
in ridicule of the protest made by twelve very distinguished men against the Queen's recent decision concerning the sacrament of baptism, contrasts "logical
dreams" and "obscure and perplexing questions of
dogmatic theology" with "the promise" in the Establishment of a large family "of daughters, spread round

the earth, shining and brightening every year." Now,
I grant that it has a narrow and technical appearance to
decide the Catholicity of a religious body by particular
words, or deeds, or measures, resulting from the temper
of a particular age, accidentally elicited, and accomplished in minutes or in days. I allow it and feel it;—
that a particular vote of parliament, endured or tacitly
accepted by bishops and clergy, or by the Metro-
politans, or a particular appointment, or a particular
omission, or a particular statement of doctrine, should
at once change the spiritual character of the body, and
ipso facto cut it off from the centre of unity and the
source of grace, is almost incredible. In spite of such
acts, surely the Anglican Church might be to-day
what it was yesterday, with an internal power and
a supernatural virtue, provided it had not already
forfeited them, and would go about its work as of
old time. It would be to-day pretty much what it
was yesterday, though in the course of the night it
had allowed an Anglo-Prussian See to be set up
in Jerusalem, and had disavowed the Athanasian
Creed.

This is the common sense of the matter, to which the
mind recurs with satisfaction, after zeal and ingenuity
have done their utmost to prove the contrary. Of
course, I am not saying that individual acts do not
tend towards, and a succession of acts does not issue in,
the most serious spiritual consequences; but it is so

D

difficult to determine the worth of each ecclesiastical
act, and what its position is relatively to acts before
and after it, that I have no intention of urging any
argument deduced from such acts in particular. A gene
ration may not be long enough for the completion of
an act of schism or heresy. Judgments admit of repeal
or reversal; enactments are liable to flaws and infor-
malities; laws require promulgation; documents admit
of explanation; words must be interpreted either by
context or by circumstances; majorities may be analysed; responsibilities may be shifted. I admit the
remark of another writer in the present controversy,
though I do not accept his conclusion: "The Church's
motion," he says, "is not that of a machine, to be
calculated with accuracy, and predicted beforehand;
where one serious injury will disturb all regularity, and
finally put a stop to action. It is that of a living body,
whose motions will be irregular, incapable of being
exactly arranged and foretold, and where it is nearly
impossible to say how much health may co-exist with
how much disease." And he speaks of the line of
reasoning which he is opposing, as being "too logical
to be real. Men," he observes, "do not, in the practical affairs of life, act on such clear, sharp, definite
theories. Such reasoning can never be the cause of
any one leaving the Church of England. But it looks
well on paper, and therefore may, perhaps, be put
forward as a theoretical argument by those who, from

some other feeling, or fancy, or prejudice, or honest conviction, think fit to leave us." [1]

Truly said, except in the imputation conveyed in the concluding words. I will grant that it is by life without us, by life within us, by the work of grace in our communion and in ourselves, that we are all of us accustomed practically to judge whether that communion be Catholic or not; not by this or that formal act or historical event. I will grant it, though of course it requires some teaching, and some discernment, and some prayer, to understand what spiritual life is, and what is the working of grace. However, at any rate, let the proposition pass;—I will here allow it, at least for argument's sake; for, my brethren, I am not here going to look out, in the last twenty years, for dates when, and ways in which, the Establishment fell from Catholic unity, and lost its divine privileges. No; the question before us is nothing narrow or technical; it has no cut-and-dried premisses, and peremptory conclusions; it is not whether this or that statute or canon at the time of the Reformation, this or that "further and further encroachment" of the State this or that "Act of William IV.," constituted the Establishment's formal separation from the Church; not whether the Queen's recent decision binds it to heresy; but, whether these acts, and abundant others, are not one and all evidences, in one out of a hundred

[1] Neal's Few Words of Hope, pp. 11, 12.

heads of evidence, that, whatever were the acts which
constituted, or the moment which completed the schism,
or rather the utter disorganisation of the National
Church, cut off and disorganised it is. No sober man
I suppose, dreams of denying, that, if that Church be
un-apostolical and impure now, it has had no claim to
be called "pure and apostolical" last year, or twenty
years back, or for any part of the period since the
Reformation.

We have, then, this simple question before us:
What evidence is there, that the doctrines and principles proclaimed to the world in 1833 had then, or have
now, any congeniality with the Establishment in which
they were propagated, and that they could or can live
in that Establishment; whether they can move or
work, whether they can breathe and live in it, better
than a being with lungs in an exhausted receiver? It
was doubted, as we have seen, by their first preachers;
how has it been determined by the event? Now,
then, to give one or two specimens and illustrations
of a fact too certain, as I think, to need much dwelling on.

6.

We know that it is the property of life to be impatient of any foreign substance in the body to which it
belongs. It will be sovereign in its own domain, and
it conflicts with what it cannot assimilate into itself,
and is irritated and disordered till it has expelled it.

Such expulsion, then, is, emphatically, a test of uncongeniality, for it shows that the substance ejected, not only is not one with the body that rejects it, but cannot be made one with it; that its introduction is not only useless, or superfluous, or adventitious, but that it is intolerable. For instance, it is usual for High Churchmen to speak of the Establishment as patient, in matter of fact, both of Catholic and Protestant principles;—truly said as regards Protestant, and it will illustrate my point to give instances of it. No one will deny, then, that neither Lutheranism nor Calvinism is the exact doctrine of the Church of England, and yet either heresy readily coalesces with it in matter of fact. Persons of Lutheran and Calvinistic, and Luthero-Calvinist bodies, are and have been chosen without scruple by the English people for husbands and wives, for sponsors, for missionaries, for deans and canons, without any formal transition from communion to communion. The Anglican Prelates write complimentary letters to what they call the foreign Protestant Churches, and they attend, with their clergy and laity, Protestant places of worship abroad. William III. was called to the throne, though a Calvinist, and George I., though a Lutheran, and that in order to exclude a family who adhered to the religion of Rome. The national religion, then, has a congeniality with Lutheranism and Calvinism, which it has not, for instance, with the Greek religion, or the Jewish. Other

religions, as they come, whatever they be, are not indifferent to it; it takes up one, it precipitates another;
it, as every religion, has a life, a spirit, a genius of its
own, in which doctrines lie implicit, out of which they
are developed, and by which they are attracted into it
from without, and assimilated to it.

There is a passage in Moehler's celebrated work on
Symbolism, so much to the point here, that I will quote
it: " Each nation," he says, " is endowed with a peculiar
character, stamped on the deepest, most hidden parts of
its being, which distinguishes it from all other nations,
and manifests its peculiarity in public and domestic
life, in art and science; in short, in every relation. In
every general act of a people, the national spirit is
infallibly expressed; and should contests, should selfish
factions occur, the element destructive to the vital
principle of the whole will most certainly be detected
in them, and the commotion excited by an alien spirit
either miscarries or is expelled; as long as the community preserves its self-consciousness, as long as its
peculiar genius yet lives and works within it. .   .   .
Let us contemplate the religious sect founded by Luther
himself. The developed doctrines of his Church, consigned as they are in the symbolical books, retain, on
the whole, so much of his spirit, that, at the first view,
they must be recognised by the observer as genuine
productions of Luther. With a sure vital instinct, the
opinions of the Majorists, the Synergists, and others.

were rejected as deadly, and indeed (from Luther's point of view) as untrue, by that community whose soul, whose living principle, he was." [1]

We have the most vivid and impressive illustrations of the truth of these remarks in the history of the Church. The religious life of a people is of a certain quality and in a certain direction, and this quality and this direction are tested by the mode in which it encounters the various opinions, customs, and institutions which are submitted to it. Drive a stake into a river's bed, and you will at once ascertain which way it is running, and at what speed; throw up even a straw upon the air, and you will see which way the wind blows; submit your heretical and your Catholic principle to the action of the multitude, and you will be able to pronounce at once whether that multitude is imbued with Catholic truth or with heretical falsehood.

7.

Take, for example, a passage in the history of the fourth century; let the place be Milan; the date the Lent of 384, 385; the reigning powers Justina and her son Valentinian, and St. Ambrose the Archbishop. The city is in an uproar; there is a mob before the imperial residence; the soldiery interferes in vain, and Ambrose is despatched by the court to disperse the people. A month elapses; Palm Sunday is come; the Archbishop

[1] Robertson's Transl., vol. ii. pp. 36-39.

is expounding the Creed to the catechumens, when he is
told that the people are again in commotion. A second
message comes, that they have seized one of the
empress's priests. The court makes reprisals on the
tradesmen, some of whom are fined, some thrown into
prison, while men of higher rank are threatened. We
are arrived at the middle of Holy Week, and we find
soldiers posted before one of the churches, and Ambrose
has menaced them with excommunication. His threat
overcomes them, and they join the congregation to
whom he is preaching. The court gives way, the guards
are withdrawn to their quarters, and the fines are re-
mitted. What does all this mean? There evidently
has been a quarrel between the court and the Archbishop, and the Archbishop, aided by the popular
enthusiasm, has conquered. A year passes, and there
is a second and more serious disturbance. Soldiers
have surrounded the same church; yet, dreading an
excommunication, they let the people enter, but refuse
to let them pass out. Still the people keep entering;
they fill the church, the courtyard, the priests'
lodgings; and there they remain with the Archbishop
for two or three days, singing psalms, till the soldiers,
overcome by the music, sing psalms too, and the
blockade melts away, no one knows how. And now,
what was the cause of so enthusiastic, so dogged an
opposition to the court, on the part of the population
of Milan? The answer is plain; it was because they

loved Christ so well, and were so sensitive of the doctrine of His divinity, that they would not allow the reigning powers to take a church from them, and bestow it on the Arians. I conceive, then, that Catholicism was emphatically the religion of Milan, or that the life of the Milanese Church was a Catholic life.

And so, in like manner, when in St. Giles' Church, Edinburgh, in July 1635, the dean of the city opened the service-book, in the presence of Bishop and Privy Council, and "a multitude of the meanest sort, most of them women," clapped their hands, cursed him, cried out, "A pope! a pope! antichrist! stone him;" [1] and one flung a stool at the Bishop, and others threw stones at doors and windows, and at Privy-seal and Bishop on their return, and this became the beginning of a movement which ended in obtaining the objects at which it aimed,—this, I consider, shows clearly enough that the religious life at Edinburgh at that day was not Catholic, not Anglican, but Presbyterian and Puritan.

And, to take one more instance, when the seven Bishops were committed to the Tower, and were proceeding "down the river to their place of confinement, the banks were covered with spectators, who, while they knelt and asked their blessing, prayed themselves for a blessing on them and their cause. The very soldiers who guarded them, and some even of the officers to

[1] Hume. Charles the First.

whose charge they were committed, knelt in like
manner before them, and besought their benediction."
When they were brought before the Court of King's
Bench, they "passed through a line of people who
kissed their hands and their garments, and begged
their blessing;" and when they were admitted to bail,
"bonfires were made in the streets, and healths drunk
to the Seven Champions of the Church." Lastly,
when they were acquitted, the verdict "was received
with a shout which seemed to shake the hall. . . . All
the churches were filled with people: the bells rang
from every tower, every house was illuminated, and
bonfires were kindled in every street. Medals were
struck in honour of the event, and portraits hastily
published and eagerly purchased, of men who were
compared to the seven golden candlesticks, and called
the seven stars of the Protestant Church." [1] Now here
again are signs of life, religious life, doubtless, but
they have nothing to do with Catholicism; they are
indubitable, unequivocal tokens what the national
religion was and is, affording a clear illustration of the
congeniality existing between the spirit and character
of a system and its own principles, and not with their
opposites.

8.

Let a people, then, Catholic or not, be little versed
in doctrine—let them be a practical, busy people, full of

[1] Southey's Book of the Church.

their secular matters—let them have no keen analytical
view of the principles which govern them,—yet they
will be spontaneously attracted by those principles and
irritated by their contraries, in such sort as they can be
attracted or irritated by no other. Their own principles
or their contraries, when once sounded in their ears,
thrill through them with a vibration, pleasant or painful, with sweet harmony or with grating discord; under
which they cannot rest quiet, but relieve their feelings
by gestures and cries, and startings to and fro, and
expressions of sympathy or antipathy towards others,
and at length by combination, and party manifestos,
and vigorous action. When, then, the note of Catholicism, as it may be called, was struck seventeen years
since, and while it has sounded louder and louder on
the national ear, what has been the response of the
national sentiment? It had many things surely in
its favour; it sounded from a centre which commanded
attention—it sounded strong and full; nor was it
intermitted, or checked, or lowered by the opposition
nor drowned by the clamour, which it occasioned
while, at length, it was re-echoed and repeated from
other centres with zeal, and energy, and sincerity, and
effect, as great as any cause could even desire or could
ask for. So far, no movement could have more advantages attendant on it than it had; and, as it proceeded,
it did not content itself with propagating an abstract
theology, but it took a part in the public events of the

day; it interfered with court, with ministers, with University matters, and with counter-movements of whatever kind.

And, moreover, which is much to the purpose, it appealed to the people, and that on the very ground that it was Apostolical in its nature. It made the experiment of this appeal the very test of its Apostolicity. "I shall offend many men," said one of its organs, "when I say, we must look to the people; but let them give me a hearing. Well can I understand their feelings. Who, at first sight, does not dislike the thoughts of gentlemen and clergymen depending for their maintenance and their reputation on their flocks? of their strength, as a visible power, lying, not in their birth, the patronage of the great, or the endowments of the Church, as hitherto, but in the homage of a multitude? But, in truth, the prospect is not so bad as it seems at first sight. The chief and obvious objection to the clergy being thrown on the people lies in that probable lowering of Christian views, and that adulation of the vulgar, which would be its consequence; and the state of dissenters is appealed to as an evidence of the danger. But let us recollect that we are an Apostolical body; we were not made, nor can be unmade, by our flocks; and, if our influence is to depend on them, yet the Sacraments are lodged with us. We have that with us which none but ourselves possess, the mantle of the Apostles; and this, properly understood and cherished, will ever keep us from being the creatures of a population."[1]

Here, then, was a challenge to the nation to decide between the movement and its opponents; and how did the nation meet it? When clergymen of Latitudinarian theology were promoted to dignities, did the faithful of the diocese, or of the episcopal city, rise in insurrection? Did parishioners blockade a church's doors to keep out a new incumbent, who refused to read the Athanasian Creed? Did vestries feel an instinctive reverence for the altar-table, as soon as that reverence was preached? Did the organs of public opinion pursue with their invectives those who became dissenters or Irvingites? Was it a subject of popular indignation, discussed and denounced in railway trains and omnibuses and steamboats, in clubs and shops, in episcopal charges and at visitation dinners, if a clergyman explained away the baptismal service, or professed his intention to leave out portions of it in ministration? Did it rouse the guards or the artillery to find that the Bishop, where they were stationed, was a Sabellian? Was it a subject for public meetings if a recognition was attempted of foreign Protestant ordinations? Did animosity to heretics of the day go so far as to lead speakers to ridicule their persons and their features, amid the cheers of sympathetic hearers? Did petitions load the

[1] Church of the Fathers.

tables of the Commons from the mothers of England
or Young Men's Associations, because the Queen went
to a Presbyterian service, or a high minister of state
was an infidel? Did the Bishops cry out and stop their
ears on hearing that one of their body denied original
sin or the grace of ordination? Was there nothing in
the course of the controversy to show what the nation
thought of that controversy, and of the parties to it?

9.

Yes, I hear a cry from an episcopal city; I have
before my eyes one scene, and it is a sample and an
earnest of many others. Once in a way, there were
those among the authorities of the Establishment who
made certain recommendations concerning the mode of
conducting divine worship: simple these in themselves,
and perfectly innocuous, but they looked like the
breath, the shadow of the movement; they seemed an
omen of something more to come; they were the
symptoms of some sort of ecclesiastical favour bestowed
in one quarter on its adherents. The newspapers, the
organs of the political, mammon-loving community,
of those vast multitudes of all ranks who are allowed
by the Anglican Church to do nearly what they will
for six, if not seven days in the week,—who, in spite of
the theological controversies rolling over their heads,
could, if they would, buy, and sell, and manufacture,
and trade at their pleasure,—who might be unconcerned,

and go their own way, for no one would interfere with
them, and might "live and let live,"—the organs, I
say, of these multitudes kindle with indignation, and
menace, and revile, and denounce, because the Bishops
in question suffer their clergy to deliver their sermons,
as well as the prayers, in a surplice. It becomes a
matter of popular interest. There are mobs in the
street, houses are threatened, life is in danger, because
only a gleam of Apostolical principles, in their faintest,
wannest expression, is cast inside a building which is
the home of the national religion. The very moment
that Catholicism ventures out of books, and cloisters,
and studies, towards the national house of prayer, when
it lifts its hand or its very eyebrow towards this people
so tolerant of heresy, at once the dull and earthly mass
is on fire. It would be little or nothing though the
minister baptized without water, though he chucked
away the consecrated wine, though he denounced fasting, though he laughed at virginity, though he inter-
changed pulpits with a Wesleyan or a Baptist, though
he defied his Bishop; he might be blamed, he might
be disliked, he might be remonstrated with; but he
would not touch the feelings of men; he would not
inflame their minds;—but, bring home to them the
very thought of Catholicism, hold up a surplice, and
the religious building is as full of excitement and
tumult as St. Victor's at Milan in the cause of orthodoxy, or St. Giles', Edinburgh, for the Kirk

"The uproar commenced," says a contemporary
account, "with a general coughing down; several persons then moved to the door making a great noise in
their progress; a young woman went off in a fit of
hysterics. uttering loud shrieks, whilst a mob outside
besieged the doors of the building. A cry of 'fire' was
raised, followed by an announcement that the church
doors were closed, and a rush was made to burst them
open. Some cried out, 'Turn him out,' 'Pull it off
him.' In the galleries the uproar was at its height,
whistling, cat-calls, hurrahing, and such cries as
are heard in theatres, echoed throughout the edifice.
The preacher still persisted to read his text, but was
quite inaudible; and the row increased, some of the
congregation waving their hats, standing on the seats,
jumping over them, bawling, roaring, and gesticulat-
ing, like a mob at an election. The reverend gentleman, in the midst of the confusion, despatched a
message to the mayor, requesting his assistance, when
one of the congregation addressed the people, and also
requested the preacher to remove the cause of the ill-
feeling which had been excited. Then another addressed
him in no measured terms, and insisted on his leaving
the pulpit. At length the mayor, the superintendent
of the police, several constables, also the chancellor and
the archdeacon, arrived. The mayor enforced silence,
and, after admonishing the people, requested the clergyman to leave the pulpit for a few minutes, which he

declined to do,—gave out his text, and proceeded with his discourse. The damage done to the interior of the church is said to be very considerable." I believe I am right in supposing that the surplice has vanished from that pulpit from that day forward. Here, at length, certainly are signs of life, but not the life of the Catholic Church.

And now to draw my conclusion from what I have been following out, if I have not sufficiently done so already. If, my brethren, your reason, your faith, your affections, are indissolubly bound up with the holy principles which you have been taught, if you know they are true, if you know their life and their power, if you know that nothing else is true; surely you have no portion or sympathy with systems which reject them. Seek those principles in their true home. If your Church rejects your principles, it rejects you ;— nor dream of indoctrinating it with them by remaining; everything has its own nature, and in that nature is its identity. You cannot change your Establishment into a Church without a miracle. It is what it is, and you have no means of acting upon it; you have not what Archimedes looked for, when he would move the world, —the fulcrum of his lever,—while you are one with it. It acts on you, while you act on it; you cannot employ it against itself. If you would make England Catholic, you must go forth on your mission *from* the Catholic

E

Church. You *have* duties towards the Establishment; it is the duty, not of owning its rule, but of converting its members. Oh, my brethren! life is short, waste it not in vanities; dream not; halt not between two opinions; wake from a dream, in which you are not profiting your neighbour, but imperilling your own souls.

LECTURE III.

*THE LIFE OF THE MOVEMENT OF 1833 NOT DERIVED
FROM THE NATIONAL CHURCH.*

I.

I AM proposing, my brethren, in these Lectures, to
answer several of the objections which are urged
against quitting the National Communion for the
Catholic Church. It has been a very common and
natural idea of those who belong to the movement of
1833, as it was the idea of its originators, that, the
Nation being on its way to give up revealed truth, all
those who wish to receive that truth in its fulness, and
to resist its enemies, are called on to make use of the
National Church, to which they belong, whose formularies they receive, as their instrument for that purpose.
I answer them, that their attempt is hopeless, because
the National Church is strictly part of the Nation, in
the same way that the Law or the Parliament is part
of the Nation; and therefore, as the Nation changes, so
will the National Church change. That Church, then,
cannot be used against the spirit of the age, except as
a drag on a wheel; for nothing can really resist the

Nation, except what stands on a basis independent of
the Nation. It must say and will say just what the
Nation says, though it may be some time in saying it.
Next, having thus shown that the National Church is
absolutely one with the Nation, I proceeded further to
show that, on the other hand, the National Church is
absolutely heterogeneous from the Apostolic or Anglo-
Catholic party of 1833; so that, while the National
Church is part of the Nation, the movement, on the
contrary, has no part or place in the National Church.
To aim, then, at making the Nation Catholic by means
of the Church of England, was something like evan-
gelizing Turkey by means of Islamism; and, as the
Turks would feel serious resentment at hearing the
Gospel in the mouths of their Muftis and Mollahs, so
was, and is, the English Nation provoked, not persuaded, by Catholic preaching in the Establishment.

And I rest the proof of these two statements on
incontrovertible facts going on during the last twenty
years, and now before our eyes; for, first, the National
Church *has* changed and *is* changing with the Nation;
and secondly, the Nation and Church have been indignant, and are indignant, with the movement of
1833. I conceive that, except in imagination and in
hope, there are no symptoms whatever of the National
Church preventing those changes of Progress, as it is
called, whether in the Nation or in itself, though it
may retard them: nor any symptoms whatever of its

welcoming those retrograde changes, to which it is invited under the name of primitive and Apostolical truth. The National Church is the slave of the Nation, and it is the opponent of the Movement; which, after all, has done no more than form a party in the one to the annoyance of the other.

And now I come to a second objection, which shall be my subject to-day. An inquirer, then, may say, "This is a very unfair and one-sided view of the matter. I grant—indeed I cannot deny—that the movement has but formed a party in the National Church. I grant it has no hold on the Church, that it does not coalesce with it, that it hangs loose of it: nay, I grant that this want of congeniality comes out clearer and clearer year by year, so that the Anglican party has never appeared more distinct from the Establishment, and foreign to it, than at this moment, when State and Bishops and people have cast it off, and its efforts, whether to alter the constitution of the Establishment, or to preserve its doctrine, have failed and are failing. I grant all this; I am forced in fairness to grant it;—or rather, whether I grant it or no, it will be taken for granted by all men without waiting for my granting. But still, so far is undeniable, that that movement of 1833 issued forth *from* the National Church; this, at least, is an incontrovertible fact: whatever light, life, or strength it has possessed, or possesses, from the National Church was it derived.

To the Sacraments, to the ordinances, to the teaching of the national Church, the movement owes its being and its continuance; and, if it be its offspring, it belongs to it, it is cognate to it, and cannot be really alien from it; and great sin and undutifulness, ingratitude, presumption, and cruelty, there must be committed by those who, belonging to the movement, abandon the Church." This is a consideration which is urged with great force against affectionate and diffident minds, and acts as an insurmountable difficulty in the way of their becoming Catholics. It is pressed upon them— "The National Church is the Church of your baptism, and therefore to leave it is to abandon your Mother."

Now, then, let us examine what is the real state of the case.

2.

We see then, certainly, a multitude of men all over the country, who, in the course of the last twenty years, have been roused to a religious life by the influence of certain principles professing to be those of the Primitive Church, and put forth by certain of the National Clergy. Every year has added to their number; nor has it been a mere profession of opinion which was their characteristic, or certain exercises of the intellect; not a fashion or taste of the hour, but a rule of life. They have subjected their wills, they have chastened their hearts, they have subdued their affections, they have submitted their reason. Devotions, com-

munions, fastings, privations, almsgiving, pious mu-
nificence, self-denying occupations, have marked the
spread of the principles in question; which have, moreover, been adorned and recommended in those who
adopted them by a consistency, grace, and refinement
of conduct nowhere else to be found in the National
Church. Such are the characteristics of the party in
question; and, moreover, its members themselves expressly attribute their advancement in the religious life
to the use of the ordinances of that National Church.

They have found, they say, as a matter of fact, that
as they attended those ordinances, they became more
strong in obedience and dutifulness, had more power
over their passions, and more love towards God and
man. "If, then," they may urge, "you confront us
with those external facts, which have formed the subjects of your first and second Lectures, here are our
internal facts to meet them; our own experience,
serious, sober, practical, outweighs a hundredfold representations which may be logical, dazzling, irrefragable;
but which still, as we ourselves know better than any
one, whatever be the real explanation of them, are,
after all, fallacious and untrue."

Here, then, we are brought to the question of the
internal evidence, which is alleged in favour of a real,
however recondite, connection of the (so-called) Anglo-
Catholic party with the National Church. It is said
that, however you are to account for it, there is the

fact of a profound intimate relationship, a spiritual
bond, between the one and the other; that party has
actually risen out of what seems so earthly, so inconsistent, so feeble, and is sustained by it; and, in fact
does but illustrate the great maxim of the Gospel,
that the weak shall be strong, and the despised shall
be glorious.   Taking their stand on this evangelical
promise and principle, the persons of whom I speak
are quite careless of argument, which silences them
without touching them.   "Their opponents may triumph, if they will; but, after all, there certainly
must be some satisfactory explanation of the difficulties
of their own position, if they did but know what it
was. The question is deeper than argument, while it
is very easy to be captious and irreverent. It is not
to be handled by intellect and talent, or decided by
logic. They are undoubtedly in a very anomalous
state of things, a state of transition; but they must
submit for a time to be without a theory of the Church,
without an intellectual basis on which to plant themselves. It would be an utter absurdity for them to leave
the Establishment, merely because they do not at the
moment see how to defend their staying in it.   Such
accidents will from time to time happen in large and
complicated questions; they have light enough to guide
them practically,—first, because even though they
wished to move ever so much, they see no place to
move into; and next, because, however it comes to

pass, however contrary it may seem to be to all the rules of theology and the maxims of polemics, to Apostles, Scripture, Fathers, Saints, common-sense, and the simplest principles of reason,—though it ought not to be so in the way of strict science,—still, so it is, they are, in matter of fact, abundantly blest where they are.

"Certainly it is vexatious that the Privy Council should have decided as it has done; vexatious not to know what to say about the decision; vexatious, inconvenient, perplexing, but nothing more. It is not a real difficulty, but only an annoyance, to be obliged to say something to quiet their people, and not to have a notion what. However, they must do their best; and, though it is true one of their friends uses one argument, another another, and these arguments are inconsistent with one another, still that is an accidental misery of their position, and it will not last for ever. Brighter times are coming; meanwhile they must, with resignation, suffer the shame, scorn of man, and distrust of friends, which is their present portion; a little patience, and the night will be over; their Athanasius will come at length, to defend and to explain the truth, and their present constancy will be their future reward.'

3.

Now, as truth is the object which I set before me in the inquiry which I am prosecuting, I will not follow their example in considering only one side of the question. I will not content myself, on my part, with insisting merely upon the external view of it, which is against them, leaving them in possession of that argument from the inward evidences of grace, on which they especially rely. I have no intention at all of evading their position,—I mean to attack it. I feel intimately what is strong in it, and I feel where it halts; so, to state their argument fairly, I will not extemporize words of my own, but I will express it in the language of a writer, who, when he so spoke, belonged to the Established Church.

"Surely," he says, "as the only true religion is that which is seated within us,—a matter not of words, but of things, so the only satisfactory test of religion is something within us. If religion be a personal matter, its reasons also should be personal. Wherever it is present in the world or in the heart, it produces an effect, and that effect is its evidence. When we view it as set up in the world, it has its external proofs; when as set up in our hearts, it has its internal; and that, whether we are able to elicit them ourselves, and put them into shape, or not. Nay, with some little limitation and explanation, it might be said, that the very fact of a religion taking root within us is a proof so far that it is true. If it were not true, it would not take root. Religious men have, in their own religiousness, an evidence of the truth of their religion. That religion is true which has power, and so far as it has power;

nothing but what is divine can renew the heart. And this is the secret reason *why* religious men believe,—whether they are adequately conscious of it or no,—whether they can put it into words or no—viz., their past experience that the doctrine which they hold is a reality in their minds, not a mere opinion, and has come to them, 'not in word but in power.' And in this sense the presence of religion in us is its own evidence." [1]

Again :—

"If, then, we are asked for 'a reason of the hope that is in us,' why we are content, or rather thankful, to be in that Church in which God's providence has placed us, would not the reasons be some one or other of these, or rather all of them, and a number of others besides, which these may suggest, deeper than they?

"First, I suppose a religious man is conscious that God has been with him, and given him whatever he has of good within him. He knows quite enough of himself to know how fallen he is from original righteousness, and he has a conviction, which nothing can shake, that without the aid of his Lord and Saviour, he can do nothing aright. I do not say he need recollect any definite season when he turned to God, and gave up the service of sin and Satan; but in one sense, every season, every year, is such a time of turning. I mean, he ever has experience, just as if he had hitherto been living in the world, of a continual conversion; he is

---

[1] The author's Sermons on Subjects of the Day, pp. 345, 346.

ever taking advantage of holy seasons, and new provi-
dences, and beginning again. The elements of sin are
still alive within him; they still tempt and influence
him, and threaten when they do no more ; and it is
only by a continual fight against them that he prevails;
and what shall persuade him that his power to fight is
his own, and not from above ? And this conviction of
a divine presence with him is stronger, according to the
length of time during which he has served God, and to
his advance in holiness. The multitude of men, nay,
a great number of those who think themselves religious, do not aim at holiness, and do not advance in
holiness ; but consider, what a great evidence it is that
God is with us, so far as we have it! Religious men,
really such, cannot but recollect in the course of years
that they have become very different from what they
were. . . . In the course of years a religious person
finds that a mysterious unseen influence has been
upon and changed him. He is indeed very different
from what he was. His tastes, his views, his judgments are different. You will say that time changes
a man as a matter of course ; advancing age, outward
circumstances, trials, experience of life. It is true;
and yet I think a religious man would feel it little less
than sacrilege, and almost blasphemy, to impute the
improvement of his heart and conduct, in his moral
being, with which he has been favoured in a certain
sufficient period, to outward or merely natural causes.

He will be unable to force himself to do so—that is to say, he has a conviction, which it is a point of religion with him not to doubt, which it is a sin to deny, that God has been with him. And this is, of course, a ground of hope to him that God will be with him still; and if he, at any time, fall into religious perplexity, it may serve to comfort him to think of it."[1]

And again:—

"I might go on to mention a still more solemn subject, viz., the experience, which, at least, certain religious persons have of the awful sacredness of our sacraments and other ordinances. If these are attended by the presence of Christ, surely we have all that a Church can have in the way of privilege and blessing. The promise runs, 'Lo, I am with you always, even unto the end of the world.' That is a Church where Christ is present; this is the very definition of the Church. The question sometimes asked is, Whether our services, our holy seasons, our rites, our sacraments, our institutions, really have with them the presence of Him who thus promised? If so, we are part of the Church; if not, then we are but performers in a sort of scene or pageant, which may be religiously intended, and which God in His mercy may visit; but if He visits, will in visiting go beyond His own promise. But observe, as if to answer to the challenge, and put herself on trial, and to give us a test of her Catholicity, our Church

---

[1] Ibid., pp. 348-350.

boldly declares of her most solemn ordinance, that he who profanes it incurs the danger of judgment. She seems, like Moses, or the Prophet from Judah, or Elijah, to put her claim to issue, not so openly, yet as really, upon the fulfilment of a certain specified sign. Now she does not speak to scare away the timid, but to startle and subdue the unbelieving, and withal to assure the wavering and perplexed; and I conceive that in such measure as God wills, and as is known to God, these effects follow. I mean, that we really have proofs among us, though, for the most part, they will be private and personal, from the nature of the case, of clear punishment coming upon profanations of the holy ordinance in question; sometimes very fearful instances, and such as serve, while they awe beholders, to comfort them;—to comfort them, for it is plain, if God be with us for judgment, surely He is with us for mercy also; if He punishes, why is it but for profanation? And how can there be profanation if there is nothing to be profaned? Surely He does not manifest His wrath except where He has first vouchsafed His grace?"[1]

I might quote much more to the same purpose; if I do not, it is not that I fear the force of the argument. but the length to which it runs.

4.

Now in this preference of internal evidences to those

[1] Ibid., pp. 353-355.

which are simply outward, there is a great principle of truth; it requires much guarding, indeed, and explaining, but I suppose, in matter of fact, that the notes of the Church, as they are called, *are* chiefly intended, as this writer says, as guides and directions into the truth, for those who are as yet external to it, and that those who are within it have *primâ facie* evidences of another and more personal kind. I grant it, and I make use of my admission; for one inward evidence at least Catholics have, which this writer had not,—certainty. I do not say, of course, that what seems like certainty is a sufficient evidence to an individual that he has found the truth, for he may mistake obstinacy or blindness for certainty; but, at any rate, the *absence* of certainty is a clear proof that a person has *not* yet found it, and at least a Catholic knows well, even if he cannot urge it in argument, that the Church is able to communicate to him that gift. No one can read the series of arguments from which I have quoted, without being struck by the author's clear avowal of *doubt,* in spite of his own reasonings, on the serious subject which is engaging his attention. He longed to have faith in the National Church, and he could not. "What *want we,*" he exclaims, "*but* faith in our Church? With faith we can do everything; without faith we can do nothing." [1] So all these inward notes which he enumerates, whatever their *primâ facie* force,

[1] Ibid., p. 380.

did not reach so far as to implant conviction even in his own breast; they did not, after all, prove to him that connection between the National Church and the spiritual gifts which he recognised in his party, which he fain would have established, and which they would fain establish to whom I am now addressing myself.

But to come to the gifts themselves. You tell me, my brethren, that you have the clear evidence of the influences of grace in your hearts, by its effects sensible at the moment or permanent in the event. You tell me, that you have been converted from sin to holiness, or that you have received great support and comfort under trial, or that you have been carried over very special temptations, though you have not submitted yourselves to the Catholic Church. More than this, you tell me of the peace, and joy, and strength which you have experienced in your own ordinances. You tell me, that when you began to go weekly to communion you found yourselves wonderfully advanced in purity. You tell me that you went to confession, and you never will believe that the hand of God was not over you at the moment when you received absolution. You were ordained, and a fragrance breathed around you; you hung over the dead, and you all but saw the happy spirit of the departed. This is what you say, and the like of this; and I am not the person, my dear brethren, to quarrel with the truth of what you say. I am not the person to be jealous of such facts, nor to wish you to contradict your own memory and your own nature, nor am I so ungrateful to God's former mercies to myself, to have the heart to deny them in you. As to miracles, indeed, if such you mean, that of course is a matter which might lead to dispute; but if you merely mean to say that the supernatural grace of God, as shown either at the time or by consequent fruits, has overshadowed you at certain times, has been with you when you were taking part in the Anglican ordinances, I have no wish, and a Catholic has no anxiety, to deny it.

Why should I deny to your memory what is so pleasant in mine? Cannot I too look back on many years past, and many events, in which I myself experienced what is now your confidence? Can I forget the happy life I have led all my days, with no cares, no anxieties worth remembering; without desolateness, or fever of thought, or gloom of mind, or doubt of God's love to me and providence over me? Can I forget,—I never can forget,—the day when in my youth I first bound myself to the ministry of God in that old church of St. Frideswide, the patroness of Oxford? nor how I wept most abundant, and most sweet tears, when I thought what I then had become; though I looked on ordination as no sacramental rite, nor even to baptism ascribed any supernatural virtue? Can I wipe out from my memory, or wish to wipe out, those happy Sunday mornings, light or dark, year after year, when

F

I celebrated your communion-rite, in my own church
of St. Mary's; and in the pleasautness and joy of it
heard nothing of the strife of tongues which surrounded
its walls? When, too, shall I not feel the soothing
recollection of those dear years which I spent in retirement, in preparation for my deliverance from Egypt,
asking for light, and by degrees gaining it, with less of
temptation in my heart, and sin on my conscience,
than ever before? O my dear brethren, my Anglican
friends! I easily give you credit for what I have experienced myself. Provided you be in good faith, if
you are not trifling with your conscience, if you are re-
solved to follow whithersoever God shall lead, if the ray
of conviction has not fallen on you, and you have shut
your eyes to it; then, anxious as I am about you for the
future, and dread as I may till you are converted, that
perhaps, when conviction comes, it will come in vain
yet still, looking back at the past years of my own life,
I recognise what you say, and bear witness to its truth.
Yet what has this to do with the matter in hand? I
admit your fact; do you, my brethren, admit, in turn,
my explanation of it. It is the explanation ready provided by the Catholic Church, provided in her general
teaching, quite independently of your particular case, not
made for the occasion, only applied when it has arisen;
—listen to it, and see whether you admit it or not as
true if it be not sufficiently probable, or possible if you

will, to invalidate the argument on which you so confidently rely.

5.

Surely you ought to know the Catholic teaching on the subject of grace, in its bearing on your argument, without my insisting on it :—*Spiritus Domini replevit orbem terrarum.* Grace is given for the merits of Christ all over the earth; there is no corner, even of Paganism, where it is not present, present in each heart of man in real sufficiency for his ultimate salvation. Not that the grace presented to each is such as at once to bring him to heaven; but it is sufficient for a beginning. It is sufficient to enable him to plead for other grace; and that second grace is such as to impetrate a third grace; and thus the soul may be led from grace to grace, and from strength to strength, till at length it is, so to say, in very sight of heaven, if the gift of perseverance does but complete the work. Now here observe, it is not certain that a soul which has the first grace will have the second; for the grant of the second at least depends on its use of the first. Again, it may have the first and second, and yet not the third; from the first on to the nineteenth, and not the twentieth. We mount up by steps towards God, and alas! it is possible that a soul may be courageous and bear up for nineteen steps, and stop and faint at the twentieth. Nay, further than this, it is possible to conceive a soul going forward till it arrives at the very grace of contrition—a contrition so loving, so sin-renouncing, as to bring it at once into a state of reconciliation, and clothe it in the vestment of justice; and yet it may yield to the further trials which beset it, and fall away.

Now all this may take place even outside the Church; and consider what at once follows from it. This follows, in the first place, that men there may be, not Catholics, yet really obeying God and rewarded by Him—nay, I might say (at least by way of argument), in His favour, with their sins forgiven, and in the enjoyment of a secret union with that heavenly kingdom to which they do not visibly belong—who are, through their subsequent failure, never to reach it. There may be those who are increasing in grace and knowledge, and approaching nearer to the Catholic Church every year, who are not in the Church, and never will be. The highest gifts and graces are compatible with ultimate reprobation. As regards, then, the evidence of sanctity in members of the National Establishment, on which you insist, Catholics are not called on to deny them. We think such instances are few, nor so eminent as you are accustomed to fancy; but we do not wish to deny, nor have any difficulty in admitting such facts as you have to adduce, whatever they be. We do not think it necessary to carp at every instance of supernatural excellence among Protestants when it comes before us, or to explain it away; all we know is, that the grace

given them is intended ultimately to bring them into
the Church, and if it is not tending to do so, it will not
ultimately profit them; but we as little deny its presence in their souls as they do themselves; and as the
fact is no perplexity to us, it is no triumph to them.

And, secondly, in like manner, whatever be the comfort or the strength attendant upon the use of the
national ordinances of religion, in the case of this or
that person, a Catholic may admit it without scruple,
for it is no evidence to him in behalf of those ordinances themselves. It is the teaching of the Catholic
Church from time immemorial, and independently of
the present controversy, that grace is given in a
sacred ordinance in two ways, viz.—to use the scholastic distinction, *ex opere operantis*, and *ex opere operato*.
Grace is given *ex opere operato*, when, the proper dispositions being supposed in the recipient, it is given
through the ordinance itself; it is given *ex opere
operantis*, when, whether there be outward sign or no,
the inward energetic act of the recipient is the instrument of it. Thus Protestants say that justification, for
instance, is gained by faith as by an instrument—*ex
opere operantis;* thus Catholics also commonly believe
that the benefit arising from the use of holy water
accrues, not *ex opere operato*, or by means of the
element itself, but, *ex opere operantis*, through the
devout mental act of the person using it, and the prayers
of the Church. So again, the Sacrifice of the Mass

benefits the person for whom it is offered *ex opere operato*, whatever be the character of the celebrating priest; but it benefits him more or less, *ex opere operantis*, according to the degree of sanctity which the priest has attained, and the earnestness with which he offers it. Again, baptism, whether administered by man or woman, saint or sinner, heretic or Catholic, regenerates an infant *ex opere operato;* on the other hand, in the case of the baptism of blood, as it was anciently called (that is, the martyrdom of unbaptized persons desiring the sacrament, but unable to obtain it), a discussion has arisen, whether the martyr was justified *ex opere operato* or *ex opere operantis*—that is, whether by the physical act of his dying for the faith, considered in itself, or by the mental act of supreme devotion to God, which caused and attended it. So again, contrition of a certain kind is sufficient as a disposition or condition, or what is called matter, for receiving absolution in Penance *ex opere operato* or by virtue of the sacrament; but it may be heightened and purified into so intense an act of divine love of hatred and sorrow for sin, and of renunciation of it, as to cleanse and justify the soul, without the sacrament at all, or *ex opere operantis*. It is plain from this distinction, that, if we would determine whether the Anglican ordinances are attended by divine grace, we must first determine whether the effects which accompany them arise *ex opere operantis* or *ex opere operato*—whether out of the religious acts, the prayers, aspirations, resolves of the recipient, or by the direct power of the ceremonial act itself,—a nice and difficult question, not to be decided by means of those effects themselves, whatever they be.

Let me grant to you, then, that the reception of your ordinances brings peace and joy to the soul; that it permanently influences or changes the character of the recipient. Let me grant, on the other hand, that their profanation, when men have been taught to believe in them, and in profaning are guilty of contempt of that God to whom they ascribe them, is attended by judgments; this properly shows nothing more than that, by a general law, lying, deceit, presumption, or hypocrisy are punished, and prayer, faith, contrition rewarded. There is nothing to show that the effects would not have been precisely the same on condition of the same inward dispositions, though another ordinance, a love-feast or a washing of the feet, with no pretence to the name of a Sacrament, had been in good faith adopted. And it is obvious to any one that, for a member of the Establishment to bring himself to confession, especially some years back, required dispositions of a very special character, a special contrition and a special desire of the Sacrament, which, as far as we may judge by outward signs, were a special effect of grace, and would fittingly receive from God's bounty a special reward, some further and higher grace, and

even, at least I am not bound to deny it, remission of
sins. And again, when a member of the Establishment, surrounded by those who scoffed at the doctrine,
accepted God's word that He would make Bread His
Body, and honoured Him by the fact that he accepted
it, is it wonderful, is it not suitable to God's mercy, if
He rewards such a special faith with a *quasi* sacramental
grace, though the worshipper unintentionally offered to
a material substance that adoration which he intended
to pay to the present, but invisible, Lamb of God?

6.

But this is not all, my dear brethren; I must allow to
others what I allow to you. If I let you plead the
sensible effects of supernatural grace, as exemplified in
yourselves, in proof that your religion is true, I must
allow the plea to others to whom by your theory you
are bound to deny it. Are you willing to place yourselves on the same footing with Wesleyans? yet what
is the difference? or rather, have they not more remarkable phenomena in their history, symptomatic of
the presence of grace among them, than you can show
in yours? Which, then, is the right explanation of
your feelings and your experience,—mine, which I
have extracted from received Catholic teaching; or
yours, which is an expedient for the occasion, and cannot be made to tell for your own Apostolical authority
without telling for those who are rebels against it?

Survey the rise of Methodism, and say candidly, whether those who made light of your ordinances abandoned them, or at least disbelieved their virtue, have not had among them evidences of that very same grace which you claim for yourselves, and which you consider a proof of your acceptance with God. Really I am obliged in candour to allow, whatever part the evil spirit had in the work, whatever gross admixture of earth polluted it, whatever extravagance there was to excite ridicule or disgust, whether it was Christian virtue or the excellence of unaided man, whatever was the spiritual state of the subjects of it, whatever their end and their final account, yet there were higher and nobler vestiges or semblances of grace and truth in Methodism than there have been among you. I give you credit for what you are, grave, serious, earnest, modest, steady, self-denying, consistent; you have the praise of such virtues; and you have a clear perception of many of the truths, or of portions of the truths, of Revelation. In these points you surpass the Wesleyans; but if I wished to find what was striking, extraordinary, suggestive of Catholic heroism—of St. Martin, St. Francis, or St. Ignatius—I should betake myself far sooner to them than to you. "In our own times," says a writer in a popular Review, speaking of the last-mentioned Saint and his companions, "in our own times much indignation and much alarm are thrown away on innovators of a very different stamp. From the ascetics

of the common room, from men whose courage rises
high enough only to hint at their unpopular opinions,
and whose belligerent passions soar at nothing more
daring than to worry some unfortunate professor, it is
almost ludicrous to fear any great movement on the
theatre of human affairs. When we see these dainty
gentlemen in rags, and hear of them from the snows of
the Himalaya, we may begin to tremble." Now such
a diversion from the course of his remarks upon St.
Ignatius and his companions, I must say, was most
uncalled for in this writer,[1] and not a little ill-natured;
for we had never pretended to be heroes at all, and
should have been the first to laugh at any one who
fancied us such; but they will serve to suggest the
fact, which is undeniable, that even when Anglicans
approach in doctrine nearest to the Catholic Church,
still heroism is not the line of their excellence. The
Established Church may have preserved in the country
the idea of sacramental grace, and the movement of
1833 may have spread it; but if you wish to find the
shadow and the suggestion of the supernatural qualities
which make up the notion of a Catholic Saint, to Wesley you must go, and such as him. Personally I do not
like him, if it were merely for his deep self-reliance and
self-conceit; still I am bound, in justice to him, to ask,
and you in consistency to answer, what historical per-
sonage in the Establishment, during its whole three

[1] Sir James Stephen.

centuries, has approximated in force and splendour of
conduct and achievements to one who began by innov-
ating on your rules, and ended by contemning your
authorities ? He and his companions, starting amid
ridicule at Oxford, with fasting and praying in the cold
night air, then going about preaching, reviled by the
rich and educated, and pelted and dragged to prison by
the populace, and converting their thousands from sin
to God's service—were it not for their pride and eccen-
tricity, their fanatical doctrine and untranquil devotion,
they would startle us, as if the times of St. Vincent
Ferrer or St. Francis Xavier were come again in a
Protestant land.

Or, to turn to other communions, whom have you with
those capabilities of greatness in them, which show
themselves in the benevolent zeal of Howard the phil-
anthropist, or Elizabeth Fry ? Or consider the almost
miraculous conversion and subsequent life of Colonel
Gardiner. Why, even old Bunyan, with his vivid
dreams when a child, his conversion, his conflicts with
Satan, his preachings and imprisonments, however inferior to you in discipline of mind and knowledge of
the truth, is, in the outline of his history, more Apostolical than you. "Weep not for me," were his last
words, as if he had been a Saint, "but for yourselves.
I go to the Father of our Lord Jesus Christ, who doubtless, through the mediation of His Son, will receive
me, though a sinner, when we shall erelong meet, to

sing the new song and be happy for ever!" Consider
the deathbeds of the thousands of those, in and out of
the Establishment, who, with scarcely one ecclesiastical
sentiment in common with you, die in confidence of
the truth of their doctrine, and of their personal safety.
Does the peace of their deaths testify to the divinity of
their creed or of their communion? Does the extreme
earnestness and reality of religious feeling, exhibited
in the sudden seizure and death of one who was as
stern in his hatred of your opinions as admirable in
his earnestness, who one evening protested against the
sacramental principle, and next morning died nobly
with the words of Holy Scripture in his mouth—does
it give any sanction to that hatred and that protest?[1]
And there is another, a Calvinist, one of whose special
and continual prayers in his last illness was for perseverance in grace, who cried, "O Lord, abhor me not, though
I be abhorrible, and abhor myself!" and who, five
minutes before his death, by the expression of his
countenance, changing from prayer to admiration and
calm peace, impressed upon the bystanders that the veil
had been removed from his eyes, and that, like Stephen,
he saw things invisible to sense;—did he, by the circumstances of his death-bed, bear evidence to the truth
of what you, as well as I, hold to be an odious heresy?[2]
"Mr. Harvey resigned his meek soul into the hands of
his Redeemer, saying, 'Lord, now lettest Thou Thy ser-

[1] Dr Arnold.   [2] Mr Scott of Ashton Sandford.

vant depart in peace.'" "Mr. Walker, before he expired, spoke nearly these words: 'I have been on the wings of the cherubim; heaven has in a manner been opened to me; I shall be there soon.'" "Mr. Whitfield rose at four o'clock on the Sabbath day, went to his closet, and was unusually long in private; laid himself on his bed for about ten minutes, then went on his knees and prayed most fervently he might that day finish his Master's work." Then he sent for a clergyman, "and before he could reach him, closed his eyes on this world without a sigh or groan, and commenced a Sabbath of everlasting rest."[1] Alas! there was another, who for three months " lingered," as he said, " in the face of death." " O my God," he cried, " I know Thou dost not overlook any of Thy creatures. Thou dost not overlook me. So much torture . . . . to kill a worm ! have mercy on me! I cry to Thee, knowing I cannot alter Thy ways. I cannot if I would, and I would not if I could. If a word would remove these sufferings, I would not utter it." " Just life enough to suffer," he continued; "but I submit, and not only submit, but rejoice." One morning he woke up, "and with firm voice and great sobriety of manner, spoke only these words: 'Now I die!' He sat as one in the attitude of expectation; and about two hours afterwards, it was as he had said." And he was a professed infidel, and worse than an infidel—an apostate priest!

[1] Sidney's Life of Hill.

7.

No, my dear brethren, these things are beyond us. Nature can do so much, and go so far; can form such rational notions of God and of duty, without grace, or merit, or a future hope; good sense has such an instinctive apprehension of what is fitting; intellect, imagination, and feeling can so take up, develop, and illuminate what nature has originated; education and intercourse with others can so insinuate into the mind what really does not belong to it; grace, not effectual, but inchoate, can so plead, and its pleadings look so like its fruits; and its mere visitations may so easily be mistaken for its in-dwelling presence, and its vestiges, when it has departed, may gleam so beautifully on the dead soul, that it is quite impossible for us to conclude, with any fairness of argument, that a certain opinion is true, or a religious position safe, simply on account of the confidence or apparent excellence of those who adopt it. Of course, we think as tenderly of them as we can; and may fairly hope that what we see is, in particular instances, the work of grace, wrought in those who are not responsible for their ignorance; but the claim in their behalf is unreasonable and exorbitant, if it is to the effect that their state of mind is to be taken in evidence, not only of promise in the individual, but of truth in his creed.

And should this view of the subject unsettle and

depress you, as if it left you no means at all of ascertaining whether God loves you, or whether anything is true, or anything to be trusted, then let this feeling answer the purpose for which I have impressed it on you. I wish to deprive you of your undue confidence in self; I wish to dislodge you from that centre in which you sit so self-possessed and self-satisfied. Your fault has been to be satisfied with but a half evidence of your safety; you have been too well contented with remaining where you found yourselves, not to catch at a line of argument, so indulgent, yet so plausible. You have thought that position impregnable; and growing confident, as time went on, you have not only said it was a sin to ascribe your good thoughts, and purposes, and aspirations to any but God (which you were right in saying), but you have presumed to pronounce it blasphemy against the Holy Ghost to doubt that they came into your hearts by means of your Church and by virtue of its ordinances. Learn, my dear brethren, a more sober, a more cautious tone of thought. Learn to fear for your souls. It is something, indeed, to be peaceful within, but it is not everything. It may be the stillness of death. The Catholic, and he alone, has within him that union of external with internal notes of God's favour, which sheds the light of conviction over his soul, and makes him both fearless in his faith and calm and thankful in his hope.

LECTURE IV.

I.

IT is scarcely possible to fancy that an event so distinctive in its character as the rise of the so-called
Anglo-Catholic party in the course of the last twenty
years, should have no scope in the designs of Divine
Providence. From beginnings so small, from elements
of thought so fortuitous, with prospects so unpromising,
that in its germ it was looked upon with contempt, if
it was ever thought of at all, it suddenly became a
power in the National Church, and an object of alarm
to her rulers and friends. Its originators would have
found it difficult to say what they aimed at of a practical kind; rather they put forth views and principles
for their own sake, because they were true, as if they
were obliged to say them; and though their object
certainly was to strengthen the Establishment, yet it
would have been very difficult for them to state precisely
the intermediate process, or definite application, by

which, in matter of fact, their preaching was to arrive at that result. And, as they might be themselves surprised at their earnestness in proclaiming, they had as great cause to be surprised at their success in propagating, the doctrines which have characterised their school. And, in fact, they had nothing else to say but that those doctrines were in the air; that to assert was to prove, and that to explain was to persuade; and that the movement in which they were taking part, was the birth of a crisis rather than of a place. I do not mean to say, that they did not use arguments on the one hand, nor attempt to associate themselves with things as they were on the other; but that, after all, their doctrine went forth rather than was delivered, and spoke rather than was spoken; that it was a message rather than an argument; that it was the master, not the creature of its proclaimers, and seemed to be said at random, because uttered with so indistinct an aim; and so, with no advantage except that of position, which of course is not to be undervalued, it spread and was taken up no one knew how. In a very few years a school of opinion was formed, fixed in its principles, indefinite and progressive in their range; and it extended into every part of the country. If, turning from the contemplation of it from within, we inquire what the world thought of it, we have still more to raise our wonder; for, not to mention the excitement it caused in England, the movement and its party-

G

names were known to the police of Italy and the back-
woodsmen of America. So it proceeded, getting stronger
and stronger every year, till it has come into collision
with the Nation, and that Church of the Nation, which
it began by professing especially to serve ; and now its
upholders and disciples have to look about, and ask
themselves where they are, and which way they are to
go, and whither they are bound.

Providence does nothing in vain; so much earnestness, zeal, toil, thought, religiousness, success, as has
a place in the history of that movement, must surely
have a place also in His scheme, and in His dealings
towards His Church in this country, if we could discern
what that place was. He has excited aspirations,
matured good thoughts, and prospered pious undertakings arising out of them : not for nothing surely
—then for what ? Wherefore ?

The movement certainly is one and the same to all
who have been influenced by it; the principles and
circumstances, which have made them what they are,
are one and the same ; the history of one of you, my
brethren, is pretty much the history of another—the
history of all. Is it meant that you should each of
you end in his own way, if your beginnings have been
the same ? The duty of one of you, is it not the duty
of another ? Are you not to act together ? In other
words, may I not look at the movement as integrally
one, and thus investigate what is its bearing and its

legitimate issue? and may not, in consequence, that
direction and scope of the movement, if such can be
ascertained, be taken as a suggestion to you how you
should act, distinct from, and in addition to, the intimations of God's will, which come home to you personally and individually? The movement has affected
us in a certain way: at one time we have felt urged
perhaps, with some of those who took part in it, to go
forward; at another, to remain where we are; then to
retire into lay-communion, if we were in the Established
ministry; then to collapse into a sect external to its
pale. We have tried to have faith in the sacraments
of the National Church; for a time we have succeeded,
and then we have failed; we have felt ourselves drawn,
we have felt ourselves repelled by the Catholic Church;
—we have felt difficulties in her faith, counter-diffi-
culties in rejecting it, complications of difficulty on difficulty, concurrent or antagonist, till we could ascertain
neither their mutual relation nor their combined issue,
and could neither change nor remain where we were
without scruple.

Under such a trial it would be some guidance, a
sort of token or note of the course destined for us by
Providence, if the movement itself, whose principles
we have drunk in, with which we are so intimately one,
had, from the nature of the case, its own natural and
necessary termination. Before now, when a Protestant,
I have said more or less to others who were in anxiety,

"Watch the movement; it is made up of individuals, but it has an objective being, proceeds on principles, is governed by laws, and is swayed and directed by external facts. We are apt to be attracted or driven this way or that; each thinks for himself and judges differently from others; each fears to decide; but may we not ascertain and follow the legitimate and divinely intended course of that, whose children we are?" A great Saint was accustomed to command his sons, when they had to determine some point relatively to themselves and their Society, to throw themselves in imagination out of themselves, and to look at the question externally, as if it were not personal to them, and they were deciding for a stranger. In like manner it has been sometimes recommended in the solution of public questions, to look at them as they will show in history, and as they will be judged of by posterity. Now in some such way should I wish, at this moment, to regard the movement of 1833, and to discover what is its proper, suitable, legitimate termination. This, then, is the question I shall consider in the present Lecture;—here is a great existing fact before our eyes—the movement and its party. What is to become of it? What ought to become of it? Is it to melt away as if it had not been? Is it merely to subserve the purposes of Liberalism, in breaking up establishments by weakening them, and in making dogma ridiculous by multiplying sects? or is it of too positive a character, both in its principles and its members, to anticipate for it so disappointing an issue.

2.

I say, it has been definite in its principles, though vague in their application and their scope. It has been formed on one idea, which has developed into a body of teaching, logical in the arrangement of its portions, and consistent with the principles on which it originally started. That idea, or first principle, was ecclesiastical liberty; the doctrine which it especially opposed was in ecclesiastical language, the heresy of Erastus, and in political, the Royal Supremacy. The object of its attack was the Establishment, considered simply as such.

When I thus represent the idea of the movement of which I am speaking, I must not be supposed to overlook or deny to it its theological, or its ritual, or its practical aspect; but I am speaking of what may be called its *form.* If I said that the one doctrine of Luther was justification by faith only, or of Wesley the doctrine of the new birth, I should not be denying that those divines respectively taught many other doctrines but merely should mean that the one doctrine or the other gave a shape and character to its teaching. In like manner, the writers of the Apostolical party of 1833 were earnest and copious in their enforcement of the high doctrines of the faith, of dogmatism, of the sacramental principle, of the sacraments (as far as the

Anglican Prayer Book admitted them), of ceremonial
observances, of practical duties, and of the counsels of
perfection; but, considering all those great articles of
teaching to be protected and guaranteed by the independence of the Church, and in that way alone, they
viewed sanctity, and sacramental grace, and dogmatic
fidelity, merely as subordinate to the mystical body of
Christ, and made them minister to her sovereignty,
that she might in turn protect them in their prerogatives. Dogma would be maintained, sacraments
would be administered, religious perfection would be
venerated and attempted, if the Church were supreme
in her spiritual power; dogma would be sacrificed to
expedience, sacraments would be rationalized, perfection would be ridiculed if she was made the slave of
the State. Erastianism, then, was the one heresy which
practically cut at the root of all revealed truth; the
man who held it would soon fraternise with Unitarians,
mistake the bustle of life for religious obedience, and
pronounce his butler to be as able to give communion
as his priest. It destroyed the supernatural altogether, by making most emphatically Christ's kingdom a
kingdom of the world. Such was the teaching of the
movement of 1833. The whole system of revealed
truth was, according to it, to be carried out upon the
anti-Erastian or Apostolical basis. The independence
of the Church is almost the one subject of three out of
four volumes of Mr. Froude's Remains; it is, in one

shape or other, the prevailing subject of the early numbers of the "Tracts for the Times," as well as of other
publications which might be named. It was for this
that the writers of whom I speak had recourse to Antiquity, insisted upon the Apostolical Succession, exalted
the Episcopate, and appealed to the people, not only because these things were true and right, but in order to
shake off the State; they introduced them, in the first
instance, as means towards the inculcation of the idea of
the Church, as constituent portions of that great idea,
which, when it once should be received, was a match
for the world.

"Our one tangible object," it was said, in a passage
too long to be extracted at length, "is to restore the
connection, at present broken, between Bishops and
people; for in this everything is involved, directly or
indirectly, for which it is a duty to contend. . . . . We
wish to maintain the faith, and bind men together in
love. We are aiming, with this view, at that commanding moral influence which attended the early Church,
which made it attractive and persuasive, which manifested itself in a fascination sufficient to elicit out of
Paganism and draw into itself all that was noblest and
best from the mass of mankind, and which created an
internal system of such grace, beauty, and majesty, that
believers were moulded thereby into martyrs and
evangelists. . . . . If master-minds are ever granted to
us, they must be persevering in insisting on the Epis-

copal system, the Apostolical Succession, the ministerial
commission, the power of the keys, the duty and desir-
ableness of Church discipline, the sacredness of Church
rites and ordinances. But, you will say, how is all this
to be made interesting to the people? I answer, that
the topics themselves which they are to preach are of
that attractive nature, which carries with it its own
influence. The very notion that representatives of the
Apostles are now on earth, from whose communion
we may obtain grace, as the first Christians did from
the Apostles, is surely, when admitted, of a most trans-
porting and persuasive character. Clergymen are at
present subject to the painful experience of losing the
more religious portion of their flocks, whom they have
tutored and moulded as children, but who, as they come
into life, fall away to the Dissenters. Why is this?
They desire to be stricter than the mass of Churchmen,
and the Church gives them no means; they desire to
be governed by sanctions more constraining than those
of mere argument, and the Church keeps back those
doctrines, which, to the eye of faith, give reality and
substance to religion. One who is told that the Church
is the treasure-house of spiritual gifts, comes for a
definite privilege. . . . . Men know not of the legitimate priesthood, and, therefore, are condemned to hang
upon the judgment of individuals and self-authorised
preachers; they put up with legends of private
Christians, in the place of the men of God, the meek

martyrs, the saintly pastors, the wise and winning teachers of the Catholic Church." [1]

3.

Passages such as this, which is but a portion of a whole, show to me, my brethren, clearly enough, that these men understood the nature of the Church far better than they understood the nature of the religious communion which they sought to defend. They saw in that religion, indeed, a contrariety to their Apostolic principles, but they seem to have fancied that such contrariety was an accident in its constitution, and was capable of a cure. They did not understand that the Established Religion [2] was set up in Erastianism, that Erastianism was its essence, and that to destroy Erastianism was to destroy the religion. The movement, then, and the Establishment, were in simple antagonism from the first, although neither party knew it; they were logical contradictories; they could not be true together; what was the life of the one was the death of the other. The sole ambition of the Establishment was to be the creature of Statesmen; the sole aspiration of the movement was to force it to act for itself. The movement went forth on the face of the country; it read, it preached, it published; it addressed

[1] British Magazine, April 1836—[Discussions and Arguments, pp. 34-38.]
[2] We must not forget, however, Mr. Froude's upas-tree.

itself to logic and to poetry; it was antiquary and
architect; only to do for the Establishment what the
Establishment considered the most intolerable of dis-
services. Every breath, every sigh, every aspiration,
every effort of the movement was an affront or an
offence to the Establishment. In its very first tract, it
could wish nothing better for the Bishops of the Establishment than martyrdom; and, as the very easiest
escape, it augured for them the loss of their temporal
possessions. It was easy to foresee what response the
Establishment would make to its officious defenders, as
soon as it could recover from its surprise; but experience was necessary to teach this to men who knew
more of St. Athanasius than of the Privy Council or
the Court of Arches.

"Why should any man in Britain," asks a Tract,
"fear or hesitate boldly to assert the authority of the
Bishops and pastors of the Church on grounds strictly
evangelical and spiritual?" "Reverend Sir," answered
the Primate to a protest against a Bishop-elect, accused
of heresy, "it is not within the bounds of any authority
possessed by me to give you an opportunity of proving
your objections; finding, therefore, nothing in which
I could act in compliance with your remonstrance, I
proceeded, in the execution of my office, to obey Her
Majesty's mandate for Dr. Hampden's consecration in
the usual form."

"Are we contented," asks another Tract, "to be

accounted the mere creation of the State, as school-masters and teachers may be, as soldiers, or magistrates, or other public officers? Did the State make us? Can it unmake us? Can it send out missionaries? Can it arrange dioceses?" "William the Fourth," answers the first magistrate of the State, "by the grace of God, of the united kingdom of Great Britain, and Ireland, King, Defender of the Faith, to all to whom these presents shall come, greeting: We, having great con-fidence in the learning, morals, and probity of our well-beloved and venerable William Grant Broughton, do name and appoint him to be Bishop and ordinary pastor of the see of Australia, so that he shall be, and shall be taken to be, Bishop of the Bishop's see, and may, by virtue of this our nomination and appoint-ment, enter into and possess the said Bishop's see as the Bishop thereof, without any let or impediment of us; and we do hereby declare, that if we, our heirs and successors, shall think fit to recall or revoke the appoint-ment of the said Bishop of Australia, or his successors, that every such Bishop shall, to all intents and purposes, cease to be Bishop of Australia."

"Confirmation is an ordinance," says the Tract, "in which the Bishop witnesses for Christ. Our Lord and Saviour confirms us with the spirit of all goodness; the Bishop is His figure and likeness when he lays his hands on the heads of children. Then Christ comes to them, to confirm in them the grace of baptism.'

"And we do hereby give and grant to the said Bishop of Australia," proceeds His Majesty, "and his successors, Bishops of Australia, full power and authority to confirm those that are baptized and come to years of discretion, and to perform all other functions peculiar and appropriate to the office of Bishop within the limits of the said see of Australia."

"Moreover," says the Tract, "the Bishop rules the Church here below, as Christ rules it above; and is commissioned to make us clergymen God's ministers. He is Christ's instrument." "And we do by these presents give and grant to the said Bishop and his successors, Bishops of Australia, full power and authority to admit into the holy orders of deacon and priest respectively, any person whom he shall deem duly qualified, and to punish and correct chaplains, ministers, priests, and deacons, according to their demerits."

"The Bishop speaks in me," says the Tract, " as Christ wrought in him, and as God sent Christ; thus the whole plan of salvation hangs together;—Christ the true Mediator; His servant the Bishop His earthly likeness; mankind the subjects of His teaching; God the author of salvation." And the Queen answers, "We do hereby signify to the Most Reverend Father in God, William, Lord Archbishop of Canterbury, our nomination of the said Augustus, requiring, and, by the faith and love whereby he is bound unto us, com-

manding the said Most Reverend Father in God, to
ordain and consecrate the said Augustus." And the
consecrated prelate echoes from across the ocean,
"Augustus, by the grace of God and the favour of
Queen Victoria, Bishop."

"You will, in time to come," says the Tract,
"honour us with a purer honour than men do now, as
those who are intrusted with the keys of heaven and
hell, as the heralds of mercy, as the denouncers of
woe to wicked men, as intrusted with the awful and
mysterious privilege of dispensing Christ's Body and
Blood." And a first Episcopal Charge replies in the
words of the Homily, "Let us diligently search the
well of life, and not run after the stinking puddles of
tradition, devised by man's imagination." A second,
"It is a subject of deep concern that any of our body
should prepare men of ardent feelings and warm
imaginations for a return to the Roman Mass-book.'
And a third, "Already are the foundations of apostasy
laid; if we once admit another Gospel, Antichrist is at
the door. I am full of fear; everything is at stake;
there seems to be something judicial in the rapid
spread of these opinions." And a fourth, "It is impossible not to remark upon the subtle wile of the
Adversary; it has been signally and unexpectedly
exemplified in the present day by the revival of errors
which might have been supposed buried for ever."
And a fifth, "Under the spurious pretence of deference

to antiquity and respect for primitive models, the
foundations of our Protestant Church are undermined
by men who dwell within her walls, and those who sit
in the Reformer's seat are traducing the Reformation."
"Our glory is in jeopardy," says a sixth. "Why all
this tenderness for the very centre and core of cor-
ruption?" asks a seventh. "Among other marvels of
the present day," says an eighth, "may be accounted
the irreverent and unbecoming language applied to the
chief promoters of the Reformation in this land. The
quick and extensive propagation of opinions, tending
to exalt the claims of the Church and of the Clergy,
can be no proof of their soundness." "Reunion with
Rome has been rendered impossible," says a ninth,
"yet I am not without hope that more cordial union
may, in time, be effected among all Protestant Churches."
"Most of the Bishops," says a tenth, "have spoken in
terms of disapproval of the 'Tracts for the Times,
and I certainly believe the system to be most perni
cious, and one which is calculated to produce the most
lamentable schism in a Church already fearfully dis-
united."

"Up to this moment," says an eleventh, "the movement is advancing under just the same pacific professions, and the same imputations are still cast upon all
who in any way impede its progress. Even the English
Bishops, who have officially expressed any disappro-
bation of the principles or proceedings of the party,

have not escaped such animadversions." "Tractarian-
ism is the masterpiece of Satan," says a twelfth.

4.

But there was a judgment more cruel still, because it
practically told in their favour; but it was the infeli-
city of the agents in the movement, that, the National
Church feeling both in its rulers and its people as
it did, their teaching could not escape animadversion
except at the expense of their principles. "A Bishop's
lightest word, *ex Cathedrâ*, is heavy," said a writer
of the "Tracts for the Times." "His judgment on
a book cannot be light; it is a rare occurrence." And
an Archbishop answered from the other side of St.
George's Channel, "Many persons look with considerable interest to the declarations on such matters that
from time to time are put forth by Bishops in their
Charges, or on other occasions. But on most of the
points to which I have been alluding, a Bishop's
declarations have no more weight, except what they
derive from his personal character, than any anonymous
pamphlet would have. The points are mostly such as
he has no official power to decide, even in reference to
his own diocese; and as to legislation for the Church,
or authoritative declarations on many of the most important matters, neither any one Bishop, nor all collec-
tively, have any more right of this kind, than the

ordinary magistrates have to take on themselves the functions of Parliament."

However, it is hardly necessary to prolong the exhibition of the controversy, or to recall to your recollection the tone of invective in which each party relieved the keen and vehement feelings which its opponents excited;—how the originators of the movement called Jewell "an irreverent Dissenter;" were even "thinking worse and worse of the Reformers;" "hated the Reformation and the Reformers more and more;" thought them the false prophets of the Apocalypse; described the National Church as having "blasphemed Tradition and the Sacraments;" were "more and more indignant at the Protestant doctrine of the Eucharist;" thought the principle on which it was founded "as proud, irreverent, and foolish, as that of any heresy, even Socinianism;" and considered the Establishment their "upas-tree," "an incubus on the country;" and its reformed condition, "a limb badly set, which must be broken before it could be righted." And how they were called in turn, "superstitious," "zealots," "mystical," "malignants," "Oxford heretics," "Jesuits in disguise," 'tamperers with Popish idolatry," "agents of Satan,' "a synagogue of Satan," "snakes in the grass," "walking about our beloved Church, polluting the sacred edifice, and leaving their slime about her altars;" "whose head," it was added, "may God crush!"

Is it not then abundantly plain, that, whatever be

the destiny of the movement of 1833, there is no tendency in it towards a coalition with the Establishment? It cannot strengthen it, it cannot serve it, it cannot obey it. The party may be dissolved, the movement may die—that is another matter; but it and its idea cannot live, cannot energize, in the National Church. If St. Athanasius could agree with Arius, St. Cyril with Nestorius, St. Dominic with the Albigenses, or St. Ignatius with Luther, then may two parties coalesce, in a certain assignable time, or by certain felicitously gradual approximations, or with dexterous limitations and concessions, who mutually think light darkness and darkness light. "Delenda est Carthago;" one or other must perish. Assuming, then, that there is a scope and limit to the movement, we certainly shall not find it in the dignities and offices of the National Church.

5.

If, then, this be not the providential direction of the movement, let us ask, in the next place, is it intended to remain just what it is at present, not in power or authority, but as a sort of principle or view of religion, found here and there with greater or less distinctness, with more or fewer followers, scattered about or concentrated, up and down the Establishment; with no exact agreement between man and man in matters of detail or in theoretical basis, but as an influence, sleeping or rousing, victorious or defeated, from time to

H

time, as the case may be? This state of things is
certainly supposable, at least for a time, for a generation; and various arguments may be adduced in its
behalf. It may be urged, "that if you cannot do any
positive good to the nation, yet at least in this way you
may prevent evil; that to be a drag upon the career of
unbelief, if you are nothing else, is a mission not to
be despised; moreover, if it be not a heroic course of
action, or look well in history, still so much the more
does such an office become those who are born in a
fallen time, and who wish to be humble."

Again, though it is good to be humble, still, on the
other hand, "there is a chance," it may be whispered
by others, "of a nobler and higher function opening on
you, if you are but patient and dutiful for a time." This
is the suggestion of those who cannot, will not, look at
things as they are; who think objects feasible because
they are desirable, and to be attempted because they
are tempting. These persons go on dwelling upon the
thought of the wonderful power of the British people,
at this day, all over the world, till at length they begin
to conjecture what may possibly be the design of Providence in raising it up. They feel that Great Britain
would be a most powerful instrument of good, if it could
be directed aright; and then they argue that if it *is* to
be influenced, what else ought naturally and obviously
to influence it but the National Church? The National
Church, then, is to be God's instrument for the conver-

sion of the world. But in order to this, of course it is indispensable that the National Church should have a clear and sufficient hold of Apostolical doctrine and usage; but then, who is to instruct the National Church in these necessary matters, but that Apostolical movement to which they themselves belong? And thus, by a few intermediate steps, they have attained the conclusion, that, because the nation is so powerful, the movement must succeed. Accordingly, they bear any degree of humiliation and discomforture; nay, any argumentative exposure, any present stultification of their principles, any, however chronic, disorganization, with an immovable resolve, as a matter of duty and merit, because they are sanguine about the future. They seem to feel that the whole cause of truth, the reform of the Establishment, the catholicizing of the nation, the conversion of the world, depends at this moment on their faithfulness to their position; on their own steadfastness the interests of humanity are at stake, and where they now are, there they will live and die. They have taken their part, and to that part they will be true.

Moreover, there are those among them who have very little grasp of principle, even from the natural temper of their minds. They see that this thing is beautiful, and that is in the Fathers, and a third is expedient, and a fourth pious; but of their connection one with another, their hidden essence and their life, and the bearing of external matters upon each and upon all, they have no perception or even suspicion. They do not look at things as parts of a whole, and often will sacrifice the most important and precious portions of their creed, or make irremediable concessions in word or in deed, from mere simplicity and want of apprehension.[1] This was in one way singularly exemplified in the beginning of the movement itself. I am not saying that every word that was used in the " Tracts for the Times " was matter of principle, or that the doctrines to be enforced were not sometimes unnecessarily coloured by the vehemence of the writer; but still it not seldom happened that readers took statements which contained the very point of the argument, or the very heart of the principle, to be mere intemperate expressions, and suggested to the authors their removal. They said "they went a great way with us, but they really could not go such lengths. Why speak of the Apostolic Succession, instead of Evangelical truth and Apostolical order ? It gave offence, it did no manner of good. Why use the word 'altar,' if it displeased weak brethren ? The word ' sacrifice ' was doubtless a misprint for ' sacrament ;' and to talk with Bishop Bull of ' making the body of Christ,' was a most extravagant, unjustifiable way of describing the administration of the Lord's Supper."

[1] Since writing the above, the author finds it necessary to observe, that, in writing it, it had no reference to persons, and he would be pained if it seemed to refer to actual passages in the controversy now in progress.

Things are changed now at the end of twenty years, but characters and intellects are the same. Such persons, at the present moment, do not formally profess any intention of giving up any of the doctrines of the movement; but they think it possible and expedient to divide portion from portion, and are rash and inconsistent in their advice and their conduct, from mere ignorance of what they are doing. So, too, they think it a success, and are elated accordingly, if any measure whatever, which happens to have been contemplated by the movement, is in any shape conceded by the Establishment or by the State; heedless altogether whether such measure be capable or not of coalescing with a foreign principle, and whether, instead of modifying, it has not been changed into that against which, in the minds of the writers of the Tracts, it was directed. For instance, the movement succeeded in gaining an increase in the number of Episcopal sees at home and abroad; well, a triumph this certainly is, if any how to succeed in a measure which one has advocated may be called by that name. But, be it recollected, measures derive their character and their worth from the principle which animates them; they have little meaning in themselves; they are but material facts, unless they include in them their scope and enforce their object; nay, they readily assume the *animus* and drift, and are taken up into the *form*, of the system by which they are adopted. If the Apostolical movement desired to increase the Episcopate, it was with a view to its own Apostolical principles; it had no wish merely to increase the staff of Government officers in England or in the colonies, the patronage of a ministry, the erection of country palaces, or the Latitudinarian votes in Parliament. Has it, for instance, done a great achievement at Manchester, if it has planted there a chair of liberalism, and inaugurated an anti-Catholic tradition?

6.

A policy, then, resting on such a temper of mind as I have been describing,—viz., a determination to act as if the course of events itself would, in some way or other, work for Apostolical truth, sooner or later, more or less; to let things alone, to do nothing, to make light of every triumph of the enemy from within or without, to waive the question of ecclesiastical liberty, to remain where you are, and go about your work in your own place, either contented to retard the course of events, or sanguine about an imaginary future,—this is simply to abandon the cause of the movement altogether. It is simply to say that there is no providential destiny or object connected with it at all. You may be right, my brethren; this may be the case; perhaps it is so. You have a right to this opinion, but understand what you are doing. Do not deceive yourselves by words; it is not a biding your time, as you may fancy, if you sur-

render the idea and the main principle of the movement; it is the abandonment of your cause. You
remain, indeed, in your place, but it is no moral, no
intellectual, but a mere secular, visible position which
you occupy. Great commanders, when in war they are
beaten back from the open country, retire to the mountains and fortify themselves in a territory which is their
own. You have no place of refuge from the foe; you
have no place from which to issue in due season, no
hope that your present concessions will bring about a
future victory. Your retreat is an evacuation. You
will remain in the Establishment in your own persons,
but your principles will be gone.

I know how it will be—a course as undignified as it
will be ineffectual. A sensation and talk whenever
something atrocious is to be done by the State against
the principles you profess; a meeting of friends here or
there, an attempt to obtain an archidiaconal meeting;
some spirited remarks in two or three provincial newspapers; an article in a review; a letter to some Bishop;
a protest signed respectably; suddenly the news that
the anticipated blow has fallen, and *causa finita est.* A
pause, and then the discovery that things are not so
bad as they seemed to be, and that after all your
Apostolical Church has come forth from the trial even
stronger and more beautiful than before. Still a secret
dissatisfaction and restlessness; a strong sermon at a
visitation; and a protest after dinner, when his lord-

ship is asked to print his Charge; a paragraph to your
great satisfaction in a hostile newspaper, saying how
that most offensive proceedings are taking place in such
and such a Tractarian parish or chapel, how that there
were flowers on the table, or that the curate has ton-
sured himself, or has used oil and salt in baptizing, or
has got a cross upon his surplice, or that in a benefit
sermon the bigoted Rector unchurched the Society of
Friends, or that Popery is coming in amain upon our
venerable Establishment, because a parsonage has been
built in shape like a Trappist monastery. And then
other signs of life; the consecration of a new church,
with Clergy walking in gown and bands, two and two,
and the Bishop preaching on decency and order, on the
impressive performance of divine Service, and the due
decoration of the house of God. Then a gathering in
the Christian Knowledge Rooms about some new book
put upon the Society's list, or some new liberalizing
regulation; a drawn battle, and a compromise. And
every now and then a learned theological work, doctrinal
or historical, justifying the ecclesiastical principles on
which the Anglican Church is founded, and refuting
the novelties of Romanism. And lastly, on occasion of
a contested election or other political struggle, theology
mingled with politics; the liberal candidate rejected by
the aid of the High-Church Clergy on some critical
question of religious policy; the Government annoyed
or embarrassed; and a sanguine hope entertained of a

ministry more favourable to Apostolical truth. My
brethren, the National Church has had experience of
this, *mutatis mutandis*, once before : I mean in the conduct of the Tory Clergy at the end of the seventeenth,
and beginning of the following century. Their proceedings in Convocation were a specimen of it; their
principles were far better than those of their Bishops;
yet the Bishops show to advantage and the Clergy look
small and contemptible in the history of that contest.
Public opinion judged, as it ever judges, by such broad
and significant indications of right and wrong; the
Government party triumphed, and the meetings of the
Convocation were suspended.

It is impossible, in a sketch such as this, to complete
the view of every point which comes into consideration ;
yet I think I have said enough to suggest the truth of
what I am urging to those who carefully turn the matter in their minds. Is the influence of the movement
to be maintained adequately to its beginnings and its
promise? Many, indeed, will say—certainly many of
those who hated or disapproved of it—that it was a
sudden ebullition of feeling, or burst of fanaticism, or
reaction from opposite errors; that it has had its day,
and is over. It may be so; but I am addressing those
who, I consider, are of another opinion; and to them
I appeal, whether I have yet proposed anything plausible about the providential future of the movement.
It is surely not intended, either to rise into the high

places of the Establishment, or to sink into a vague, amorphous faction at the foot of it. It cannot rise and it ought not to sink.

7.

And now I am in danger of exceeding the limits which I have proposed to myself, though another more important head of consideration lies before me, could I hope to do justice to it. I have urged that you will be most inconsistent, my brethren, with your principles and views, if you remain in the Establishment; I say with your principles and views, for you may give them up, and then you will not be inconsistent. You may say, "I do not hold them so strongly as to make them the basis and starting-point of any course of action whatever. I have believed in them, it is true; but I have never contemplated the liabilities you are urging upon me. I cannot, under any supposition, contemplate an abandonment of the National Church. I am not that knight-errant to give up my position, which surely is given me by Providence, on a theory. I am what I am. I am where I am. My reason has followed the teaching of the movement, and I have assented to it; so far I grant. But it is a new idea to me quite, which I have never contemplated at starting, which I cannot contemplate now, that possibly it might

involve the most awful, most utter of sacrifices.
I have ten thousand claims upon me, urging me to
remain where I am. They are real, tangible, habitual,
immutable; nothing can shake or lessen them from
within. A distinct call of God from without would, of
course, overcome them, but nothing short of it. Am I
as sure of those Apostolical principles which I have
embraced as I am of these claims? Moreover, I am
doing good in my parish and in my place. The day
passes as usual. Sunday comes round once a week;
the bell rings, the congregation is met, and service is
performed. There is the same round of parochial
duties and charities; sick people to be visited, the
school to be inspected. The sun shines, and the rain
falls, the garden smiles, as it used to do; and can some
one definite, external event have changed the position
of this happy scene of which I am the centre? Is
not that position a self-dependent, is it a mere relative
position? What care I for the Privy Council or the
Archbishop, while I can preach and catechize just as
before? I have my daily service and my Saints' day
sermons, and I can tell my people about the primitive
Bishops and martyrs, and about the grace of the Sacraments, and the power of the Church, how that it is
Catholic, and Apostolic, and Holy, and One, as if nothing had happened; and I can say my hours, or use
my edition of Roman Devotions, and observe the days

of fasting, and take confessions, if they are offered, in spite of all gainsayers."

It is true, my dear brethren, you *may* knowingly abandon altogether what you have once held, or you may profess to hold truths without being faithful to them. Well, then, you are of those who think that the movement has come to an end; if in your conscience you think so—that it was a mere phantom, or deceit, or unreality, or dream, which has taken you in, and from which you have awakened,—I have not a word to say. If, however, as I trust is the case, God has not in vain unrolled the pages of antiquity before your eyes, but has stamped them upon your hearts; if He has put into your minds the perception of the truth which, once given, can scarcely be lost, once possessed, will ever be recognized; if you have by His grace been favoured in any measure with the supernatural gift of faith, then, my brethren, I think too well of you, I hope too much of you, to fancy that you can be untrue to convictions so special and so commanding. No; you are under a destiny, the destiny of truth—truth is your master, not you the master of truth—you must go whither it leads. You can have no trust in the Establishment or its Sacraments and ordinances. You must leave it, you must secede; you must turn your back upon, you must renounce, what has—not suddenly become, but has now been proved to you to have ever been—an imposture. You must take up your cross and you must go hence. But whither? That is the question which it follows to ask, could I do justice to it. But you will rather do justice to it in your own thoughts. You must betake yourselves elsewhere—and "to whom shall you go?"

LECTURE V.

I.

I KNOW how very difficult it is to persuade others
of a point which to one's self may be so clear as to
require no argument at all; and, therefore, I am not
at all sanguine, my brethren, that what I said in my
last Lecture has done as much as I wished it to do. It
is not an easy thing to prove to men that their duty
lies just in the reverse direction to that in which they
have hitherto placed it; that all they have hitherto
learned and taught, that all their past labours, hopes,
and successes, that their boyhood, youth, and manhood,
that their position, their connections, and their influence,
are, in a certain sense, to go for nothing; and that life
is to begin with them anew. It is not an easy thing
to attain to the conviction, that, with the Apostle, their
greatest gain must be counted loss; and that their glory
and their peace must be found in what will make them
for a while the wonder and the scorn of the world. It

is true I may have shown you that you cannot coalesce
with the National Church; that you cannot wed yourselves to its principles and its routine, and that it, in
turn, has no confidence at all in you;—and, again, that
you cannot consistently hang about what you neither
love nor trust, cumbering with your presence what you
are not allowed to serve; but still, nevertheless, you
will cling to the past and present, and will hope for the
future against hope; and your forlorn hope is this, that
it is, perhaps, possible to remain as an actual party in
the Establishment, nay, an avowed party; not, on the
one hand, rising into ecclesiastical power, yet not, on
the other, disorganized and contemptible; but availing
yourselves of your several positions in it individually,
and developing, with more consistency and caution, the
principles of 1833. You may say that I passed over
this obvious course in my foregoing Lecture, and decided it in the negative without fair examination; and
you may argue that such a party is surely allowable in
a religious communion like the Establishment, which, as
the Committee of Privy Council implies, is based upon
principles so comprehensive, exercises so large a toleration, and is so patient of speculatists and innovators,
who are even further removed from its professed principles than yourselves.

Thus I am led to take one more survey of your present
position; yet I own I cannot do so without an apology
to others, who may think that I am trifling with a

serious subject and a clear case, and imagining objections in order to overthrow them. Such persons certainly there may be; but these I would have consider, on the other hand, that my aim is to bring before those I am addressing, really and vividly, where they are standing; that this cannot be done, unless they are induced steadily to fix their minds upon it; that the discussion of imaginary cases brings out principles which they cannot help recognizing, when they are presented to them, and the relation, moreover, of those principles to their own circumstances and duty; and that even where a view of a subject is imaginary, if taken as a whole and in its integral perfection, yet portions of it may linger in the mind, unknown to itself, and influence its practical decisions.

With this apology for a proceeding which some persons may feel tedious, I shall suppose you, my brethren, to address me in the following strain: "The movement has been, for nearly twenty years, a party, and why should it not continue a party as before? It has avowedly opposed a contrary party in the National Church; it has had its principles, its leaders, its usages, its party signs, its publications: it may have them still. It was once, indeed, a point of policy to deny our party character, or we tried to hide the truth from ourselves, but a party we were. The National Church admits of private judgment, and where there is private judgment, there must be parties. We are, of course, under a dis advantage now, which then did not lie upon us; we have, at the present time, the highest ecclesiastical authorities in distinct and avowed opposition to our doctrines and our doings; but we knew their feelings before they expressed them. This misfortune is nothing new; we always reckoned on an uphill game; it is better that every one should speak out; we now know the worst; we know now where to *find* our spiritual rulers; they are not more opposed to us than before, but they have been obliged openly to commit themselves, which we always wished them to do, though, of course, we should have preferred their committing themselves on our side. But, anyhow, we cannot be said to be in a worse case than before ; and, if we were allowably and hopefully a party before, we surely have as ample allowance to agitate, and not less hope of success, now."

2.

You think, then, my brethren, that to-day can be as yesterday, that you were a party then and can remain a party now, that your present position is your old one, that you can be faithful to the movement, yet continue just what you were. My brethren, you do not bear in mind that a movement is a thing that moves ; you cannot be true to it and remain still. The single question is, What is the limit or scope of that which once had a beginning and now has a progress ? Your principles,

I

indeed, are fixed, but circumstances are not what they were. If you would be true to your principles, you must remove from a position in which it is not longer possible for you to fulfil them.

Observe :—your movement started on the ground of maintaining ecclesiastical authority, as opposed to the Erastianism of the State. It exhibited the Church as the one earthly object of religious loyalty and venera- tion, the source of all spiritual power and jurisdiction, and the channel of all grace. It represented it to be the interest, as well as the duty, of Churchmen, the bond of peace and the secret of strength, to submit their judgment in all things to her decision. And it taught that this divinely founded Church was real- ised and brought into effect in our country in the Na- tional Establishment, which was the outward form or development of a continuous dynasty and hereditary power which descended from the Apostles. It gave, then, to that Establishment, in its officers, its laws, its usages, and its worship, that devotion and obedience which are correlative to the very idea of the Church. It set up on high the bench of Bishops and the Book of Common Prayer, as the authority to which it was itself to bow, with which it was to cow and overpower an Erastian State.

It is hardly necessary to bring together passages from the early numbers of the "Tracts for the Times" in support of this statement. Each Tract, I may say,

is directed, in one way or other, to the defence of the
existing documents or regulations of the National
Church. No abstract ground is taken in these com-
positions; conclusions are not worked out from philosophical premisses, nor conjectures recommended by
poetical illustrations, nor a system put together out of
eclectic materials; but emphatically and strenuously it
is maintained, that whatever is is right, and must be
obeyed. If the Apostolic succession is true, it is not
simply because St. Ignatius and St. Cyprian might
affirm it, though Fathers are adduced also, but because
it is implied in the Ordination Service. If the Church
is independent of the State in things spiritual, it is not
simply because Bishop Pearson has extolled her powers
in his Exposition of the Creed, though divines are
brought forward as authorities too; but by reason of
"the force of that article of our belief, the one Catholic
and Apostolic Church." If the mysterious grace of the
Episcopate is insisted on, it is not merely as contained
in Holy Scripture, though Scripture is appealed to again
and again; but as implied in "that ineffable mystery,
called in the Creed, the Communion of Saints." Scripture was copiously quoted, the Fathers were boldly invoked, and Anglican divines were diligently consulted;
but the immediate, present, and, as the leaders of the
movement hoped, the living authority, on which they
based their theological system, was what was called the
"Liturgy," or Book of Common Prayer.

This "Liturgy," as the instrument of their teaching, was, on that account, regarded as practically infallible. "Attempts are making to get the Liturgy altered," says a Tract; "I beseech you consider with me, whether you ought not to resist the alteration of even one jot or tittle of it." Then as to the burial service: "I frankly own," says another Tract, "it is sometimes distressing to use it; but this must ever be in the nature of things, wherever you draw the line." Again, it was said that "there was a growing feeling that the Services were too long," and ought to be shortened but it was to be "arrested" by "certain considerations" offered in a third. "There were persons who wished certain Sunday Lessons removed from the Service;" but, according to a fourth, there was reason the other way, in the very argument which was "brought in favour of the change." Another project afloat was that of leaving out "such and such chapters of the Old Testament," and "assigning proper Lessons to every Sunday from the New;" but it was temperately and ingeniously argued in a fifth, that things were best just as they were. And as the Prayer Book, so too was the Episcopate invested with a sacred character, which it was a crime to affront or impair. "Exalt our Holy Fathers," said a sixth Tract, "as the representatives of the Apostles, and the Angels of the Churches." "They stand in the place of the Apostles," said a seventh, "as far as the office of ruling is concerned; and he that despiseth them despiseth the Apostles."

3.

Now, why do I refer to these passages? Not for their own sake, but to show that the movement was based on submission to a definite existing authority, and that private judgment was practically excluded. I do not mean to say that its originators thought the Prayer Book inspired, any more than the Bishops infallible, as if they had nothing to do but accept and believe what was put into their hands. They had too much common sense to deny the necessary exercise of private judgment, in one sense or another. They knew that the Catholic Church herself admitted it, though she directed and limited it to a decision upon the question of the organ of revelation; and they expressly recognized what they had no wish to deny. "So far," they said, "all parties must be agreed, that without private judgment there is no responsibility . . . even though an infallible guidance be accorded, a man must have a choice of resisting it or not."[1] But still, not denying this as an abstract truth, they determined that, as regards the teaching of the Liturgy, or the enunciations of the Bishops—which is the point immediately under our consideration—all differences of opinion existing between members of the Establishment could

[1] Proph. Off., p. 157.

be but minor ones, which might profitably, and without
effort, be suppressed; that is, these were such as ought
to be inwardly discredited and rejected, as less probable
than the authoritative rule or statement, or at most
must only be entertained at home, not published or
defended. The matters in debate could not be more
than matters of opinion, not of doctrine. Thus, with
respect to alterations in the Prayer Book, the Tract
says, "Though most of you would wish some immaterial points altered, yet not many of you agree in those
points, and not many of you agree what is and what is
not immaterial. If all your respective emendations
are taken, the alterations in the Service will be extensive; and, though each will gain something he wishes,
he will lose more in consequence of those alterations
which he did not wish. How few would be pleased by
any given alterations, and how many pained!" Though,
then, the Prayer Book was not perfect, it had a sort of
practical perfection; and, though it was not unerring,
it was a sure and sufficient safeguard against error. It
was dangerous to question any part of it. "A taste
for criticism grows upon the mind," said a Tract.
"This unsettling of the mind is a frightful thing, both
for ourselves, and more so for our flocks." The principle, then, of these writers was this: An infallible
authority is necessary; we have it not, for the Prayer
Book is all we have got; but since we have nothing
better, we must use it as if infallible. I am not justi-

fying the logic of this proceeding; but if it be deficient, much more clearly does it, for that very reason, bring out the strength with which they held the principle of authority itself, when they would make so great an effort to find for it a place in the National Religion, and would rather force a conclusion than give up their premiss.

The Prayer Book, then, according to the first agents in the movement, was the arbiter, and limit, and working rule of the ten thousand varying private judgments of which the community was made up, which could not all be satisfied, which could not all be right, which were, every one of them, less likely to be right than it. It was the immediate instrument by means of which they professed to make their way, the fulcrum by which they were to hoist up the Establishment, and set it down securely on the basis of Apostolical Truth. And thus it was accepted by the party, not only as essentially and substantially true, but also as eminently expedient and necessary for the time.

"To do anything effectually," said a speaker in a dialogue of mine, who is expressing the philosophy (so to call it) of the movement in answer to a Romanizing friend, "we must start from recognized principles and customs. Any other procedure stamps a person as wrong-headed, ill-judging, or eccentric, and brings upon him the contempt and ridicule of those sensible men by whose opinions society is necessarily governed. Putting aside the question of truth and falsehood (which, of course, is the main consideration), even as aiming at success, we must be aware of the great error of making changes on no more definite basis than their abstract fitness, alleged scripturalness, or adoption by the ancients. Such changes are rightly called innovations; —those which spring from existing institutions, opinions, and feelings, are called developments, and may be recommended, without invidiousness, as improvements. I adopt then, and claim as my own, that position of yours, that 'we must take and use what is ready to our hands.' To do otherwise is to act the *doctrinaire*, and to provide for failure. For instance, if we would enforce observance of the Lord's Day, we must not, at the outset, rest it on any theory, however just, of Church authority, but on the authority of Scripture. If we would oppose the State's interference with the distribution of Church property, we shall succeed, not by urging any doctrine of Church independence, or by citing decrees of general councils, but by showing the contrariety of that measure to existing constitutional and ecclesiastical precedents among ourselves. Hildebrand found the Church provided with certain existing means of power ; he vindicated them, and was rewarded with the success which attends, not on truth as such, but on this prudence and tact in conduct. St. Paul observed the same rule, whether in preaching at Athens or persuading his countrymen. It was the gracious condescension of our Lord Himself, not to substitute Christianity for Judaism by any violent revolution, but to develope Judaism into Christianity, as the Jews might bear it."[1]

4

Now all this was very well, if expedience was the end, and not merely a reason, of their extolling the Episcopate and the Prayer Book; but if it was a question of truth (and as such they certainly considered it), then it was undeniable, that Prayer Book and Episcopate could not support themselves, but required some intellectual basis; and what was that to be? Here again, as before (and this is the point to which all along I wish to direct your attention), these writers professed to go by authority, not by private judgment; for they fell back upon the divines of the Anglican Church, as their channels for ascertaining both what Anglicanism taught and why. It is scarcely necessary to remind any one who has followed the movement in its course, how careful and anxious they were, as soon as they got (what may be called) under weigh, at once to collect and arrange Catenas of Anglican authorities, on whom their own teaching might be founded, and under whose name it might be protected. Accordingly the doctrines, especially of the Apostolical succession, of Baptismal Regeneration, of the Euchar-

[1] British Mag., April 1836.

istic sacrifice, and of the Rule of Faith, were made the
subject of elaborate collections of extracts from the
divines of the Establishment. And so in like manner,
when a formal theory or idea was attempted of the
Anglican system, the writer said, and believed, that "he
had endeavoured, in all important points of doctrine,
to guide himself by our standard divines; and, had
space admitted, would have selected passages from their
writings, in evidence of it. Such a collection of testimonies," he continued, "is almost a duty on the part
of every author, who professes, not to strike out new
theories, but to build up and fortify what has been
committed to us." [1]

5.

But now a further question obviously arises: by
what rule will you determine what divines are authoritative, and what are not? for it is obvious, unless you
can adduce such, private judgment will come in at last
upon your ecclesiastical structure, in spite of your
success hitherto in keeping it out. This answer, too,
was ready:—Scripture itself suggested to them the rule
they should follow, and it was a rule external to themselves. They professed, then, to take simply those as
authorities whom "all the people accounted prophets." [2]

[1] Proph. Off. p. vi.
[2] Viz., the text prefixed to the Catenas, Tract 74. There was another
obvious rule also, but still not a private one. They had recourse to those
Anglican divines who alone contemplated, and professed to provide, an

As it was no private judgment, but the spontaneous
sentiment of a whole people, that canonized the Baptist, as the ancient saints are raised over our altars by
the acclamation of a universal immemorial belief; so,
according to these writers, the popular voice was to be
consulted, and its decision simply recorded and obeyed,
in the selection of the divines on whom their theology
was to be founded. They professed to put aside individual liking; they might admire Hooker, or they
might think him obscure ; they might love Taylor, or
they might feel a secret repugnance to him; they might
delight in the vigour of Bull, or they might be repelled
by his homeliness and his want of the supernatural
element; these various feelings they had, but they did
not wish to select their authorities by any such private
taste or reason, in which they would differ from each
other, but by the voice of the community. For instance,
Davenant is a far abler writer than Hammond, but how
few have heard of him ? Horne or Wilson is far inferior in learning, power, or originality to Warburton,
yet their works have a popularity which Warburton's
have not, and have, in consequence, a higher claim to
the formal title of Anglican divinity. Such was the
principle of selection on which the authors of the
movement proceeded; and if you say they were untrue
to their principles in the Catenas they drew out, and,

idea, theory, or *intellectual position* for their Church, as Laud and Stillingfleet.

after all, selected partially, and on private judgment,
I repeat, so much the more for my purpose. How
clearly must the principle of an ecclesiastical and
authoritative, not a private judgment, have been the
principle of the movement, when those who belonged
to it were obliged to own that principle, at the very
time that it was inconvenient to them, and when they
were driven, whether consciously or not, to misuse or
evade it!

6.

Such, then, was the principle on which they professed
to select the authorities they were to follow; nor was
their anxiety in consulting them less than their care-
fulness in ascertaining them. Here again, I am not
going into the question whether they deceived themselves in consulting, as well as in ascertaining these
divines; whether they followed them where they agreed
with themselves, and, where they stopped short, went
forward without them: I am not aware that they did,
but, whether they did or no, they tried not to do so;
they wished to make the Anglican divines real vouchers
and sanctions of their own teaching, and they used
their words rather than their own. They shrank from
seeming to speak without warrant, even on matters
which in no sense were matters of faith, and I can
adduce an instance of it, which is more to the point,
for the very reason it was singularly misunderstood;

and, though it may seem to require some apology that I should again refer to an author from whom I have made several extracts already, I mean myself, I have an excuse for doing so in the circumstance, that I naturally know his works better than those of others, and I can quote him without misrepresenting him or hurting his feelings. In a Retractation, then, which he published in the year 1843, of some strong statements which he had made against the Catholic Church, these words occur:—" If you ask me how an individual could venture, *not simply to hold but to publish* such views of a communion so ancient, so wide-spreading, so fruitful in Saints, I answer, that I said to myself, ' *I am not speaking my own words,* I am but following almost a *consensus* of the divines of my Church. They have ever used the strongest language against Rome, even the most able and learned of them. I wish to throw myself into their system. While I say what they *say,* I am safe. Such views, too, are necessary for our position.' " Now, this passage has been taken to mean, that the writer spoke from expediency what he did not believe; but this is false in fact, and inaccurate in criticism. He spoke what he felt, what he thought, what at the time he held, and nothing but what he held with an internal assent; but still, though he internally thought it, he would not have dared to *say* it — he would have shrunk, as well he might, from standing up, *on his own private judgment,* an accuser

against the great Roman communion, and unless in
doing so he felt he had been doing simply what his own
Church *required* of him, and what was *necessary* for his
Church's cause, and what all his Church's divines had
ever done before him. This being the case, he " could
venture, not simply to *hold* but to *publish*; " he was
not " speaking his own *words*," though he *was* expressing his own *thoughts*; and, as using those words, he was
behind " a system " received by his Church, as well as
by himself. He felt " safe," because he spoke after, and
" throwing himself into," he was sheltering himself
according to its teaching and its teachers. It had, indeed,
been one sin that he had thought ill of the Catholic
Church; it had been another and greater, that he
had uttered what he thought; and there was just this
alleviation of his second sin, that he had not said it
wantonly, and that he had said what others had said
before him. There is nothing difficult or unnatural,
surely, in this state of mind; but it is not wonderful
that to the mass of Protestants it was incomprehensible
that any one should shrink from the display of that
private judgment in which they themselves so luxu-
riated, that any one should think of clearing himself
from what in their eyes was simply a virtue, or should be
shocked at having the credit given him of making use
of a special privilege.

7.

But I have not yet arrived at the ultimate resolution of faith, in the judgment of the theological party of 1833: the Anglican divines, it seems, were to be followed, but, after all, were they inspired more than the Prayer Book? else, on what are we to say that their authority in turn depended? Again, the answer was ready: The Anglican divines are sanctioned by that authority, to which they themselves refer, the Fathers of the Church. Thus spoke the party: now at length, you will say, they are brought to a point, when private judgment must necessarily be admitted; for who shall ascertain what is in the Fathers and what is not, without a most special and singular application of his own powers of mind, and his own personal attainments, to the execution of so serious an undertaking? But not even here did they allow themselves to be committed to the Protestant instrument of inquiry, though this point will require some little explanation. It must be observed, then, that they were accustomed to regard theology generally, much more upon its anti-Protestant side than upon its anti-Roman; and, from the circumstances in which they found themselves, were far more solicitous to refute Luther and Calvin than Suarez or Bellarmine. Protestantism was a present foe; Catholicism, or Romanism as they called it, was but a possible adversary; " it was not likely," they said, "that

Romanism should ever again become formidable in
England;" and they engaged with it accordingly, not
from any desire to do so, but because they could not
form an ecclesiastical theory without its coming in
their way, and challenging their notice.   It was "necessary for their position" to dispose of Catholicism, but
it was not a task of which they acquitted themselves
with the zeal or interest which was so evident in their
assaults upon their Protestant brethren.   "Those who
feel the importance of that article of the Creed," the
holy Catholic Church, says a work several times quoted,
"and yet are not Romanists, are *bound* on several
accounts to show why they are not Romanists, and how
they differ from them.   They are bound to do so, in
order to remove the prejudice with which an article of
the Creed is at present encompassed.   From the circumstances, then, of the moment, the following Lectures
are chiefly engaged in examining and exposing certain
tenets of Romanism."[1] The author's feeling, then, seems
to have been,—I should have a perfect case against this

[1] Proph. Office, p. 7. I am not unmindful of the following "ground"
for publishing the Translations of the Fathers, contained in the prospectus:—" II. The great danger in which the Romanists are of lapsing into
secret infidelity, not seeing how to escape from the palpable errors of
their own Church, without falling into the opposite errors of ultra-Pro-
testants.   It appeared an act of especial charity to point out to such of
them as are dissatisfied with the state of their own Church, a body of
ancient Catholic truth, free from the errors alike of modern Rome, and
of ultra-Protestantism." I have nothing to say in explanation, but that
this passage was not written by me, and that I do not consider it to
have expressed my own feelings, or those of the movement.

Protestantism but for these inconvenient "Romanists," whose claims I do not admit indeed, but who, controversially, stand in my way.

But now, with this explanation, to the point before us:—The consequence of this state of mind was, that the persons in question were not very solicitous (if I dare speak for others) *how far* the Fathers *seemed* to tell for the Church of Rome or not; on the whole, they were sure they did not tell materially for her; but it was no matter, though they partially seemed to do so; for their great and deadly foe, their scorn, and their laughing-stock, was that imbecile, inconsistent thing called Protestantism; and there could not be a more thorough refutation of its foundation and superstructure than was to be found in the volumes of the Fathers. There was no mistaking that the principles professed, and doctrines taught by those holy men, were utterly anti-Protestant; and, being satisfied of this, which was their principal consideration, it did not occur to them accurately to determine the range and bounds of the teaching of the early Church, or to reflect that, perhaps, they had as yet a clearer view of what it did not sanction, than of what it did. They saw, then, that there simply was no opportunity at all for private judgment, if one wished to exercise it ever so much, as regards the question of the anti-Protestantism of the Fathers; it was a patent fact, open to all, written on the face of their works, that they were anti-Protestant; you might

K

defer to them, you might reject them, but you could as
little deny that they were essentially anti-Protestant,
as you could deny that "the Romanists" were anti-
Protestants. It was a matter of fact, a matter of sense,
which Protestants themselves admitted or rather maintained; and here, in this public and undeniable fact,
we have arrived at what the movement considered the
ultimate resolution of its faith. It argued, for instance,
"A private Christian may put what meaning he pleases
on many parts of Scripture, and no one can hinder him.
If interfered with, he can promptly answer, that it is his
own opinion, and may appeal to his right of private
judgment. But he cannot so deal with Antiquity:
history is a record of facts; and facts, according to the
proverb, are stubborn things."[1]   And accordingly, these
writers represented the Church as they conceived of it,
as having no power whatever over the faith; her Creed
was simply a public matter of fact, which needed as
little explanation, as little interpretation, as the fact of
her own existence. Hence they said: "The humblest
and meanest among Christians may defend the faith
against the whole Church, if the need arise. He has
as much stake in it, and as much right to it, as Bishop
or Archbishop; . . . . all that learning has to do for
him is to ascertain the fact, what is the meaning of the
Creed in particular points, since matter of opinion it is

[1] Proph. Office, p. 45.

not, any more than the history of the rise and spread
of Christianity itself."[1]

Accordingly, as their first act, when they were once
set off, had been to publish Catenas of the Anglican
divines, so their second was to publish translations of
the Fathers—viz., in order to put the matter out of
their own hands, and throw the decision upon the *private* judgment of no one, but on the common judgment
of the whole community, Anglicans and Protestants at
once. They considered that the Fathers had hitherto
been monopolised by controversialists, who treated
them merely as magazines of passages which might be
brought forward in argument, mutilated and garbled
for the occasion; and that the greatest service to their
own cause was simply to publish them.[2] "A main
reason," it was said, "of the jealousy with which
Christians of this age and country adhere to the notion
that truth of doctrine can be gained from Scripture by
individuals is this, that they are unwilling, as they say,
to be led by others blindfold. They can possess and
read the Scriptures; whereas, of traditions they are not
adequate judges, and they dread priestcraft. I am not
here to enter into the discussion of this feeling, whether
praiseworthy or the contrary. However this be, it does
seem a reason for putting before them, if possible, the

[1] P. 292.
[2] See this brought out in an article on the Apostolical Fathers, in the
British Critic of January 1839. [*Vide* the author's "Essays: Critical
and Historical," No. 5.]

principal works of the Fathers, translated as Scripture
is; that they may have by them what, whether used or
not, will at least act as a check upon the growth of an
undue dependence on the word of individual teachers,
and will be a something to consult, if they have reason
to doubt the Catholic character of any tenet to which
they are invited to accede." [1]

By way, then, of rescuing the faith from private
teaching on the one hand, and private judgment on
the other, it was proposed to publish a Library of the
Fathers translated into English. And let it be observed, in pursuance of this object, the Translations
were to be presented to the general reader without note
or comment. It was distinctly stated in the Prospectus,
that "the notes shall be limited to the explanation of
obscure passages, or the removal of any misapprehen-
sion which might not improbably arise." And this
was so strictly adhered to at first, that the translation
of St. Cyril's Catechetical Lectures was criticised in
a Catholic Review on this very ground; [2] and it was
asked why his account of the Holy Eucharist was not
reconciled by the Editor with the Anglican formularies,
when the very idea of the Editor had been to bring out

---

[1] Proph. Office, p. 203. This passage, moreover, negatives the charge,
sometimes advanced against the agents in the movement, that they
wished *every individual Christian* to gain his faith for himself by study
of the Fathers. They have enough to bear without our imagining
absurdities.

[2] Viz., the "Dublin Review." The rule of publishing without note
or comment was, in consequence of such objections, soon abandoned.

facts, and leave the result to a judgment more authoritative than his own, and favourable on the whole, as he hoped, in the event, to the Church to which he belonged. "We can do no more," he had said in the Preface, "than have patience, and recommend patience to others; and with the racer in the Tragedy, look forward steadily and hopefully to the event, 'in the end relying,' when, as we trust, all that is inharmonious and anomalous in the details, will at length be practically smoothed."[1]

8.

Such, then, was the clear, unvarying line of thought, as I believed it to be, on which the movement of 1833 commenced and proceeded, as regards the questions of Church authority and private judgment. It was fancied that no opportunity for the exercise of private judgment could arise in any public or important matter. The Church declared, whether by Prayer Book or Episcopal authority, what was to be said or done; and private judgment either had no objection which it could make good, or only on those minor matters where there was a propriety in its yielding to authority. And the present Church declared what her divines had declared; and her divines had declared what the Fathers had declared; and what the Fathers had declared was no matter of private judgment at all, but a matter of fact,

[1] Page xi.

cognizable by all who chose to read their writings.
Their testimony was as decisive and clear as Pope's
Bull or Definition of Council, or catechisings or direction of any individual parish priest. There was no
room for two opinions on the subject; and, as Catholics
consider that the truth is brought home to the soul
supernaturally, so that the soul sees it and no longer
depends on reason, so in some parallel way it was supposed, in the theology of the movement, that that same
truth, as contained in the Fathers, was a natural fact,
recognised by the natural and ordinary intelligence
of mankind, as soon as that intelligence was directed
towards it.

The idea, then, of the divines of the movement
was simply and absolutely submission to an external
authority; to such an authority they appealed, to it
they betook themselves; there they found a haven of
rest; thence they looked out upon the troubled surge
of human opinion and upon the crazy vessels which
were labouring, without chart or compass, upon it.
Judge then of their dismay, when, according to the
Arabian tale, on their striking their anchors into the
supposed soil, lighting their fires on it, and fixing in it
the poles of their tents, suddenly their island began to
move, to heave, to splash, to frisk to and fro, to dive,
and at last to swim away, spouting out inhospitable jets
of water upon the credulous mariners who had made it
their home. And such, I suppose, was the undeniable

fact: I mean, the time at length came, when first of
all turning their minds (some of them, at least) more
carefully to the doctrinal controversies of the early
Church, they saw distinctly that in the reasonings of
the Fathers, elicited by means of them, and in the
decisions of authority, in which they issued, were contained at least the rudiments, the anticipation, the
justification of what they had been accustomed to consider the corruptions of Rome. And if only one, or a
few of them, were visited with this conviction, still even
one was sufficient, of course, to destroy that cardinal
point of their whole system, the objective perspicuity
and distinctness of the teaching of the Fathers. But
time went on, and there was no mistaking or denying
the misfortune which was impending over them. They
had reared a goodly house, but their foundations were
falling in. The soil and the masonry both were bad.
The Fathers *would* protect "Romanists" as well as
extinguish Dissenters. The Anglican divines *would*
misquote the Fathers, and shrink from the very doctors
to whom they appealed. The Bishops of the seventeenth century were shy of the Bishops of the fourth;
and the Bishops of the nineteenth were shy of the
Bishops of the seventeenth. The ecclesiastical courts
upheld the sixteenth century against the seventeenth,
and, regardless of the flagrant irregularities of Protestant clergymen, chastised the mild misdemeanours of
Anglo-Catholic. Soon the living rulers of the Establish-

ment began to move. There are those who, reversing
the Roman's maxim,[1] are wont to shrink from the con-
tumacious, and to be valiant towards the submissive;
and the authorities in question gladly availed themselves of the power conferred on them by the movement against the movement itself. They fearlessly
handselled their Apostolic weapons upon the Apostolical party. One after another, in long succession, they
took up their song and their parable against it. It
was a solemn war-dance, which they executed round
victims, who by their very principles were bound hand
and foot, and could only eye with disgust and perplexity this most unaccountable movement, on the
part of their " holy Fathers, the representatives of the
Apostles, and the Angels of the Churches." It was the
beginning of the end.

My brethren, when it was at length plain that primitive Christianity ignored the National Church, and that
the National Church cared little for primitive Christianity, or for those who appealed to it as her foundation ;
when Bishops spoke against them, and Bishops' courts
sentenced them, and Universities degraded them, and
the people rose against them, from that day their
" occupation was gone." Their initial principle, their

---

1 " Parcere subjectis, et debellare superbos." It may be right here to
say, that the author never can forget the great kindness which Dr. Bagot,
at that time Bishop of Oxford, showed him on several occasions. He
also has to notice the courtesy of Dr. Thirwall's language, a prelate whom
he has never had the honour of knowing.

basis, external authority, was cut from under them; they had "set their fortunes on a cast;" they had lost; henceforward they had nothing left for them but to shut up their school, and retire into the country. Nothing else was left for them, unless, indeed, they took up some other theory, unless they changed their ground, unless they ceased to be what they were, and became what they were not; unless they belied their own principles, and strangely forgot their own luminous and most keen convictions; unless they vindicated the right of private judgment, took up some fancy-religion, retailed the Fathers, and jobbed theology. They had but a choice between doing nothing at all, and looking out for truth and peace elsewhere.

9.

And now, at length, I am in a condition to answer the question which you have proposed for my consideration. You ask me whether you cannot now continue what you were. No, my brethren, it is impossible, you cannot recall the past; you cannot surround yourselves with circumstances which have simply ceased to be. In the beginning of the movement you disowned private judgment, but now, if you would remain a party, you must, with whatever inconsistency, profess it;— then you were a party only externally, that is, not in your wishes and feelings, but merely because you were seen to differ from others in matter of fact, when the

world looked at you, whether you would or no; but
now you will be a party knowingly and on principle,
intrinsically, and will be erected on a party basis. You
cannot be what you were. You will no longer be
Anglo-Catholic, but Patristico-Protestants. You will
be obliged to frame a religion for yourselves, and then
to maintain that it is that very truth, pure and celestial,
which the Apostles promulgated. You will be induced
of necessity to put together some speculation of your
own, and then to fancy it of importance enough to din
it into the ears of your neighbours, to plague the world
with it, and, if you have success, to convulse your own
Communion with the imperious inculcation of doctrines
which you can never engraft upon it.

For me, my dear brethren, did I know myself well,
I should doubtless find I was open to the temptation,
as well as others, to take a line of my own, or, what is
called, to set up for myself; but whatever might be my
real infirmity in this matter, I should, from mere common sense and common delicacy, hide it from myself,
and give it some good name in order to make it palat-
able. I never could get myself to say, " Listen to me,
for I have something great to tell you, which no one
else knows, but of which there is no manner of doubt."
I should be kept from such extravagance from an intense
sense of the intellectual absurdity, which, in my feelings,
such a claim would involve ; which would shame me as
keenly, and humble me in my own sight as utterly, as

some moral impropriety or degradation. I should feel
I was simply making a fool of myself, and taking on
myself in figure that penance, of which we read in the
Lives of the Saints, of playing antics and making faces
in the market-place. Not religious principle, but even
worldly pride, would keep me from so unworthy an
exhibition. I can understand, my brethren, I can sym-
pathise with those old-world thinkers, whose commen-
tators are Mant and D'Oyly, whose theologian is Tomline,
whose ritualist is Wheatly, and whose canonist is Burns;
who are proud of their Jewels and their Chillingworths,
whose works they have never opened, and toast Cranmer
and Ridley, and William of Orange, as the founders of
their religion. In these times three hundred years is a
respectable antiquity; and traditions, recognized in law
courts, and built into the structure of society, may
well without violence be imagined to be immemorial.
Those also I can understand, who take their stand upon
the Prayer Book; or those who honestly profess to
follow the *consensus* of Anglican divines, as the voice of
authority and the standard of faith. Moreover, I can
quite enter into the sentiment with which members of
the liberal and infidel school investigate the history and
the documents of the early Church. They profess a
view of Christianity, truer than the world has ever had;
nor, on the assumption of their principles, is there
anything shocking to good sense in this profession.
They look upon the Christian Religion as something

simply human; and there is no reason at all why a
phenomenon of that kind should not be better understood, in its origin and nature, as years proceed.   It is,
indeed, an intolerable paradox to assert, that a revelation, given from God to man, should lie unknown or
mistaken for eighteen centuries, and now at length
should be suddenly deciphered by individuals; but it
is quite intelligible to assert, and plausible to argue,
that a human fact should be more philosophically
explained than it was eighteen hundred years ago, and
more exactly ascertained than it was a thousand.   History is at this day undergoing a process of revolution;
the science of criticism, the disinterment of antiquities,
the unrolling of manuscripts, the interpretation of
inscriptions, have thrown us into a new world of
thought; characters and events come forth transformed
in the process; romance, prejudice, local tradition,
party bias, are no longer accepted as guarantees of
truth; the order and mutual relation of events are
readjusted; the springs and the scope of action are
reversed.   Were Christianity a mere work of man, it,
too, might turn out something different from what it
has hitherto been considered; its history might require
re-writing, as the history of Rome, or of the earth's
strata, or of languages, or of chemical action.   A
Catholic neither deprecates nor fears such inquiry,
though he abhors the spirit in which it is too often
conducted.   He is willing that infidelity should do its

work against the Church, knowing that she will be found just where she was, when the assault is over. It is nothing to him, though her enemies put themselves to the trouble of denying everything that has hitherto been taught, and begin with constructing her history all over again, for he is quite sure that they will end at length with a compulsory admission of what at first they so wantonly discarded. Free thinkers and broad thinkers, Laudians and Prayer-Book Christians, high-and-dry and Establishment-men, all these he would understand; but what he would feel so prodigious is this,—that such as you, my brethren, should consider Christianity given from heaven once for all, should protest against private judgment, should profess to transmit what you have received, and yet from diligent study of the Fathers, from your thorough knowledge of St. Basil and St. Chrysostom, from living, as you say, in the atmosphere of Antiquity, that you should come forth into open day with your new edition of the Catholic faith, different from that held in any existing body of Christians anywhere, which not half-a-dozen men all over the world would honour with their *imprimatur;* and then, withal, should be as positive about its truth in every part, as if the voice of mankind were with you instead of being against you.

You are a body of yesterday; you are a drop in the ocean of professing Christians; yet you would give the

law to priest and prophet; and you fancy it an humble
office, forsooth, suited to humble men, to testify the very
truth of Revelation to a fallen generation, or rather to
almost a long bi-millenary, which has been in unallevi-
ated traditionary error. You have a mission to teach
the National Church, which is to teach the British empire, which is to teach the world; you are more learned
than Greece; you are purer than Rome; you know
more than St. Bernard; you judge how far St.
Thomas was right, and where he is to be read with
caution, or held up to blame. You can bring to
light juster views of grace, or of penance, or of invocation of saints, than St. Gregory or St. Augustine,—

"qualia vincunt
Pythagoran, Anytique reum, doctumque Platona."

This is what you can do; yes, and when you have
done all, to what have you attained? to do just what
heretics have done before you, and, as doing, have
incurred the anathema of Holy Church. Such was
Jansenius; for of him we are told, "From the commencement of his theological studies, when he began
to read, with the schoolmen, the holy Fathers, and
especially Augustine, he at once saw, as he confessed,
that most of the schoolmen went far astray from that
holy Doctor's view, in that capital article of grace and
free will. He sometimes owned to his friends, that he
had read over more than ten times the entire works of
Augustine, with lively attention and diligent annota-

tion, and his books against the Pelagians at least thirty times from beginning to end. He said that no mind, whether Aristotle or Archimedes, or any other under the heavens, was equal to Augustine. . . . I have heard him say more than once, that life would be most delightful to him, though on some ocean-isle or rock, apart from all human society, had he but his Augustine with him. In a word, after God and Holy Scripture, Augustine was his all in all. However, for many years he had to struggle with his old opinions, before he put them all off, and arrived at the intimate sense of St. Augustine. . . . For this work, he often said, he was specially born; and that, when he had finished it, he should be most ready to die."[1] Such, too, was another nearer home, on whom Burnet bestows this panegyric:—"Cranmer," says he, "was at great pains to collect the sense of ancient writers upon all the heads of religion, by which he might be directed in such an important matter. I have seen two volumes in folio, written with his own hand, containing, upon all the heads of religion, a vast heap of places of Scripture, and quotations out of ancient Fathers, and later doctors and schoolmen, by which he governed himself in that work."

10.

And now, my brethren, will it not be so, as I have said, of simple necessity, if you attempt at this time to

[1] Synops, Vit. ap. Opp. 1643.

perpetuate in the National Church a form of opinion
which the National Church disowns? You do not
follow its Bishops; you disown its existing traditions;
you are discontented with its divines; you protest
against its law courts; you shrink from its laity; you
outstrip its Prayer Book. You have in all respects an
eclectic or an original religion of our own. You dare
not stand or fall by Andrewes, or by Laud, or by Hammond, or by Bull, or by Thorndike, or by all of them
together. There is a *consensus* of divines, stronger than
there is for Baptismal Regeneration or the Apostolical
Succession, that Rome is, strictly and literally, an anti-
Christian power:—Liberals and High Churchmen in
your Communion in this agree with Evangelicals; you
put it aside. There is a *consensus* against Transubstantiation, besides the declaration of the Article; yet
many of you hold it notwithstanding. Nearly all your
divines, if not all, call themselves Protestants, and you
anathematize the name. Who makes the concessions
to Catholics which you do, yet remains separate from
them? Who, among Anglican authorities, would speak
of Penance as a Sacrament, as you do? Who of them
encourages, much less insists upon, auricular confession,
as you? or makes fasting an obligation? or uses the
crucifix and the rosary? or reserves the consecrated
bread? or believes in miracles as existing in your communion? or administers, as I believe you do, Extreme
Unction? In some points you prefer Rome, in others

Greece, in others England, in others Scotland; and
of that preference your own private judgment is the
ultimate sanction.

What am I to say in answer to conduct so preposterous? Say you go by any authority whatever, and I
shall know where to find you, and I shall respect you.
Swear by any school of Religion, old or modern, by
Ronge's Church, or the Evangelical Alliance, nay, by
yourselves, and I shall know what you mean, and will
listen to you. But do not come to me with the latest
fashion of opinion which the world has seen, and protest to me that it is the oldest. Do not come to me at
this time of day with views palpably new, isolated,
original, *sui generis*, warranted old neither by Christian
nor unbeliever, and challenge me to answer what I
really have not the patience to read. Life is not long
enough for such trifles. Go elsewhere, not to me, if
you wish to make a proselyte. Your inconsistency,
my dear brethren, is on your very front. Nor pretend
that you are but executing the sacred duty of defending
your own Communion : your Church does not thank you
for a defence, which she has no dream of appropriat-
ing. You innovate on her professions of doctrine, and
then you bid us love her for your innovations. You
cling to her for what she denounces; and you almost
anathematise us for taking a step which you would
please her best by taking also. You call it restless,
impatient, undutiful in us, to do what she would have

L

us do; and you think it a loving and confiding course
in her children to believe, not her, but you. She is to
teach, and we are to hear, only according to your own
private researces into St. Chrysostom and St. Augustine. "I began myself with doubting and inquiring,"
you seem to say; "I departed from the teaching I
received; I was educated in some older type of Anglicanism; in the school of Newton, Cecil, and Scott, or
in the Bartlett's-Building School, or in the Liberal Whig
School. I was a Dissenter, or a Wesleyan, and by study
and thought I became an Anglo-Catholic. And then
I read the Fathers, and I have determined what works
are genuine, and what are not; which of them apply to
all times, which are occasional; which historical, and
which doctrinal; what opinions are private, what
authoritative; what they only seem to hold, what they
ought to hold; what are fundamental, what ornamental.
Having thus measured and cut and put together my
creed by my own proper intellect, by my own lucubra-
tions, and differing from the whole world in my results,
I distinctly bid you, I solemnly warn you, not to do as
I have done, but to accept what I have found, to revere
that, to use that, to believe that, for it is the teaching
of the old Fathers, and of your Mother the Church of
England. Take my word for it, that this is the very
truth of Christ; deny your own reason, for I know
better than you, and it is as clear as day that some
moral fault in you is the cause of your differing from

me. It is pride, or vanity, or self-reliance, or fulness
of bread. You require some medicine for your soul;
you must fast; you must make a general confession;
and look very sharp to yourself, for you are already
next door to a rationalist or an infidel."

Surely, I have not exaggerated, my brethren, what
you will be obliged to say, if you take the course which
you are projecting; but the point immediately before
us is something short of this; it is, whether a party in
the Establishment formed on such principles (and as
things are now it can be formed on no other) can in
any sense be called a genuine continuation of the
Apostolical party of twenty years ago? The basis of
that party was the professed abnegation of private
judgment; your basis is the professed exercise of it.
If you are really children of it as it was in 1833, you
must have nothing to say to it as it is in 1850

LECTURE VI.

I.

THERE are persons who may think that the line of thought which I pursued in my last two Lectures had somewhat of a secular and political cast, and was deficient in that simplicity which becomes an inquiry after religious truth. We are inquiring, you may say, whether the National Church is in possession of the Sacraments. whether we can obtain the grace of Christ, necessary for our salvation, at its hands? On this great question depends our leaving its communion or not; but you answer us by simply bidding us consider which course of action will look best, what the world expects of us, how posterity will judge of us, what termination is most logically consistent with our commencement, what are to be the historical fortunes in prospect of a large body of men, variously circumstanced, and subject to a variety of influences from without and within. It is a personal, an individual, question to each inquirer; but you would have us view it as a political game, in which each side makes moves, and just now it is our turn, not, as it really is, a matter of religious conviction, duty, and responsibility.

But thus to speak is mistaking the argument altogether. First, I am not addressing those who have no doubt whatever about the divine origin of the Established Church. I am not attempting to rouse, or, as some would call it, unsettle them. If there be such—for, to tell the truth, I almost doubt their existence—I pass them by. I am contemplating that not inconsiderable number, who are, in a true sense, though in various degrees, and in various modes, inquirers; who, on the one hand, have no doubt at all of the great Apostolical principles which are stamped upon the face of the early Church, and were the life of the movement of 1833; and who, on the other hand, have certain doubts about those principles being the property and the life of the National Church—who have fears, grave anxieties or vague misgivings, as the case may be, lest that communion be not a treasure-house and fount of grace—and then all at once are afraid again, that, after all, perhaps it *is,* and that it is their own fault that they are blind to the fact, and that it is undutifulness in them to question it;—who, after even their most violent doubts, have seasons of relenting and compunction; and who at length are so perplexed by

reason of the clear light pouring in on them from
above, yet by the secret whisper the while, that they
ought to doubt their own perceptions, because (as they
are told) they are impatient, or self-willed, or excited,
or dreaming, and have lost the faculty of looking at
things in a natural, straightforward way, that at length
they do not know what they hold and what they do not
hold, or where they stand, and are in conflict within,
and almost in a state of anarchy and recklessness.

2.

Now, to persons in this cruel strife of thought, I offer
the consideration on which I have been dwelling, as a
sort of diversion to their harassed minds; as an argument of fact, external to themselves, and over which
they have no power, which is of a nature to arbitrate
and decide for them between their own antagonist
judgments.   You wish to know whether the Establishment is what you began by assuming it to be — the
grace-giving Church of God.   If it be, you and your
principles will surely find your position there and your
home.   When you proclaim it to be Apostolical, it will
smile on you; when you kneel down and ask its blessing, it will stretch its hands over you; when you would
strike at heresy, it will arm you for the fight; when
you wind your dangerous way with steady tread between Sabellius, Nestorius, and Eutyches, between
Pelagius and Calvin, it will follow you with anxious

eyes and a beating heart; when you proclaim its relationship to Rome and Greece, it will in transport embrace you as its own dear children; you will sink happily into its arms, you will repose upon its breast, you will recognise your mother, and be at peace. If, however, on the contrary, you find that the more those great principles which you have imbibed from St. Athanasius and St. Augustine, and which have become the life and the form of your moral and intellectual being, vegetate and expand within you, the more awkward and unnatural you find your position in the Establishment, and the more difficult its explanation; if there is no lying, or standing, or sitting, or kneeling, or stooping there, in any possible attitude; if, as in the tyrant's cage, when you would rest your head, your legs are forced out between the Articles, and when you would relieve your back, your head strikes against the Prayer Book; when, place yourselves as you will, on the right side or the left, and try to keep as still as you can, your flesh is ever being punctured and probed by the stings of Bishops, laity, and nine-tenths of the Clergy buzzing about you; is it not as plain as day that the Establishment is not your place, since it is no place for your principles? Those principles are not there professed, they are not there realised. That mystical sacramental system on which your thoughts live, which was once among men, as you know well—and therefore must be always with them—is not the inheritance of

Anglicanism, but must have been bequeathed to others.
it must be sought elsewhere. You have doubts on the
point already; well, here is the confirmation of them.
I have no wish, then, to substitute an external and
political view for your personal serious inquiry. I am
but assisting you in that inquiry; I am deciding existing doubts, which belong to yourselves, by an external
fact, which is as admissible, surely, in such a matter, as
the allegation of miracles would be, or any other evidence of the kind ; for the same God who works in you
individually, is working in the public and historical
course of things also.

I think, then, that in my last Lectures I have proved,
not adequately, for it would take many words to do
justice to a proof so abundant in materials, but as far
as time allowed, and as was necessary for those who
would pursue the thought, that the movement to which
you and I belong, looks away from the Establishment,
that "Let us go hence" is its motto. I cannot doubt
you would agree with me in this, did you not belong to
it, did you disbelieve its principles, were you merely
disinterested, dispassionate lookers-on; in that case you
would decide that you must join some other communion: judge then as disbelieving, act as believing.
If the movement be a providential work, it has a providential scope; if that scope be not in the direction of
the Establishment, as I have been proving, in what
direction is it ? Does it look towards Greece, or towards

America, or towards Scotland, or towards Rome? This is the subject which has next to be considered, and to which, in part, I shall address myself to-day.

Here then, when you are investigating whither you shall go for your new succession and your new priesthood, I am going to offer you a suggestion which, if it approves itself to you, will do away with the opportunity, or the possibility, of choice altogether. It will reduce the claimants to one. Before entering, then, upon the inquiry, whither you shall betake yourselves, and what you shall be, bear with me while I give you one piece of advice; it is this :—While you are looking about for a new Communion, have nothing to do with a "Branch Church." You have had enough experience of branch churches already, and you know very well what they are. Depend upon it, such as is one, such is another. They may differ in accidents certainly; but, after all, a branch is a branch, and no branch is a tree. Depend on it, my brethren, it is not worth while leaving one branch for another. While you are doing so great a work, do it thoroughly; do it once for all; change for the better. Rather than go to another branch, remain where you are; do not put yourselves to trouble for nothing; do not sacrifice this world without gaining the next. Now let us consider this point attentively.

3.

By a Branch Church is meant, I suppose, if we
interpret the metaphor, a Church which is separate
from its stem; and if we ask what is meant by the
stem, I suppose it means the "Universal Church," as
you are accustomed to call it. The Catholic Church,
indeed, as understood by Catholics, is one kingdom or
society, divisible into parts, each of which is in intercommunion with each other and with the whole, as the
members of a human body. This Catholic Church, as
I suppose you would maintain, has ceased to exist, or
at least is in *deliquium*, for you will not give the name
to us, nor do you take it yourselves, and scarcely ever
use the phrase at all, except in the Creed; but a
"Universal Church" you think there really is, and you
mean by it the whole body of professing Christians all
over the world, whatever their faith, origin, and traditions, provided they lay claim to an Apostolical Succession, and this whole is divisible into portions or
branches, each of them independent of the whole, dis-
cordant one with another in doctrine and in ritual, des-
titute of mutual intercommunion, and more frequently
in actual warfare, portion with portion, than in a state
of neutrality. Such is pretty nearly what you mean by
a Branch, allowing for differences of opinion on the subject; such, for instance, is the Russian Branch, which
denounces the Pope as a usurper; such the Papal,
which anathematises the Protestantism of the Anglican;

such the Anglican, which reprobates the devotions and scorns the rites of the Russian; such the Scotch, which has changed the Eucharistic service of the Anglican; such the American, which has put aside its Athanasian Creed.

Such, I say, is a Branch Church, and, as you will see at once, it is virtually synonymous with a National; for though it may be in fact and at present but one out of many communions in a nation, it is intended, by its very mission, as preacher and evangelist, to spread through the nation; nor has it done its duty till it has so spread, for it must be supposed to have the promise of success as well as the mission. On the other hand, it cannot extravagate beyond the nation, for the very principle of demarcation between Branch and Branch is the distinction of Nation or State; to the Nation, then, or State it is limited, and beyond the Nation's boundaries it cannot properly pass. Thus it is the normal condition of a Branch Church to be a National Church; it tends to nationality as its perfect idea; till it is national it is defective, and when it is national it is all it can be, or was meant to be. Since, then, to understand what any being is, we must contemplate it, not in its rudiments or commencements, any more than in its decline, but in its maturity and its perfection, it follows that, if we would know what a Branch Church is, we must view it as a National Church, and we shall form but an erroneous estimate of its nature and its characteristics, unless we investigate its national form.

Recollect, then, that a Branch Church is a National Church, and the reason why I warn you against getting your orders from such a Church, or joining such a Church, as, for instance, the Greek, the Russian, or some Monophysite Church, is that you are in a National Church already, and that a National Church ever will be and must be what you have found your own to be,—an Erastian body. You are going to start afresh. Well, then, I assert, that if you do not get beyond the idea of Nationalism in this your new beginning, you are just where you were. Erastianism, the fruitful mother of all heresies, will be your first and your last. You will have left Erastianism to take Erastianism up again,—that heresy which is the very badge of Anglicanism, and the abomination of that theological movement from which you spring.

I here assert, then, that a Branch or National Church is necessarily Erastian, and cannot be otherwise, till the nature of man is other than it is; and I shall prove this from the state of the case, and from the course of history, and from the confession, or rather avowal, of its defenders. The English Establishment is nothing extraordinary in this respect; the Russian Church is Erastian, so is the Greek; such was the Nestorian; such would be the Scotch Episcopal, such the Anglo-American, if ever they became commensurate

with the nation. And now for my reasons for saying
so.

4

You hold, and rightly hold, that the Church is a
sovereign and self-sustaining power, in the same sense
in which any temporal State is such. She is sufficient
for herself; she is absolutely independent in her own
sphere; she has irresponsible control over her subjects
in religious matters; she makes laws for them of her
own authority, and enforces obedience on them as the
tenure of their membership with her. And you know,
in the next place, that the very people, who are her
subjects, are in another relation the State's subjects.
and that those very matters which in one aspect are
spiritual, in another are secular. The very same persons and the very same things belong to two supreme
jurisdictions at once, so that the Church cannot issue
any order, but it affects the persons and the things of
the State: nor can the State issue any order, without
its affecting the persons and the things of the Church.
Moreover, though there is a general coincidence between the principles on which civil and ecclesiastical
welfare respectively depend, as proceeding from one
and the same God, who has given power to the Magistrate as well as to the Priest, still there is no necessary
coincidence in their particular application and resulting
details, in the one and in the other polity, just as the
good of the soul is not always the good of the body;

and much more is this the case, considering there is no divine direction promised to the State, to preserve it from human passion and human selfishness. You will, I think, agree with me in judging, that under these circumstances it is morally impossible that there should not be continual collision, or chance of collision, between the State and the Church; and, considering the State has the power of the sword, and the Church has no arms but such as are spiritual, the problem to be considered by us is, how the Church may be able to do her divinely appointed work without let or hindrance from the physical force of the State.

And a difficulty surely it is, and a difficulty which Christianity for the most part brought into the world. It can scarcely be said to have existed before; for, if not altogether in Judaism, yet certainly in the heathen polities, the care of public worship, of morals, of education, was mainly committed, as well as secular matters, to the civil magistrate. There was once no independent jurisdiction in religion; but, when our Lord came, it was with the express object of introducing a new kingdom, distinct and different from the kingdoms of the world, and He was sought after by Herod, and condemned by Pilate, on the very apprehension that His claims to royalty were inconsistent with their prerogatives. Such was the Church when first introduced into the world, and her subsequent history has been after the pattern of her commencement; the State has ever been jealous of her, and has persecuted her from without and bribed her from within.

I repeat, the great principles of the State are those of the Church, and, if the State would but keep within its own province, it would find the Church its truest ally and best benefactor. She upholds obedience to the magistrate; she recognises his office as from God; she is the preacher of peace, the sanction of law, the first element of order, and the safeguard of morality, and that without possible vacillation or failure; she may be fully trusted; she is a sure friend, for she is indefectible and undying. But it is not enough for the State that things should be done, unless it has the doing of them itself; it abhors a double jurisdiction, and what it calls a divided allegiance; *aut Cæsar aut nullus*, is its motto, nor does it willingly accept of any compromise. All power is founded, as it is often said, on public opinion; for the State to allow the existence of a collateral and rival authority, is to weaken its own; and, even though that authority never showed its presence by collision, but never concurred and co-operated in the acts of the State, yet the divinity with which the State would fain hedge itself would, in the minds of men, be concentrated on that Ordinance of God which has the higher claim to it.

5.

Such being the difficulty which ever has attended,

and ever will attend, the claims and the position of the
Catholic Church in this proud and ambitious world,
let us see how, as a matter of history, Providence has
practically solved or alleviated it. He has done so
by means of the very circumstance that the Church *is*
Catholic, that she is one organised body, expanded over
the whole earth, and in active intercommunion part
with part, so that no one part acts without acting on
and acting with every other. He has broken the force
of the collisions, which ever must be, between Church
and State, by the circumstance that a large community,
such as the Church, necessarily moves slowly; and this
will particularly be the case when it is subject to
distinct temporal rulers, exposed to various political
interests and prepossessions, and embarrassed by such
impediments to communication (physical or moral,
mountains and seas, languages and laws) as separation
into nations involves. Added to this, the Church is
composed of a vast number of ranks and offices, so that
there is scarcely any of her acts that belongs to one
individual will, or is elaborated by one intellect, or that
is not rather the joint result of many co-operating
agents, each in his own place, and at his appointed
moment. And so fertile an idea as the Christian faith,
so happy a mother as the Catholic Church, is necessarily developed and multiplied into a thousand various
powers and functions; she has her Clergy and laity.
her seculars and regulars, her Episcopate and Prelacy,

her diversified orders, congregations, confraternities, communities, each indeed intimately one with the whole, yet with its own characteristics, its own work, its own traditions, its graceful rivalry, or its disgraceful jealousies, and sensitive, on its own ground and its own sphere, of whatever takes place anywhere else. And then again, there is the ever-varying action of the ten thousand influences, political, national, local, municipal, provincial, agrarian, scholastic, all bearing upon her; the clashing of temporal interests, the apprehension of danger to the whole or its parts, the necessity of conciliation, and the duty of temporising. Further, she has no material weapons of attack or defence, and is at any moment susceptible of apparent defeat from local misfortune or personal misadventure. Moreover, her centre is one, and, from this very circumstance, sheltered from secular inquisitiveness; sheltered, moreover, in consequence of the antiquated character of its traditions, the peculiarity of its modes of acting, the tranquillity and deliberateness of its operations, as well as the mysteriousness thrown about it both from its picturesque and imposing ceremonial, and the popular opinion of its sanctity. And further still, she has the sacred obligation on her of long-suffering, patience, charity, of regard for the souls of her children, and of an anxious anticipation of the consequences of her measures. Hence, though her course is consistent, determinate, and simple, when viewed in history, yet to those who

M

accompany the stages of its evolution from day to day as they occur, it is confused and disappointing.

How different is the bearing of the temporal power upon the spiritual! Its promptitude, decisiveness, keenness, and force are well represented in the military host which is its instrument. Punctual in its movements, precise in its operations, imposing in its equipments, with its spirits high and its step firm, with its haughty clarion and its black artillery, behold, the mighty world is gone forth to war, with what? with an unknown something, which it feels but cannot see? which flits around it, which flaps against its cheek, with the air, with the wind. It charges and it slashes, and it fires its volleys, and it bayonets, and it is mocked by a foe who dwells in another sphere, and is far beyond the force of its analysis, or the capacities of its calculus. The air gives way, and it returns again; it exerts a gentle but constant pressure on every side; moreover, it is of vital necessity to the very power which is attacking it. Whom have you gone out against? a few old men, with red hats and stockings, or a hundred pale students, with eyes on the ground, and beads in their girdle; they are as stubble; destroy them;—then there will be other old men, and other pale students instead of them. But we will direct our rage against one; he flees; what is to be done with him? Cast him out upon the wide world! but nothing can go on without him. Then bring him back! but he will give us no

guarantee for the future. Then leave him alone; his
power is gone, he is at an end, or he will take a new
course of himself : he will take part with the State or
the people. Meanwhile the multitude of interests in
active operation all over the great Catholic body rise
up, as it were, all around, and encircle the combat, and
hide the fortune of the day from the eyes of the world;
and unreal judgments are hazarded, and rash predic-
tions, till the mist clears away, and then the old man
is found in his own place, as before, saying Mass over
the tomb of the Apostles. Resentment and animosity
succeed in the minds of the many, when they find
their worldly wisdom quite at fault, and that the weak
has over-mastered the strong. They accuse the Church
of craft. But, in truth, it is her very vastness, her
manifold constituents, her complicated structure, which
gives her this semblance, whenever she wears it, of
feebleness, vacillation, subtleness, or dissimulation.
She advances, retires, goes to and fro, passes to the
right or left, bides her time, by a spontaneous, not a
deliberate action. It is the divinely-intended method
of her coping with the world's power. Even in the
brute creation, each animal which God has made has
its own instincts for securing its subsistence, and
guarding against its foes ; and, when He sent out His
own into the world, as sheep among wolves, over and
above the harmlessness and wisdom with which He
gifted them, He lodged the security of His truth in the

very fact of its Catholicity. The Church triumphs
over the world's jurisdiction everywhere, because,
though she is everywhere, for that very reason she
is in the fulness of her jurisdiction nowhere. Ten
thousand subordinate authorities have been planted
round, or have issued from, that venerable Chair where
sits the plenitude of Apostolical power. Hence, when
she would act, the blow is broken, and concussion
avoided, by the innumerable springs, if I may use the
word, on which the celestial machinery is hung. By
an inevitable law of the system, and by the nature
of the case, there are inquiries, and remonstrances,
and threatenings, and first decisions, and appeals, and
reversals, and conferences, and long delays, and arbitra-
tions, before the final steps are taken in its battle with
the State, if they cannot be avoided, and before the
proper authority of the Church shows itself, whether
in definition, or bull, or anathema, or interdict, or other
spiritual instrument; and then, if, after all, persuasion
has failed, and compromise with the civil power is
impossible, the world is prepared for the event; and even
in that case the Sovereign Pontiff, as such, is spared
any direct collision with it, for the reason that he is no
subject in matters temporal of the State with which
he is at variance, whatever it be, being temporal
Sovereign in his own home, and treating with the
States of the earth only through his secular representatives and ministers.

6.

The remarks I have been making are well illustrated
by the history of our own great St. Thomas, in his
contest with King Henry II. Deserted by his suffra-
gans, and threatened with assassination, he is forced
to escape, as he can, to the Continent. He puts his
cause before the Pope, but with no immediate result,
for the Pope is in contest with the Emperor, who has
supported a pretender to the Apostolic See. For two
years nothing is done; then the Pope begins to move,
but mediates between Archbishop and King, instead
of taking the part of the former. The King of France
comes forward on the Saint's side, and his friends
attempt to gain the Empress Matilda also. Strengthened by these demonstrations, St. Thomas excommunicates some of the King's party, and threatens the
King himself, not to say his realm, with an interdict.
Then there are appeals to Rome on the part of the
King's Bishops, alarmed at the prospect of such
extremities, while the Pope on the other hand gives
a more distinct countenance to the Saint's cause.
Suddenly, the face of things is overcast; the Pope has
anathematised the Emperor, and has his hands full
of his own matters; Henry's agents at Rome obtain a
Legatine Commission, under the presidency of a Cardinal favourable to his cause.

The quarrel lingers on; two years more have passed,
and then the Commission fails. Then St. Thomas

rouses himself again, and is proceeding with the interdict, when news comes that the King has overreached
the Pope, and the Archbishop's powers are altogether
suspended for a set time.   The artifice is detected by
the good offices of the French Bishops, the Pope sends
comminatory letters to the King, but, then again, does
not carry them out.   There is a reconciliation between
the Kings of England and France, at the expense of
St. Thomas; but, by this time, the suspension is over,
and the Saint excommunicates the Bishop of London.
In consequence, he receives a rebuke from the Pope,
who, after absolving the Bishop, takes the matter into
his own hands, himself excommunicates the Bishop,
and himself threatens the kingdom with an interdict.
Then St. Thomas returns, and is martyred, winning
the day by suffering, not by striking.

Seven years are consumed in these transactions from
first to last, and they afford a sufficient illustration of
the subject before us.   If I add the remarks made on
them by the editor of the Saint's letters, in Mr. Froude's
"Remains," it is for the sake of his general statement,
which is as just as it is apposite to my purpose, though
I may not be able to approve of the tone or the drift of
it.   Speaking of St. Thomas, he says, "His notions, both
as regarded the justice and policy to be pursued in the
treatment of Henry, had suggested this course [the
interdict] to him from the first opening of the contest;
and he seems always to have had such a measure before

him, only the interruptions occasioned by embassies from Rome, and appeals to Rome, and other temporary suspensions of his ecclesiastical powers, had prevented him from putting his purpose into effect; these having, in fact, taken up almost the whole of the time. For an embassy, it must be observed, from the first day of its appointment, suspended the Archbishop's movements, who could do nothing while special and higher judges were in office. . . . In this way, there being so much time, both before and after the actual holding of the conferences, during which the Archbishop's hands were tied, he may be said to have been almost under one sentence of suspension from the first, only rendered more harassing and vexatious from the promise afforded by his short intervals of liberty, and the alternations, in consequence, of expectation and disappointment. It was a state of confinement, which was always approaching its termination, and never realising it. With a clear line of action before him from the first, and with resolution and ability to carry it out, the Archbishop was compelled to keep pace, step by step, with a court that was absolutely deficient in both these respects; and found himself reduced throughout to a state of simple passiveness and endurance." [1]   Of course;—a Branch Church indeed, with the Catholic dogma and with Saints in it, cannot be; but, supposing the English Church had been such at the time of that contest, it

[1] Froude's Remains, vol. iv. p. 449.

would, humanly speaking, have been inevitably shat-
tered to pieces by its direct collision with the civil
power; or else, its Saints got rid of, its Erastianising
Bishops made its masters, and ultimately its dogma
corrupted, and the times of Henry VIII. anticipated;—
this would have been the case, but for its intercommunion with the rest of Christendom and the supremacy
of Rome.

7.

This, however, is what has been going on, in one
way or another, for the whole eighteen centuries of
Christian history. For even in the ante-Nicene period,
the heretic Patriarch of Antioch was protected by the
local sovereign against the Catholics, and was dispossessed by the authority and influence with the
Imperial Government of the See of Rome. And since
that time, again and again would the civil power,
humanly speaking, have taken captive and corrupted
each portion of Christendom in turn, but for its union
with the rest, and the noble championship of the
Supreme Pontiff. Our ears ring with the oft-told tale,
how the temporal sovereign persecuted, or attempted, or
gained, the local Episcopate, and how the many or the
few faithful fell back on Rome. So was it with the
Arians in the East and St. Athanasius; so with the
Byzantine Empress and St. Chrysostom; so with the
Vandal Hunneric and the Africans; so with the 130
Monophysite Bishops at Ephesus and St. Flavian; so

was it in the instance of the 500 Bishops, who, by the influence of Basilicus, signed a declaration against the Tome of St. Leo ; so in the instance of the Henoticon of Zeno ; and so in the controversies both of the Monothelites and of the Iconoclasts. Nay, in some of those few instances which are brought in controversy, as derogatory to the constancy of the Roman See, the vacillation, whatever it was, was owing to what, as I have shown, is ordinarily avoided, — the immediate and direct pressure of the temporal power. As, among a hundred Martyr and Confessor Popes, St. Peter and St. Marcellinus for an hour or a day denied their Lord, so if Liberius and Vigilius gave a momentary scandal to the cause of orthodoxy, it was when they were no longer in their proper place, as the keystone of a great system, and as the correlative of a thousand ministering authorities, but mere individuals, torn from their see and prostrated before Cæsar.

In later and modern times we see the same truth irresistibly brought out; not only, for instance, in St Thomas's history, but in St. Anselm's, nay, in the whole course of English ecclesiastical affairs, from the Conquest to the sixteenth century, and, not with least significancy, in the primacy of Cranmer. Moreover, we see it in the tendency of the Gallicanism of Louis XIV., and the Josephism of Austria. Such, too, is the lesson taught us in the recent policy of the Czar towards the United Greeks, and in the present bearing of the English Government towards the Church of Ireland. In all these instances, it is a struggle between the Holy See and some local, perhaps distant, Government, the liberty and orthodoxy of its faithful people being the matter in dispute; and while the temporal power is on the spot, and eager, and cogent, and persuasive, and dangerous, the strength of the assailed party lies in its fidelity to the rest of Christendom and to the Holy See.

Well, this is intelligible; we see why it should be so, and we see it in historical fact; but how is it possible, and where are the instances in proof, that a Church can cast off Catholic intercommunion without falling under the power of the State? Could an isolated Church do now, what, humanly speaking, it could not have done in the twelfth century, though a Saint was its champion? Do you hope to do, my brethren, what was beyond St. Thomas of Canterbury? Truly is it then called a Branch Church; for, as a branch cannot live of itself, therefore, as soon as it is lopped off from the Body of Christ, it is straightway grafted of sheer necessity upon the civil constitution, if it is to preserve life of any kind. Indeed, who could ever entertain such a dream, as that a circumscribed religious society, without the awfulness of a divine origin, the sacredness of immemorial custom, or the authority of many previous successes, while standing on its own ground, and simply subordinate as regards its constitu-

ent members to the civil power, should be able to assert
ecclesiastical claims, which are to impede the free action
of that same sovereign power, and to insult its majesty?
—a subject hierarchy, growing out of a nation's very
soil, yet challenging it, standing breast to breast against
it, breathing defiance into its very face, striking at it
full and straight,—why, as men are constituted, such
a nuisance, as they would call it, would be intoler
able. The rigid, unelastic, wooden contrivance would
be shivered into bits by the very recoil and jar of the
first blow it was rash enough to venture. But matters
would not go so far; the blandishments, the alliances,
the bribes, the strong arm of the world, would bring it
to its senses, and humble it in its own sight, ere it had
opportunity to be valiant. The world would simply
over - master the presumptuous claimant to divine
authority, and would use for its own purposes the
slave whom it had dishonoured. It would set her
to sweep its courts, or to keep the line of its
march, who had thought to reign among the stars of
heaven.

For, it is evident enough, a National or Branch
Church can be of the highest service to the State, if
properly under control. The State wishes to make its
subjects peaceful and obedient; and there is nothing
more fitted to effect this object than religion. It wishes
them to have some teaching about the next world, but
not too much: just as much as is important and bene-

ficial to the interests of the present. Decency, order, industry, patience, sobriety, and as much of purity as can be expected from human nature,—this is its list of requisites; not dogma, for it creates the *odium theologicum;* not mystery, for it only serves to exalt the priesthood. Useful, sensible preaching, activity in benevolent schemes, the care of schools, the superintendence of charities, good advice for the thoughtless and idle, and "spiritual consolation" for the dying—these are the duties of a National or Branch Church. The parochial clergy are to be a moral police; as to the Bishops, they are to be officers of a State-religion, not shepherds of a people; not mixing and interfering in the crowd, but coming forward on solemn occasions to crown, or to marry, or to baptize royalty, or to read prayers to the House of Peers, or to consecrate churches, or to ordain and confirm, or to preach for charities, and to be but little seen in public in any other way. Synods are unnecessary and dangerous, for they convey the impression that the Establishment is a distinct body, and has rights of its own. So is discipline, or any practical separation of Churchmen and Dissenters; for nationality is the real bond, and Churchmanship is but the accident, of Englishmen. Churches and churchyards are national property, and open to all, whatever their denomination, for marriage and for burial, when they will. Nor must the Establishment be in the eye of the law a corporation, even though its separate incumbents and chapters be such, lest it be looked upon as politically more than a name, or a function of State.

8.

Now, in order to show that this is no exaggeration, I will, in conclusion, refer in evidence to the celebrated work of a celebrated man, in defence of the Establishment; a work, too, which disowns Erastianism, and, in a certain sense, is written against it, and which, moreover, is, in breadth of doctrine, behind what would be maintained or taken for granted by statesmen now. For all these reasons, if I would illustrate what I have been saying of the certainty of a theoretical Branch Church becoming, in fact, and in the event, a Branch of the State, and of the liking of the State for Branch Churches and nothing else, I could not take a work fairer to the National Church, than "The Alliance of Church and State" of Bishop Warburton. A few extracts will be sufficient for my purpose.

In this Treatise he tells us, that the object of the State in this alliance is, not the propagation of the truth, but the wellbeing of society. "The true end," he says, "for which religion is established," by the State, "is not to provide for the true faith, but for civil utility."[1] This is "the key," he observes, "to open the whole mystery of this controversy, and to lead" a man "safe through all the intricacies, windings, and perplex-

[1] Bp. Warburton's "Alliance of Church and State," p. 148, ed. 1741.

ities in which it has been involved." Next, religion is
to be used for the benefit of that civil power, which, it
seems, does not in any true sense provide for religion.
"This use of religion to the State," he says, "was seen
by the learned, and felt by all men of every age and
nation. The ancient world particularly was so firmly
convinced of this truth, that the greatest secret of the
sublime art of legislation consisted in this—how best
religion might be applied to serve society."[1]

Well, so far we might tolerate him; such statements,
if not simply true, are not absolutely unheard of or
paradoxical; but next he makes a startling step in advance. "Public utility and truth coincide,"[2] he says;
nay, further still, he distinctly calls public utility "a
sure rule and measure of truth;"[3] so that he continues,
by means of it the State "will be much better enabled
to find out truth, than any speculative inquirer with all
the aid of the philosophy of the schools."[4] "From
whence it appears," he continues, "that while a State,
in union with the Church, hath so great an interest and
concern with true religion, and so great a capacity for
discovering what is true, religion is likely to thrive
much better than when left to itself." The State, then,
it would appear, out of compassion to Religion, takes
it out of the schools, and adapts it to its own purposes
to keep it pure and make it perfect.

---

[1] Bp. Warburton's "Alliance of Church and State," p. 18.
[2] Ibid. p. 147.   [3] Ibid. p. 135.   [4] Ibid.

He does not scruple to bring out this very sentiment in the most explicit statements, that there may be no mistake about his meaning. He considers conformity to objects of State, the simple rule of truth, of purity, of exaggeration, of excess, of perversity, and of dangerousness in doctrinal teaching. "Of whatever use," he says, "an alliance may be thought for preserving the being of religion, the necessity of it for preserving its *purity* is most evident. . . . . . Let us consider the danger religion runs, when left in its natural state to itself, of deviating from truth. In those circumstances, the men who have the greatest credit in the Church are such as are famed for greatest sanctity. Now, Church sanctity has been generally understood to be then most perfect, when most estranged from the world and all its habitudes and relations. But this being only to be acquired by secession and retirement from human affairs, and that secession rendering man ignorant of civil society and its rights and interests, in place of which will succeed, according to his natural temper, all the follies of superstition or fanaticism, we must needs conclude, that religion, under such directors and reformers (and God knows these are generally its lot), will deviate from truth, and *consequently* from a capacity, in proportion, of serving civil society. . .

. Such societies we have seen, whose religious doctrines are so little serviceable to civil society, that they can prosper only on the ruin and destruction of it.

such are those who preach up the sanctity of celibacy, asceticism, the sinfulness of defensive war, of capital punishments, and even of civil magistracy itself. On the other hand, when Religion is in alliance with the State, as it then comes under the magistrate's direction (those holy leaders having now neither credit nor power to do mischief), its purity must needs be reasonably well supported and preserved. For, truth and public utility coinciding, the civil magistrate, as such, will see it for his interest to seek after and promote the truth in religion; and, by means of public utility, which his office enables him so well to understand, he will never be at a loss to know where such truth is to be found." [1]

He takes delight in this view of the subject, and enforces it as follows :—" The means of attaining man's happiness here," he says, " is civil society; the means of his happiness hereafter is contemplation. If, then, opinions, the result of contemplation, obstruct the effects of civil society, it follows that they must be restrained. Accordingly, the ancient masters of wisdom, who, from these considerations, taught that man was born for action, not for contemplation, universally concurred to establish it as a maxim, founded on the nature of things, that *opinions should always give way to civil peace.*" [2] And he proceeds to defend it as follows: "God so dis-

---

[1] Bp. Warburton's " Alliance of Church and State," p. 58.
[2] Ibid. p. 126.

posed things, that the means of attaining the happiness of one state [of existence] should not cross or obstruct the means of attaining the happiness of the other. From whence we must conclude, that where the supposed means of each—viz., opinions and civil peace—do clash, there one of them is not the true means of happiness. But the means of attaining the happiness peculiar to that state in which the man at present exists, being *perfectly and infallibly known* by man, and the means of the happiness of his future existence, as far as relates to the discovery of truth, but *very imperfectly known* by him, it necessarily follows that, *wherever opinions clash with civil peace, those opinions are no means of future happiness*, or, in other words, are either no truths, or truths of no importance." Behold the principle of the reasonings of the Committee of Privy Council, and the philosophy of the Premier's satisfaction thereupon! Baptismal regeneration is determined to be true or not true, not by the text of Scripture, the testimony of the Fathers, the tradition of the Church, nay, not by Prayer Book, Articles, Jewell, Usher, Carleton, or Bullinger, but by its tendency to minister to the peace and repose of the community, to the convenience and comfort of Downing Street, Lambeth, and Exeter Hall.

If the Bishop makes doctrine depend upon political expedience, it is not wonderful that he should take the same measure of the Sacraments and Orders of his

N

Church. "Hence," he says, "may be seen the folly of those Christian sects, which, under pretence that Christianity is a spiritual religion, fancy it cannot have rites, ceremonies, public worship, a ministry or ecclesiastical policy. *Not reflecting* that *without* these *it could never have become national*, and consequently, could not have done that *service* to the State that it, of all religions, is most capable of performing." [1] And then in a note, on occasion of Burnet's statement, that "Sidney's notion of Christianity was, that it was like a divine philosophy in the mind, without public worship or anything that looked like a Church," he adds, "that an ignorant monk, who had seen no further than his cell, or a mad fanatic, who had thrown aside his reason, should talk thus is nothing; but that the great Sidney, a man so superlatively skilled in the science of human nature and civil policy, and who *so well knew* what religion *was capable* of doing for the State, should fall into this extravagant error, is, indeed, very surprising."

Accordingly, he mentions some of the details in which ecclesiastical ceremonies are serviceable to the State; and in quoting his list and reasons of them, I shall conclude my extracts from his very instructive volume. "There are peculiar junctures," he says, "when the influence of religion is more than ordinarily serviceable to the State, and these the civil magistrate only knows. Now, while a Church is in its natural state of inde-

[1] Bp. Warburton's "Alliance of Church and State," p 104.

pendency, it is not in his power to improve these con-
junctures to the advantage of the State by a proper
application of religion; but when the alliance is made,
and, consequently, the Church under his direction, he
has the authority to prescribe such public exercises of
religion, as days of humiliation, fasts, festivals, exhor-
tations and dehortations, thanksgivings and deprecia-
tions, and in such a manner as he finds the exigencies
of State require." [1]

9.

And now I think I have shown you, my brethren, as
far as I could hope to do so in the course of a Lecture,
that if your first principle be, as it was the first principle of the movement of 1833, that the Church should
have absolute power over her faith, worship, and teaching, you must not be contemplating an ecclesiastical
body, local and isolated, or what you have been accustomed to call a Branch Church. The fable of the
bundle of sticks especially applies to those who have
no weapons of flesh and blood,—to an unarmed hierarchy, who have to contend with the pride of intellect
and the power of the sword. Look abroad, my brethren,
and see whether this union of many members, divided
in place and circumstances, but one in heart, is not
most visibly the very strength of the Catholic Church
at this very time. Then only can you resist the world,

[1] Bp. Warburton's "Alliance of Church and State," p. 63.

when you belong to a communion which exists under many governments, not one; or should it ever be under some empire commensurate with itself (which is not conceivable), a communion which has, at least, an immovable centre to fall back upon. But if this be the state of the case, if you must, on the one hand, leave the existing Establishment, yet, on the other, not seek or form a Branch Church instead of it, I have brought you by a short, but I hope, not an abrupt or unsafe path, to the conclusion that you must cease to be an Anglican by becoming a Catholic. Indeed, if the movement, of which you are the children, had any providential scope at all, I do not see how you can disguise from yourselves that Catholicism is it. The Catholic Church, and she alone, from the nature of the case, is proof against Erastianism.

LECTURE VII.

THE PROVIDENTIAL COURSE OF THE MOVEMENT OF 1833 NOT IN THE DIRECTION OF A SECT.

IT was my object yesterday to show that such persons as are led by the principles of the anti-Erastian movement of 1833 to quit the Establishment, are necessarily called upon, as by one and the same act, to join the Catholic Church; for the case is not supposable in reason, of their quitting the one without their joining the other. The only other course which lies open to them is either that of joining the communion of some other National or Branch Church, or, on the other hand, that of founding a Sect; but a Branch or National Church is inevitably Erastian. This point I argued out at considerable length; and now I come to the second alternative, viz., that of founding a Sect, or as it is sometimes familiarly called, setting up for one's self. And I shall show to-day that, bad as it is for a man to take the State for his guide and master in religion, or to become an Erastian, it is worse still to become a Sectarian, that is, to be his own Doctor and his own Pope.

What is really meant by a "Church," is a religious body which has jurisdiction over its members, or which governs itself; whereas, according to the doctrine of Erastus, it has no such jurisdiction, really is not a body at all, but is simply governed by the State, and is one department of the State's operations. This is one error, and a great one; it is an error, my brethren, which you have from the first withstood; but now I wish to show you that, if you will not accept of the Catholic Church, and submit yourselves to her authority, this said Erastianism is the least and the most tolerable error you can embrace; that your best and most religious of courses, which are all bad and irreligious, is to acquiesce in Erastianism at once; to give up the principles on which you set out, and to tell the world that the movement of 1833 was a mistake, and that you have grown wiser.

I.

I would have you recollect, then, that the civil power is a divine ordinance; no one doubts it. It is prior in history to ecclesiastical power. The Jewish lawgivers, judges, prophets, kings, had some sort of jurisdiction over the priesthood, though the priesthood had its distinct powers and duties. The Jewish Church was not a body distinct from the State. In a certain sense, then, the civil magistrate is what divines call, "in possession;" the *onus probandi* lies with those who would

encroach upon his power. He was in possession in
the age when Christ came; he is in possession now
in the minds of men, and in the *primâ facie* view of
human society. He is in possession, because the benefits he confers on mankind are tangible, and obvious to
the world at large. And he is recognised and sanctioned in Scripture in the most solemn way; nay, the
very instrument of his power, by which he is strong,
the carnal weapon itself, is formally committed to him.
"Let every soul," says St. Paul, "be subject to the
higher powers; for there is no power but from God;
and those that are," the powers that be, "are ordained
of God. Therefore he that resisteth the power, resisteth the ordinance of God; and they that resist, pur-
chase to themselves damnation. For princes are not
a terror to the good work, but to the evil. Wilt thou,
then, not be afraid of the power? Do that which is
good, and thou shalt have praise from the same. For
he is God's minister to thee for good. But if thou do
that which is evil, fear, for he beareth not the sword in
vain. For he is God's minister, an avenger to execute
wrath upon him that doth evil."

It is difficult to find a passage in Scripture more
solemn and distinct than this—distinct in the duty
laid down, and in the sin of transgressing it, and
solemn in the reasons on which the duty is enforced.
The civil magistrate is a minister, or, in a certain sense,
a priest of the Most High; for, as is well known, the

word in the original Greek is one which commonly is
appropriated to denote the sacerdotal office and function. He is, moreover, "an avenger to execute wrath;"
he is the representative and image on earth of that
awful attribute of God, His justice, as fathers are types
and intimations of His tenderness and providence towards His creatures. Nor is this a solitary recognition
of the divine origin and the dignity of the civil power:
—when Divine Wisdom, in the book of Proverbs, would
enlarge upon her great works on the earth, she finds
one principal and special instance of them to consist
in her presence and operation in the rulers of the
people. "By me," she says, "kings reign, and lawgivers
decree just things: by me princes rule, and the mighty
decree justice." And let it be observed, that the function here ascribed to the civil magistrate, and requiring
a peculiar gift, is one of those which especially enters
into the idea of the times of the promised Messias.
"Behold," says the Prophet, "a king shall reign in
justice, and princes shall rule in judgment." Such is
the civil power, the representative, and oracle, and instrument, of the eternal law of God, with the power of
life and death, the awful power of continuing or cutting
short the probation of beings destined to live eternally.
To it are committed all things under heaven; it is the
sovereign lord of the wide earth and its various fruits,
and of men who till it or traverse it; and it allots, and
distributes, and maintains, the one for the benefit of the

other. And as it is sacred in its origin, so may it be considered irresponsible in its acts, and treason against it, in some sort, rebellion against the Most High.

Now, such being the office of the temporal power, and considering the manifold temporal blessings of which it is the source and channel, and the cruelty of disturbing the settled order of society, and the madness of the attempt, surely a man has to think twice, and ought to be quite sure what he is doing, and to have a clear case to produce in his behalf, before he sets up any rival society to embarrass and endanger it. Pause before you decide on such a step, and make sure of your ground. Surely it is not likely that God should undo His own work for nothing. He does not revoke His ordinances except when they have failed of their mission. He does not supersede them or innovate on them, except when He is about to commence a higher work than He has already committed to them. Judaism was supplanted by Christianity, because its law was unprofitable, and because the Gospel was a definite revelation and doctrine from above, which required a more perfect organ for its promulgation. An institution was formed upon a new idea, and to it was transferred a portion of that authority which hitherto had centred in the State, and independence was bestowed on it; but surely only because it was able to do something which ancient philosophy and statesmanship had not dreamed of. Unless the duties of the Church had been different, or if they had been but partially different. from the duties of the State, it is obvious to ask, for what conceivable reason should two societies be set up to do the work of one ? Is it likely that Almighty Wisdom would have set up a second without recalling the first ? would have continued the commission to the first, yet sent forth a second upon the same field ? Such a course would simply have been adapted to kindle perpetual strife, and, if we may judge by appearances, to defeat the very purposes for which the civil power was appointed, and therefore is, in the highest degree, improbable, prior to some very clear proof to the contrary. This surely approves itself to the common sense of mankind. Either no Church has been set up in the world, or it is not set up for nothing; it must have a mission and a message of its own. Everything is defined, or made specific by its object : if the duties of the Church, its functions, its teaching, its working, be not specially distinct from those of the State, why, it will be impossible to resist the conclusion, that it was meant to be amalgamated with the State, to join on to it, to be a part of it, to be subordinate to it. We do not form two guilds for the same trade. Either assign to the Church its own craft, or do not ask that it should be chartered. Its object is its claim.

This consideration is a sufficient exposure of the theory of Alliance between Church and State, of which I was led to speak yesterday. Warburton maintains that each power, the Church and the State, does substantially just one and the same thing; the Church preaches truth, the State pursues expediency; but Christian truth is identical with political expediency. There is no possible thesis which a preacher can put forth, or a synod could define as true, but is infallibly determined to be such ("infallible" is his word) by the political expedience and experience of the State. But if this be really so, what is the use of this second Society, which you put forth as naturally independent of the State, and as so high and mighty an ally of it? I do not say that to preach is not a function different from speaking in Parliament, or reading prayers to a congregation from sitting in a police court; the functions are different, and the functionaries will be different. But in like manner the function of a police magistrate is different from the function of a speaker in Parliament; but you do not have a distinct society, divine in its origin, independent in its constitution, to exercise jurisdiction over members of Parliament or of the Police. I repeat, unless the Church has something to say and something to do, very different from what the State says and does, Erastianism is the doctrine of common sense, and must be very clearly negatived in Scripture if it is to be discarded.

2.

I will refer to another author in illustration. There was an anonymous work published, apparently in the

character of a Scotch Episcopalian, some years before
the movement of 1833 ; which, on supposed principles
of Scripture, advocated a Branch or National Church,
though the author would I suppose, have preferred the
words, "free," "independent," or "unestablished." Judging from the internal evidence, the world identified him
with a vigorous and original thinker, whom none could
approach without being set thinking also, whether with
him or contrary to him, and who has since risen to
the very highest rank of the Anglican hierarchy.[1] He
wrote, partly in answer to Warburton, and partly to
exhibit a counter-view of his own; but, if he will
pardon me in saying it, he is an instance of the same
unreality and inconsistency which I have just been
imputing to Warburton himself.

" The supreme head on earth," he says, "of each
branch of Christ's Church should evidently be some
spiritual officer or body.   Whether the governor of the
English Church were the primate, or the convocation,
or both conjointly, or any other man or body of men,
holding *ecclesiastical* authority, not attached to any
civil office, nor in the gift of any civil governor, in
either case the non-secular character of Christ's kingdom would be preserved.   The king, in conjunction
with the other branches of the legislature, ought to
have a distinctly defined *temporal* authority over every
one of his subjects, of whatever persuasion; and, of

[1] Dr. Whately.

consequence, over the ministers and all other members, both of the Church of England and of every other religious community, Christian, Jewish, or Pagan, within his dominions; but neither he, nor any other civil power, should interfere with articles of faith, liturgy, Church discipline, or any other spiritual matters. The kingdom of Heaven has no king but Christ; and He delegated His authority to Apostles, and through them to Bishops and Presbyters; not to any secular magistrates. These, therefore, ought not, by virtue of their civil offices, to claim the appointment to any office in the Church." [1] You see, my brethren, what clear views this anonymous writer has of the jurisdiction of the Church; they are identical with your own, or rather they go beyond you.

In consequence he speaks of its "degrading" the sacred character of Articles and Liturgy, "that they should stand upon the foundation of Acts of Parliament; that the spiritual rulers cannot alter them when they may need it; and that the secular power can, whether they need it or not. And accordingly," he continues, "it is almost a proverbial reproach, that yours is a 'parliamentary religion;' that you worship the Almighty as the Act directs; and that you are bound to seek for salvation 'according to the law in that case made and provided' by kings, lords, and

---

[1] Letters on the Church, p. 181. Dr. Whately never, I believe, owned to the authorship of this work.

commons; under the directions of the ministers of State; of persons," he adds, with a prophetic eye towards 1850, "who may be eminently well fitted for their *civil* offices, and who may indeed *chance* to be not only exemplary Christians, but sound divines, but who certainly are not appointed to their respective offices with any sort of view to their spiritual functions, who cannot even pretend that any sort of qualification for the good regulation of the Church is implied by their holding such stations as they do. Can this possibly be agreeable to the designs and institutions of Christ and His Apostles? If any one will seriously answer in the affirmative, he is beyond my powers of argumentation."[1]

Presently he observes, "The English Government seems to have a delight and a pride, in not only making the clergy do as much as possible in return for the protection they enjoy, but in enforcing their services in the most harsh and mortifying way. Like the ancient Persian soldiers, they are brought into the field under the lash of perpetual penalties, which serve to keep your ministers in a state of degradation as well as of dependence on the State, which I defy you to parallel in any other Christian Church that ever existed."[2] He then compares certain of the clergy to the dog in the fable, who mistook the clog round his neck for a badge of honourable distinction. He continues, "Altogether, indeed, I cannot but say, if I must speak out, there is

[1] p. 119.   [2] p. 125.

another fable respecting a dog, of which the condition
of your Church strongly reminds me. Your American
brethren, for instance, and some others, might say to
you, as the lean and hungry wolf did to the well-fed
mastiff, 'you are fat and sleek, indeed, while I am
gaunt and half-famished, but what means that mark
round your neck?' You must do this, under a penalty;
and you must not do that under a penalty; you must
comply with the rubric, and yet, at the same time, you
must not comply with the rubric. . . . In short, you
are fettered and crippled and disabled in every joint,
by your alliance with a body of a different character,
which could not, even with the best intentions, fail
to weaken instead of aiding you; but which, in fact,
aims chiefly at making a tool of you. But some of
you seem so habituated to this dependence of the
Church on the State, and so fond of it, as to have even
solicited interference in a case which could not concern
the civil community, and which the secular magistrate
was likely to care about as little as Gallio. An English
bishop did not dare to ordain an American to officiate
in a country not under British dominion, without asking and obtaining permission of his government, which
had just as much to do with the business as the
government of Abyssinia."[1]

Now all this is very ably put, and very true; but the
question comes upon the reader, What is the meaning

[1] p. 129.

and object of the sweeping ecclesiastical changes which
are advocated by this author? We must not take to
pieces the constitution and re-write the law for nothing.
What would be gained by his recommendations practically? And what are they intended to accomplish or
secure? Is it a gymnastical display or "agonism," as
the heathen author calls it, from the Academy or the
Garden, or a clever piece of irony which he presents to
our perusal, or is it the grave and earnest sermon of
one who would practise what he preaches, and would
not partake of what he condemns? Now I will do the
writer the justice to confess, that he does not agree
with Warburton in considering that truth is measured
by political expediency. He is too honest, too generous,
too high-minded, too sensible, for so miserable a paradox; but, considering the far higher views he takes of the
position of the Church, how he frets under her humiliation, how nobly zealous he is for her liberty, certainly
he will be guilty of a different, indeed, but a not less
startling paradox himself, if he has such exalted notions
of the Church, and yet gives her nothing to do. Warburton recognises the Church in order to destroy it; he
thinks it never has existed, or rather never ought to
have existed in its proper nature, but, from its first moment of creation, ought to have been dissolved into the
constitution of the State. But our author makes much
ado about ecclesiastical rights and privileges, which he
considers divinely bestowed, and, therefore, indefeasible.

He thinks the Church so pure and celestial, as to be insulted, defiled, by any communion with things simply secular. "My kingdom is not of this world," said our Lord, and, therefore, it seems, no ecclesiastical person must, as such, have a seat in Parliament, and, on the other hand, neither King nor Parliament, as such, must be able to appoint a fast day. "It was," he says, "Satan who first proposed an alliance between the Christian Church and the State, by offering temporal advantages in exchange for giving up some of the 'things that be God's,' and which we ought to 'render unto God,'—for not 'serving Him only,' whom only we ought to serve. The next, I am inclined to think, who proposed to himself this scheme, and endeavoured to bring it about, was Judas Iscariot."[1]

Well, then, if the Church be a kingdom, or government, not of this world, I do trust you have provided for her a message, a function, not of this world,— something distinct, something special, something which the world cannot do, which "eye hath not seen, nor ear heard, nor heart of man conceived." It is not enough to give her morality to preach about; why a heaven-appointed Society for that? With the Bible in his hands, if that be all, I do not see why one man, if properly educated, should not preach morality as well as another, without any disturbance of the rights of the magistrate or the order of civil society.

[1] p. 97.

O

It is sometimes said in bitterness that the Church's work is priestcraft; I have already accepted the word; it *is* a craft, a craft in the same sense that goldsmiths' work, or architecture, or legal science is a craft; it must have its teaching, its intellectual and moral habits, its long experience, its precedents, its traditions; nay, it must have all these in a much higher sense than crafts of this world, if it is to claim to come from above. The more certainly the Church is a kingdom of heaven, and, as the author is so fond of saying, "not of this world," the more certain is it that she must have simply a heavenly work also, which the world cannot do for itself.

3.

Now, I fear, I must say, I see no symptoms at all of the writer in question intending to make his pattern-Church answer to this most reasonable expectation. There is nothing in his book to show that he entrusts his Church with any special doctrine or work of any kind. Whatever he may say, there is nothing to show why a lawyer, or a physician, or a scientific professor, or a country gentleman, or any one who has his evenings to himself, and is of an active turn, should not do everything which he ascribes to his heaven-born society. If, for instance, religion has its mysteries, if it has its fertile dogmas and their varied ramifications, if it has its theology,

if it has its long line of momentous controversies, its
careful ventilation of questions, and its satisfactory
and definite solutions; if, moreover, it has its special
work, its substantial presence in the midst of us, its
daily gifts from heaven, and its necessary ministries
thence arising, then we shall see the meaning, we
shall adore the wisdom, of the Divine Governor of
all, in having done a new thing upon the earth when
Christ came, in having withdrawn a jurisdiction He
had once given to the State, and having bestowed
it on a special ordinance created for a special purpose. But in proportion as this author fails in this
just anticipation, and disappoints the common sense
of mankind, if he has nothing better to tell us than
that one man's opinion is as good as another's; that
Fathers and Schoolmen, and the greater number of
Anglican divines, are puzzled-headed or dishonest;
that heretics have at least this good about them, that
they are in earnest, and do not take doctrines for
granted; that religion is simple, and theologians have
made it hard; that controversy is on the whole a
logomachy; that we must worship in spirit and in
truth; that we ought to love truth; that few people
love truth for its own sake; that we ought to be
candid and dispassionate, to avoid extremes, to eschew
party spirit, to take a rational satisfaction in contemplating the works of nature, and not to speculate
about "secret things;" that our Lord came to teach

us all this, and to gain us immortality by His death,
and the promise of spiritual assistance, and that this
is pretty nearly the whole of theology; and that at
least all is in the Bible, where every one may read
it for himself—(and I see no evidence whatever of
his going much beyond this round of teaching)—then,
I say, if the work and mission of Christianity be so
level in its exercise to the capacities of the State,
surely its ministry also is within the State's jurisdiction. I cannot believe that Bishops, and clergymen,
and councils, and convocations have been divinely
sent into the world, simply or mainly to broach
opinions, to discuss theories, to talk literature, to display the results of their own speculations on the text
of Scripture, to create a brilliant, ephemeral, ever-
varying theology, to say in one generation what the
next will unsay; else, why were not our debating
clubs and our scientific societies ennobled with a
divine charter also? God surely did not create the
visible Church for the protection of private judgment:
private judgment is quite able to take care of itself.
This is no day for what are popularly called "shams."
Many as are its errors, it is aiming at the destruction
of shadows and the attainment of what is either
sensibly or intellectually tangible. Why, then, should
we have so much bustle and turmoil about "supremacy," and "protection," and "alliance," and "authority," and "indefeasible rights," and "encroachments,"

and "usurpations," after the manner of this writer, if all the effort and elaboration is to be in its result but a mountain in labour, bringing forth nothing?

The State claims the allegiance of its subjects on the ground of the tangible benefits of which it is the instrument towards them. Its strength lies in this undeniable fact, and its subjects endure and maintain its coercion and its laws, because the certainty of this fact is ever present to their minds. What mean the array and the pomp which surround the Sovereign, — the strict ceremonial, the minute etiquette, the almost unsleeping watchfulness which eyes her every motion, which follows her into her garden and her chamber, which notes down every shade of her countenance and every variation of her pulse? Why do her soldiers hover about her, and officials line her ante-rooms, and cannon and illumination carry forward the tiding of her progresses among her people? Is this all a mockery? Is it done for nothing? Surely not; in her is centred the order, the security, the happiness of a great people. And, in like manner, the Church must be the guardian of a fact; she must have something to produce; she must have something to do. It is not enough to be keeper of even an inspired book: for there is nothing to show that her protection of it is necessary at this day. The State might fairly commit its custody to the art of printing, and dissolve an institution whose occupation was no more. She must, in order to have a meaning, do that which otherwise cannot be done, which she alone can do. She must have a benefit to bestow, in order to be worth her existence; and the benefit must be a fact which no one can doubt about. It must not be an opinion, or matter of opinion, but a something which is like a first principle, which may be taken for granted, a foundation indubitable and irresistible. In other words, she must have a dogma and Sacraments;—it is a dogma and Sacraments, and nothing else, which can give meaning to a Church, or sustain her against the State; for by these are meant certain facts or acts which are special instruments of spiritual good to those who receive them. As we do not gain the benefits of civil society unless we submit to its laws and customs, so we do not gain the spiritual blessings which the Church has to bestow upon us, unless we receive her dogmas and her Sacraments.

This, you know, is understood by every fanatic who would collect followers and form a sect. Who would ever dream of collecting a congregation, and having nothing to say to them? No! they think they have that to offer to the world which cannot otherwise be obtained. They do not bring forward mere opinions; they do not preach a disputable doctrine; but they assert, boldly and simply, that he who believes them will be saved. They announce, for instance, that every one must undergo the new birth, and for this they organise their society; viz., in order to preach and to testify, to realise and to perpetuate in the world this great and necessary fact,—the new birth of the soul. Or, again, they have a commission to do miracles, or they can prophesy, or they are sent to declare the end of the world. Something or other they do, which the existing establishments of Church and State do not, and cannot do.

4.

This being the state of the case, consider how entirely the reasonable anticipation of our minds is fulfilled in the professions of the Catholic Church. A Protestant wanders into one of our chapels; he sees a priest kneeling and bowing and throwing up a thurible, and boys in cottas going in and out, and a whole choir and people singing amain all the time, and he has nothing to suggest to him what it is all about; and he calls it mummery, and he walks out again. And would it not indeed be so, my brethren, if this were all? But will he think it mummery when he learns and seriously apprehends the fact, that, according to the belief of a Catholic, the Word Incarnate, the Second Person of the Eternal Trinity, is there bodily present,—hidden, indeed, from our senses, but in no other way withheld from us? He may reject what we believe; he will not wonder at what we do. And so, again, open the Missal, read the minute directions given for the celebration of Mass,—what are the fit disposi-

tions under which the Priest prepares for it, how he is
to arrange his every action, movement, gesture, utterance,
during the course of it, and what is to be done in case
of a variety of supposable accidents. What a mockery
would all this be, if the rite meant nothing! But if it
be a fact that God the Son is there offered up in human
flesh and blood by the hands of man, why, it is plain
that no rite whatever, however anxious and elaborate,
is equal to the depth of the overwhelming thoughts
which are borne in upon the mind by such an action
Thus the usages and ordinances of the Church do not
exist for their own sake; they do not stand of themselves; they are not sufficient for themselves; they do
not fight against the State their own battle; they are
not appointed as ultimate ends; but they are dependent
on an inward substance; they protect a mystery; they
defend a dogma; they represent an idea; they preach
good tidings; they are the channels of grace. They
are the outward shape of an inward reality or fact,
which no Catholic doubts, which is assumed as a first
principle, which is not an inference of reason, but the
object of a spiritual sense.

Herein is the strength of the Church; herein she
differs from all Protestant mockeries of her. She professes to be built upon facts, not opinions; on objective
truths, not on variable sentiments; on immemorial testimony, not on private judgment; on convictions or
perceptions, not on conclusions. None else but she can

make this profession. She makes high claims against
the temporal power, but she has that within her which
justifies her. She merely acts out what she says she
is. She does no more than she reasonably should do.
If God has given her a specific work, no wonder she is
not under the superintendence of the civil magistrate
in doing it. If her Clergy be Priests, if they can forgive sins, and bring the Son of God upon her altars, it
is obvious they cannot, considered as such, hold of the
State. If they were not Priests, the sooner they were
put under a minister of public instruction, and the
Episcopate abolished, the better. But she has not dis-
turbed the world for nothing. Her precision and per-
emptoriness, all that is laid to her charge as intolerance
and exclusiveness, her claim entirely to understand and
to be able to deal with her own deposit and her own
functions; her claim to reveal the unknown and to
communicate the invisible, is, in the eye of reason (so
far from being an objection to her coming from above),
the very tenure of her high mission,—just what would
be sure to characterise her if she had received such a
mission. She cannot be conceived without her message
and her gifts. She is the organ and oracle, and nothing
else, of a supernatural doctrine, which is independent
of individuals, given to her once for all, coming down
from the first ages, and so deeply and intimately embo-
somed in her, that it cannot be clean torn out of her,
even if you should try; which gradually and majesti-

cally comes forth into dogmatic shape, as time goes on and need requires, still by no private judgment, but at the will of its Giver, and by the infallible elaboration of the whole body;—and which is simply necessary for the salvation of every one of us. It is not a philosophy, or literature, cognisable and attainable at once by those who cast their eyes that way; but it is a sacred deposit and tradition, a mystery or secret, as Scripture calls it, sufficient to arrest and occupy the whole intellect, and unlike anything else; and hence requiring, from the nature of the case, organs special to itself, made for the purpose, whether for entering into its fulness, or carrying it out in deed.

5.

And now, my brethren, you may have been some time asking yourselves how all this bears upon the particular subject on which these Lectures are engaged; and yet I think it bears upon it very closely and significantly. For, perhaps, you may have said, in answer to my Lecture of yesterday, " We do not aim at forming a Branch Church; we put before us a really humble work. We have no ambition, no expectation of spreading through the nation, or of spreading at all. We do but mean to preserve for future times what we hold to be the truth. As books are consigned to some large library, with a simple view to their security, not let out to the world, and apparently useless, but yet with a definite object and benefit,—'though for no other cause, yet for this,' as Hooker says, 'that posterity may know we have not loosely through silence permitted things to pass away as in a dream,'—so, we care not to be successful in our day; we are willing to be despised; we do but aim at transmitting Catholic doctrine in its purest and most primitive form to posterity. We are willing to look like a small sect at the gate of the National Church, when really we are the heirs of the Apostles. We do not boast of this; we do not wish to inflict it upon the world; leave us to ourselves quietly and unostentatiously to transmit our burden to posterity in our own way."

I say, in reply, my brethren, that so far you are right, that you at least profess to have something to transmit; but be you sure withal that you have it, and know what it is. It will not do to have only a vague idea of it, if it is to form the basis of a communion; you must be at home with it, and must have surveyed it in its various aspects, and must be clear about it, and be prepared to state decisively to all inquirers its ground, its details, and its consequences, and must be able to say, unequivocally, that it comes from heaven;—or it will not serve your purpose. I am not sanguine that you will be able to do this even as regards the Sacrament of Baptism; differences have already risen among you as to the relative importance, at least under circumstances, of separate portions of the doctrine; and when you come

to define the consequences of sin after it, and the re-
medies of that sin, your variations and uncertainties
will be greater still. And much more of other doctrines;
there is hardly one of which you will be able to take a
clear and complete view. I say, then, Do not set up a
sect, till you are quite sure what is to be its creed.

6.

In the commencement of the movement of 1833, much
interest was felt in the Non-jurors. It was natural
that inquirers who had drawn their principles from the
primitive Church, should be attracted by the exhibition
of any portion of those principles anywhere in, or about,
an Establishment which was so emphatically opposed
to them. Therefore, in their need, they fixed their eyes
on a body of men who were not only sufferers for
conscience' sake, but held, in connection with their
political principles, a certain portion of Catholic truth.
But, after all, what *is*, in a word, the history of the Non-
jurors, for it does not take long to tell it? A party
composed of seven Bishops and some hundred Clergy,
virtuous and learned, and, as regards their leaders, even
popular, for political services lately rendered to the
nation, is hardly formed but it begins to dissolve and
come to nought, and that, simply because it had no
sufficient object, represented no idea, and proclaimed no
dogma. What should keep it together? why should it
exist? To form an association is to go out of the way,

and ever requires an excuse or an account of so preten-
tious a proceeding. Such were the ancient apologies
put forward for the Church in her first age; such the
Apologies of the Anglican Jewell, and the Quaker
Barclay. What was the apology of the Non-jurors?
Now their secession, properly speaking, was based on
no theological truth at all; it arose simply because, as
their name signifies, certain Bishops and Clergy could
not take the oaths to a new King. There is something
very venerable and winning in Bishop Ken; but this
arises in part from the very fact that he was so little
disposed to defend any position, or oppose things as they
were. He could not take the oaths, and was dispossessed;
but he had nothing special to say for himself; he had
no message to deliver; his difficulty was of a personal
nature, and he was unwilling that the Non-juring
Succession should be continued. It was against his
judgment to perpetuate his own communion. But look
at the body in its more theological aspect, and its negative and external character is brought out even more
strikingly. Its members had much more to say against
the Catholic Church, like Protestants in general, than
for themselves. They are considered especially high in
their Doctrine of the Holy Eucharist; yet, I do not
know anything in Dr. Brett's whole Treatise on the
Ancient Liturgies, which fixes itself so vividly on the
reader's mind, as his assertion, that the rubrics of the
Roman Missal are "corrupt, dangerous, superstitious,

abominably idolatrous, theatrical, and utterly unworthy
the gravity of so sacred an institution."

The Non-jurors were far less certain what they did
hold, than what they did not. They were great champions of the Sacrifice, and wished to restore the ancient
Liturgies ; yet, they could not raise their minds to anything higher than the sacrifice of the material bread and
wine, as representatives of One, who was not literally
present but absent; as symbols of His Body and Blood,
not in truth and fact, but in virtue and effect. Yet,
while they had such insufficient notions of the heavenly
gift committed to the ordinance, they could, as I have
said, be very jealous of its outward formalities, and laid
the greatest stress on a point, important certainly in its
place, but not when separated from that which gave it
meaning and life, the mixing of the water with the
wine; and upon this, and other questions, of higher
moment indeed, but not of a character specifically different, they soon divided into two communions. They
broke into pieces, not from external causes, not from
the hostility or the allurements of a court, but simply
because they had no common heart and life in them.
They were safe from the civil sword, from their insignificancy ; they had no need of falling back on a distant
centre for support; all they needed was an idea, an
object, a work to make them one.

But I have another remark to make on the Non-
jurors. You recollect, my brethren, that they are the

continuation and heirs of the traditions, so to call them, of the High-Church divines of the seventeenth century. Now, how high and imposing do the names sound of Andrewes, Laud, Taylor, Jackson, Pearson, Cosin, and their fellows ? I am not speaking against them as individuals, but viewing them as theological authorities. How great and mysterious are the doctrines which they teach! and how proudly they appeal to primitive times, and claim the ancient Fathers! Surely, as some one says, "in Laud is our Cyprian, and in Taylor is our Chrysostom, and all we want is our Athanasius." Look on, my brethren, to the history of the Non-jurors. and you will see what these Anglican divines were worth. There you will see that it was simply their position, their temporal possessions, their civil dignities, as standing round a King's throne, or seated in his great council, and not their principles, which made them what they were. Their genius, learning, faith, whatever it was, would have had no power to stand by themselves; these qualities had no substance, for, as we see, when the State abandoned them, they shrank at once and collapsed, and ceased to be. These qualities were not the stuff out of which a Church is made, though they looked well and bravely when fitted *upon* the Establishment. And, indeed, they did not, in the event, wear better in the Establishment than out of it; for since the Establishment at the Revolution had changed its make and altered its position, the old vestments would not fit it, and fell out of fashion. The Nation and the National Church had got new ideas, and the language of the ancient Fathers could not express them. There were those, who, at the era in question, took the oaths; they could secure their positions, could they secure their creed? The event answers the question. There is some story of Bull and Beveridge, who were two of the number, meeting together, I think in the House of Lords, and mourning together over the degeneracy of the times. The times certainly *were* degenerate; and if learning could have restored them, there was enough in those two heads to have done the work of Athanasius, Leo, and the seventh Gregory; but learning never made a body live. The High Church party died out within the Establishment, as well as outside of it, for it had neither dogma to rest upon, nor object to pursue.

All this is your warning, my brethren; you too, when it comes to the point, will have nothing to profess, to teach, to transmit. At present you do not know your own weakness. You have the life of the Establishment in you, and you fancy it is your own life; you fancy that the accidental *congeries* of opinions, which forms your creed, has that unity, individuality, and consistency, which allows of its developing into a system, and perpetuating a school. Look into the matter more steadily; it is very pleasant to decorate your chapels, oratories, and studies now, but you cannot be doing this for ever. It is pleasant to adopt a habit or

a vestment ; to use your office book or your beads ; but
it is like feeding on flowers, unless you have that objective vision in your faith, and that satisfaction in
your reason, of which devotional exercises and ecclesiastical regulations are the suitable expression. Such
will not last, on the long run, as are not commanded
and rewarded by divine authority ; they cannot be
made to rest on the influence of individuals. It is well
to have rich architecture, curious works of art, and
splendid vestments, when you have a present God ;
but oh! what a mockery, if you have not! If your
externals surpass what is within, you are, so far, as
hollow as your evangelical opponents who baptize, yet
expect no grace ; or, as the latitudinarian writer I have
been reviewing, who would make Christ's kingdom not
of this world, in order to do a little more than the
world's work. Thus your Church becomes, not a
home, but sepulchre ; like those high cathedrals, once
Catholic, which you do not know what to do with,
which you shut up and make monuments of, sacred
to the memory of what has passed away.

7.

Therefore, I say now,—as I have said years ago, when
others have wished still to uphold their party, after
their arguments had broken under them—Find out
first of all where you stand, take your position, write
down your creed, draw up your catechism. Tell me

why you form your party, under what conditions, how
long it is to last, what are your relations to the Establishment, and to the other branches (as you speak) of
the Universal Church, how you stand relatively to
Antiquity, what is Antiquity, whether you accept the
Via Media, whether you are zealous for "Apostolical
order," what is your rule of faith, how you prove it, and
what are your doctrines. It is easy for a while to be
doing merely what you do at present; to remain where
you are, till it is proved to you that you must go; to
refuse to say what you hold and what you do not, and
to act only on the offensive; but you cannot do this
for ever. The time is coming, or is come, when you
must act in some way or other for yourselves, unless
you would drift to some form of infidelity, or give up
principle altogether, or believe or not believe by accident. The *onus probandi* will be on your side then.
Now you are content to be negative and fragmentary in
doctrine; you aim at nothing higher than smart articles
in newspapers and magazines, at clever hits, spirited
attacks, raillery, satire, skirmishing on posts of your
own selecting; fastening on weak points, or what you
think so, in Dissenters or Catholics; inventing ingeni-
ous retorts, evading dangerous questions; parading this
or that isolated doctrine as essential, and praising this
or that Catholic practice or Catholic saint, to make up
for abuse, and to show your impartiality; and taking
all along a high, eclectic, patronising, indifferent tone;

this has been for some time past your line, and it will not suffice; it excites no respect, it creates no confidence, it inspires no hope.

And when, at length, you have one and all agreed upon your creed, and developed it doctrinally, morally, and polemically, then find for it some safe foundation, deeper and firmer than private judgment, which may ensure its transmission and continuance to generations to come. And, when you have done all this, then, last of all, persuade others and yourselves, that the foundation you have formed is surer and more trustworthy than that of Erastianism, on the one hand, and of immemorial and uninterrupted tradition, that is, of Catholicism, on the other.

PART II.

DIFFICULTIES IN ACCEPTING THE COMMUNION OF ROME
AS ONE, HOLY, CATHOLIC, AND APOSTOLIC.

LECTURE VIII.

*THE SOCIAL STATE OF CATHOLIC COUNTRIES NO
PREJUDICE TO THE SANCTITY OF THE CHURCH.*

I.

I HAVE been engaged in many Lectures in showing
that your place, my brethren, if you own the principles of the movement of 1833, is nowhere else but
the Catholic Church. To this you may answer, that,
even though I had been unanswerable, I should not
have done much, for my argument has, on the whole,
been a negative one; that there are difficulties on both
sides of the controversy; that I have been enlarging
on the Protestant difficulty, but there are not a few
Catholic difficulties also; that, to be sure, you are
not very happy in the Establishment, but you have
serious misgivings whether you would be happier

with us. Moreover, you might mention the following objection, in particular, as prominent and very practical, which weighs with you a great deal, and warns you off the ground whither I am trying to lead you. You are much offended, you would say, with the bad state of Catholics abroad, and their uninteresting character everywhere, compared with Protestants. Those countries, you say, which have retained Catholicism, are notoriously behind the age; they have not kept up with the march of civilization; they are ignorant, and, in a measure, barbarous; they have the faults of barbarians; they have no self-command; they cannot be trusted. They must be treated as slaves, or they rebel; they emerge out of their superstitions in order to turn infidels. They cannot combine and coalesce in social institutions; they want the very faculty of citizenship. The sword, not the law, is their ruler. They are spectacles of idleness, slovenliness, want of spirit, disorder, dirt, and dishonesty. There must, then, be something in their religion to account for this; it keeps them children, and then, being children, they keep to it. No man in his senses, certainly no English gentleman, would abandon the high station which his country both occupies and bestows on him in the eyes of man, to make himself the co-religionist of such slaves, and the creature of such a Creed.

I propose to make a suggestion in answer to this

objection; and, in making it, I shall consider you, my brethren, not as unbelievers, who are careless whether this objection strikes at Christianity or no; nor as Protestants proper, who have no concern about so expressing themselves, as to compromise the first centuries of the Church; but as those who feel that the Catholic Church was in the beginning founded by our Lord and His Apostles; again, that the Establishment is not the Catholic Church; that nothing *but* the Church of Rome can be; that, if the Church of Rome is not, then the Catholic Church is not to be found in this age, or in this part of the world; for this is what I have been proving in my preceding Lectures. What, then, you are saying comes, in fact, to this: We would rather deny our initial principles, than accept such a development of them as the communion of Rome, viewed as it is; we would rather believe Erastianism, and all its train of consequences, to be from God, than the religion of such countries as France and Belgium, Spain and Italy. This is what you must mean to say, and nothing short of it.

2.

I simply deny the justice of your argument, my brethren; and, to show you that I am not framing a view for the occasion, and, moreover, in order to start with a principle, which, perhaps, you yourselves have before now admitted, I will quote words which I used myself twelve years ago:—"If we were asked what was the object of Christian preaching, teaching, and instruction; what the office of the Church, considered as the dispenser of the Word of God, I suppose we should not all return the same answer. Perhaps we might say that the object of Revelation was to enlighten and enlarge the mind, to make us act by reason, and to expand and strengthen our powers: or to impart knowledge about religious truth, knowledge being power directly it is given, and enabling us forthwith to think, judge, and act for ourselves; or to make us good members of the community, loyal subjects, orderly and useful in our station, whatever it be; or to secure, what otherwise would be hopeless, our leading a religious life,—the reason why persons go wrong, throw themselves away, follow bad courses, and lose their character, being, that they have had no education, that they are ignorant. These and other answers might be given; some beside, and some short of, the mark. It may be useful, then, to consider with what end, with what expectation, we preach, teach, instruct, discuss, bear witness, praise, and blame; what fruit the Church is right in anticipating as the result of her ministerial labours. St. Paul gives us a reason . . . different from any of those which I have mentioned. He laboured more than all the Apostles. And why? Not to civilize the world, not to smooth the face of society, not to facilitate the movements of civil government, not to spread abroad knowledge, not to cultivate the reason, not for any great worldly object, but 'for the elect's sake.' . . . And such is the office of the Church in every nation where she sojourns; she attempts much; she expects and promises little." [1]

I do not, of course, deny that the Church does a great deal more than she promises: she fulfils a number of secondary ends, and is the means of numberless temporal blessings to any country which receives her. I only say, she is not to be estimated and measured by such effects; and if you think she is, my brethren, then I must rank you with such Erastians as Warburton, who, as I have shown you in a former Lecture, considered political convenience to be the test and standard of truth.

I thus begin with a consideration which, you see, I fully recognised before I was a Catholic; and now I proceed to another, which has been forced on me, as a matter of fact and experience, most powerfully ever since I was a Catholic, as it must be forced on every one who is in the communion of the Church; and which, therefore, like the former, has not at all originated in the need, nor is put forth for the occasion to meet your difficulty.

The Church, you know, is in warfare; her life here below is one long battle. But with whom is she fight-

---

[1] Paroch. Serm., vol. iv.

ing? For till we know her enemy we shall not be able
to estimate the skill of her tactics, the object of her
evolutions, or the success of her movements. We shall
be like civilians, contemplating a field of battle, and
seeing much dust, and smoke, and motion, much defil-
ing, charging, and manœuvring, but quite at a loss to
tell the meaning of all, or which party is getting the
better. And, if we actually mistake the foe, we shall
criticise when we should praise, and think that all is
a defeat, when every blow is telling. In all undertakings we must ascertain the end proposed, before we
can predicate their success or failure; and, therefore,
before we so freely speak against the state of Catholic
countries, and reflect upon the Church herself in consequence, we must have a clear view what it is that the
Church has proposed to do with them and for them
We have, indeed, a right to blame and dissent from
the end which she sets before her; we may quarrel with
the mission she professes to have received from above;
we may dispense with Scripture, Fathers, and the continuous tradition of 1800 years. That is another matter;
then, at least, we have nothing to do with the theological
movement which has given occasion to these Lectures;
then we are not in the way to join the Catholic Church;
then we must be met on our own ground: but I am
speaking to those who go a great way with me; who
admit my principles, who almost admit my conclusion;
who are all but ready to submit to the Church, but who

are frightened by the present state of Catholic countries;
—to such I say, Judge of her fruit by her principles
and her object, which you yourselves also admit; not
by those of her enemies, which you renounce.

The world believes in the world's ends as the greatest
of goods; it wishes society to be governed simply and
entirely for the sake of this world. Provided it could
gain one little islet in the ocean, one foot upon the coast,
if it could cheapen tea by sixpence a pound, or make its
flag respected among the Esquimaux or Otaheitans, at
the cost of a hundred lives and a hundred souls, it
would think it a very good bargain. What does it
know of hell? it disbelieves it; it spits upon, it abomi-
nates, it curses its very name and notion. Next, as to
the devil, it does not believe in him either. We next
come to the flesh, and it is "free to confess" that it does
not think there is any great harm in following the
instincts of that nature which, perhaps it goes on to say,
God has given. How could it be otherwise? who ever
heard of the world fighting against the flesh and the
devil? Well, then, what is its notion of evil? Evil,
says the world, is whatever is an offence to me, whatever obscures my majesty, whatever disturbs my peace.
Order, tranquillity, popular contentment, plenty, prosperity, advance in arts and sciences, literature, refinement, splendour, this is my millennium, or rather my
elysium, my swerga; I acknowledge no whole, no individuality, but my own; the units which compose me

are but parts of me; they have no perfection in themselves; no end but in me; in my glory is their bliss, and in the hidings of my countenance they come to nought.

3.

Such is the philosophy and practice of the world;—now the Church looks and moves in a simply opposite direction. It contemplates, not the whole, but the parts; not a nation, but the men who form it; not society in the first place, but in the second place, and in the first place individuals; it looks beyond the outward act, on and into the thought, the motive, the intention, and the will; it looks beyond the world, and detects and moves against the devil, who is sitting in ambush behind it. It has, then, a foe in view; nay, it has a battle-field, to which the world is blind; its proper battle-field is the heart of the individual, and its true foe is Satan.

My dear brethren, do not think I am declaiming in the air or translating the pages of some old worm-eaten homily; as I have already said, I bear my own testimony to what has been brought home to me most closely and vividly as a matter of fact since I have been a Catholic; viz., that that mighty world-wide Church, like her Divine Author, regards, consults for, labours for the individual soul; she looks at the souls for whom Christ died, and who are made over to her; and her one object, for which everything is sacrificed—appear ances, reputation, worldly triumph—is to acquit herself well of this most awful responsibility. Her one duty is to bring forward the elect to salvation, and to make them as many as she can :—to take offences out of their path, to warn them of sin, to rescue them from evil, to convert them, to teach them, to feed them, to protect them, and to perfect them. Oh, most tender loving Mother, ill-judged by the world, which thinks she is, like itself, always minding the main chance ; on the contrary, it is her keen view of things spiritual, and her love for the soul, which hampers her in her negotiations and her measures, on this hard cold earth, which is her place of sojourning. How easy would her course be, at least for a while, could she give up this or that point of faith, or connive at some innovation or irregularity in the administration of the Sacraments! How much would Gregory have gained from Russia could he have abandoned the United Greeks! how secure had Pius been upon his throne, could he have allowed himself to fire on his people!

No, my dear brethren, it is this supernatural sight and supernatural aim, which is the folly and the feebleness of the Church in the eyes of the world, and would be failure but for the providence of God. The Church overlooks everything in comparison of the immortal soul.

Good and evil to her are not lights and shades passing over the surface of society, but living powers, springing from the depths of the heart. Actions in her sight are

not mere outward deeds and words, committed by hand
or tongue, and manifested in effects over a range of
influence wider or narrower, as the case may be; but
they are the thoughts, the desires, the purposes of the
solitary responsible spirit. She knows nothing of space
or time, except as secondary to will; she knows no evil
but sin, and sin is a something personal, conscious, voluntary; she knows no good but grace, and grace again
is something personal, private, special, lodged in the
soul of the individual. She has one and one only aim
—to purify the heart; she recollects who it is who has
turned our thoughts from the external crime to the
inward imagination; who said, that "unless our justice
abounded more than that of Scribes and Pharisees, we
should not enter into the kingdom of Heaven;" and
that "out of the heart proceed evil thoughts, murders,
adulteries, fornications, thefts, false testimonies, blasphemies. These are the things that defile a man."

Now I would have you take up the sermons of any
preacher, or any writer on moral theology, who has a
name among Catholics, and see if what I have said is
not strictly fulfilled, however little you fancied so before you make trial. Protestants, I say, think that the
Church aims at appearance and effect; she must be
splendid, and majestic, and influential: fine services,
music, lights, vestments, and then again, in her dealings with others, courtesy, smoothness, cunning, dexterity, intrigue, management—these, it seems, are the

weapons of the Catholic Church. Well, my brethren, she cannot help succeeding, she cannot help being strong, she cannot help being beautiful; it is her gift; as she moves, the many wonder and adore; — "Et vera incessu patuit Dea." It cannot be otherwise, certainly; but it is not her aim; she goes forth on the one errand, as I have said, of healing the diseases of the soul. Look, I say, into any book of moral theology you will; there is much there which may startle you: you will find principles hard to digest; explanations which seem to you subtle; details which distress you; you will find abundance of what will make excellent matter of attack at Exeter Hall; but you will find from first to last this one idea—(nay, you will find that very matter of attack upon her is occasioned by her keeping it in view; she would be saved the odium, she would not have thus bared her side to the sword, but for her fidelity to it)—the one idea, I say, that sin is the enemy of the soul; and that sin especially consists, not in overt acts, but in the thoughts of the heart.

4.

This, then, is the point I insist upon, in answer to the objection which you have to-day urged against me. The Church aims, not at making a show, but at doing a work. She regards this world, and all that is in it, as a mere shadow, as dust and ashes, compared with the value of one single soul. She holds that, unless

she can, in her own way, do good to souls, it is no use
her doing anything; she holds that it were better for
sun and moon to drop from heaven, for the earth to
fail, and for all the many millions who are upon it to
die of starvation in extremest agony, so far as temporal
affliction goes, than that one soul, I will not say,
should be lost, but should commit one single venial
sin, should tell one wilful untruth, though it harmed
no one, or steal one poor farthing without excuse.
She considers the action of this world and the action
of the soul simply incommensurate, viewed in their
respective spheres; she would rather save the soul of
one single wild bandit of Calabria, or whining beggar
of Palermo, than draw a hundred lines of railroad
through the length and breadth of Italy, or carry out a
sanitary reform, in its fullest details, in every city of
Sicily, except so far as these great national works
tended to some spiritual good beyond them.

Such is the Church, O ye men of the world, and now
you know her. Such she is, such she will be; and,
though she aims at your good, it is in her own way,—
and if you oppose her, she defies you. She has her
mission, and do it she will, whether she be in rags, or
in fine linen; whether with awkward or with refined
carriage; whether by means of uncultivated intellects,
or with the grace of accomplishments. Not that, in
fact, she is not the source of numberless temporal
and moral blessings to you also; the history of ages

testifies it; but she makes no promises; she is sent to seek the lost; that is her first object, and she will fulfil it, whatever comes of it.

And now, in saying this, I think I have gone a great way towards suggesting one main solution of the difficulty which I proposed to consider. The question was this:—How is it, that at this time Catholic countries happen to be behind Protestants in civilization? In answer, I do not at all determine how far the fact is so, or what explanation there may be of the appearance of it; but anyhow the fact, granting it exists, is surely no objection to Catholicism, unless Catholicism has professed, or ought to have professed, directly to promote mere civilization; on the other hand, it has a work of its own, and this work is, first, *different* from that of the world; next, *difficult of attainment*, compared with that of the world; and, lastly, *secret* from the world in its details and consequences. If, then, Spain or Italy be deficient in secular progress, if the national mind in those countries be but partially formed, if it be unable to develope into civil institutions, if it have no moral instinct of deference to a policeman, if the national finances be in disorder, if the people be excitable, and open to deception from political pretenders, if it know little or nothing of arts, sciences, and literature; I repeat, of course, I do not admit all this, except hypothetically, because it is difficult to draw the line between what is

Q

true in it and what is not:—then all I can say is, that
it is not wonderful that civil governments, which
profess certain objects, should succeed in them better
than the Church, which does not. Not till the State is
blamed for not making saints, may it fairly be laid
to the fault of the Church that she cannot invent a
steam-engine or construct a tariff. It is, in truth,
merely because she has often done so much more than
she professes, it is really in consequence of her very
exuberance of benefit to the world, that the world is
disappointed that she does not display that exuberance
always,—like some hangers-on of the great, who come
at length to think they have a claim on their bounty.

5.

Now, let me try to bring out what I mean more in
detail; and, in doing so, I hope to be pardoned, my
brethren, if my language be now and then of a more
directly religious cast than I willingly would admit
into disquisitions such as the present; though speaking, as I do, in a place set apart for religious purposes,
I am not perhaps called upon to apologize. In religious
language, then, the one object of the Church, to which
every other object is second, is that of reconciling the
soul to God. She cannot disguise from herself, that,
with whatever advantages her children commence their
course, in spite of their baptism, in spite of their most
careful education and training, still the great multi-

tude of them require her present and continual succour
to keep them or rescue them from a state of mortal
sin. Taking human nature as it is, she knows well,
that, left to themselves, they would relapse into the
state of those who are not Catholics, whatever latent
principle of truth and goodness might remain in them,
and whatever consequent hope there might be of a
future revival. They may be full of ability and energy,
they may be men of genius, men of literature and taste,
poets and painters, musicians and architects; they may
be statesmen or soldiers; they may be in professions
or in trade; they may be skilled in the mechanical
arts; they may be a hard-working, money-making community; they may have great political influence; they
may pour out a flood of population on every side; they
may have a talent for colonization; or, on the other
hand, they may be members of a country once glorious,
whose day is past; where luxury, or civil discord, or
want of mental force, or other more subtle cause, is
the insuperable bar in the way of any national
demonstration; or they may be half reclaimed from
barbarism, or they may be a simple rural population;
they may be the cold north, or the beautiful south;
but, whatever and wherever they are, the Church
knows well, that those vast masses of population,
as viewed in the individual units of which they are
composed, are in a state of continual lapse from the
Centre of sanctity and love, ever falling under His

displeasure, and tending to a state of habitual alienation from Him. Her one work towards these many
millions is, year after year, day after day, to be raising
them out of the mire, and when they sink again to
raise them again, and so to keep them afloat, as she
best may, on the surface of that stream, which is
carrying them down to eternity. Of course, through
God's mercy, there are numbers who are exceptions
to this statement, who are living in obedience and
peace, or going on to perfection; but the word of
Christ, "Many are called, few are chosen," is fulfilled
in any extensive field of operation which the Church
is called to superintend. Her one object, through
her ten thousand organs, by preachers and by con-
fessors, by parish priests and by religious communities, in missions and in retreats, at Christmas and at
Easter, by fasts and by feasts, by confraternities and
by pilgrimages, by devotions and by indulgences, is
this unwearied, ever-patient reconciliation of the soul
to God and obliteration of sin. Thus, in the words of
Scripture, most emphatically, she knows nought else but
"Jesus Christ and Him crucified." It is her ordinary
toil, into which her other labours resolve themselves,
or towards which they are directed. Does she send
out her missionaries? Does she summon her doctors?
Does she enlarge or diversify her worship? Does she
multiply her religious bodies? It is all to gain souls
to Christ. And if she encourages secular enterprises,

studies, or pursuits, as she does, or the arts of civilization generally, it is either from their indirect bearing
upon her great object, or from the spontaneous energy
which great ideas, such as hers, exert, and the irresistible influence which they exercise, in matters and
in provinces not really their own.

Moreover, as sins are of unequal gravity in God's
judgment, though all of whatever kind are offensive
to Him, and incur their measure of punishment, the
Church's great object is to discriminate between sin
and sin, and to secure in individuals that renunciation
of evil, which is implied in the idea of a substantial
and unfeigned conversion. She has no warrant, and
she has no encouragement, to enforce upon men in
general more than those habits of virtue, the absence
of which would be tantamount to their separation
from God; and she thinks she has done a great deal,
and exults in her success, does she proceed so far; and
she bears as she may, what remains still to be done, in
the conviction that, did she attempt more, she might
lose all. There are sins which are simply incompatible
with contrition and absolution under any circumstances; there are others which are disorders and
disfigurements of the soul. She exhorts men against
the second, she directs her efforts against the first.

Now here at once the Church and the world part
company; for the world, too, as is necessary, has its
scale of offences as well as the Church; but, referring

them to a contrary object, it classifies them on quite a contrary principle; so that what is heinous in the world is often regarded patiently by the Church, and what is horrible and ruinous in the judgment of the Church may fail to exclude a man from the best society of the world. And, this being so, when the world contemplates the training of the Church and its results, it cannot, from the nature of the case, if for no other reason, avoid thinking very contemptuously of fruits, which are so different from those which it makes the standard and token of moral excellence in its own code of right and wrong.

6.

I may say the Church aims at three special virtues as reconciling and uniting the soul to its Maker:— faith, purity, and charity; for two of which the world cares little or nothing. The world, on the other hand, puts in the foremost place, in some states of society, certain heroic qualities; in others certain virtues of a political or mercantile character. In ruder ages, it is personal courage, strength of purpose, magnanimity; in more civilized, honesty, fairness, honour, truth, and benevolence:—virtues, all of which, of course, the teaching of the Church comprehends, all of which she expects in their degree in all her consistent children, and all of which she enacts in their fulness in her saints; but which, after all, most beautiful as they are, admit of being the fruit of nature as well as of grace; which do not necessarily imply grace at all: which do not reach so far as to sanctify, or unite the soul by any supernatural process to the source of supernatural perfection and supernatural blessedness. Again, as I have already said, the Church contemplates virtue and vice in their first elements, as conceived and existing in thought, desire, and will, and holds that the one or the other may be as complete and mature, without passing forth from the home of the secret heart, as if it had ranged forth in profession and in deed all over the earth. Thus at first sight she seems to ignore bodies politic, and society, and temporal interests: whereas the world, on the contrary, talks of religion as being a matter of such private concern, so personal, so sacred, that it has no opinion at all about it; it praises public men, if they are useful to itself, but simply ridicules inquiry into their motives, thinks it impertinent in others to attempt it, and out of taste in themselves to sanction it. All public men it considers to be pretty much the same at bottom; but what matter is that to it, if they do its work? It offers high pay, and it expects faithful service; but, as to its agents, overseers, men of business, operatives, journeymen, figure-servants, and labourers, what they are personally, what are their principles and aims, what their creed, what their conversation; where they live, how they spend their leisure time, whither they are

going, how they die—I am stating a simple matter of
fact, I am not here praising or blaming, I am but con-
trasting,—I say, all questions implying the existence
of the soul, are as much beyond the circuit of the
world's imagination, as they are intimately and pri-
marily present to the apprehension of the Church.

The Church, then, considers the momentary, fleeting
act of the will, in the three subject matters I have
mentioned, to be capable of guiltiness of the deadliest
character, or of the most efficacious and triumphant
merit.   Moreover, she holds that a soul laden with the
most enormous offences, in deed as well as thought, a
savage tyrant, who delighted in cruelty, an habitual
adulterer, a murderer, a blasphemer, who has scoffed
at religion through a long life, and corrupted every
soul which he could bring within his influence, who
has loathed the Sacred Name, and cursed his Saviour,
—that such a man can under circumstances, in a
moment, by one thought of the heart, by one true
act of contrition, reconcile himself to Almighty God
(through His secret grace), without Sacrament, without priest, and be as clean, and fair, and lovely, as if
he had never sinned.   Again, she considers that in a
moment also, with eyes shut and arms folded, a man
may cut himself off from the Almighty by a deliberate
act of the will, and cast himself into perdition.   With
the world it is the reverse; a member of society may
go as near the line of evil, as the world draws it, as he

will; but, till he has passed it, he is safe. Again, when he has once transgressed it, recovery is impossible; let honour of man or woman be sullied, and to restore its splendour is simply to undo the past; it is impossible.

Such being the extreme difference between the Church and the world, both as to the measure and the scale of moral good and evil, we may be prepared for those vast differences in matters of detail, which I hardly like to mention, lest they should be out of keeping with the gravity of the subject, as contemplated in its broad principle. For instance, the Church pronounces the momentary wish, if conscious and deliberate, that another should be struck down dead, or suffer any other grievous misfortune, as a blacker sin than a passionate, unpremeditated attempt on the life of the Sovereign. She considers direct unequivocal consent, though as quick as thought, to a single unchaste desire as indefinitely more heinous than any lie which can possibly be fancied, that is, when that lie is viewed, of course, in itself, and apart from its causes, motives, and consequences. Take a mere beggar-woman, lazy, ragged, and filthy, and not over-scrupulous of truth — (I do not say she had arrived at perfection) — but if she is chaste, and sober, and cheerful, and goes to her religious duties (and I am supposing not at all an impossible case), she will, in the eyes of the Church, have a prospect of

heaven, which is quite closed and refused to the
State's pattern-man, the just, the upright, the generous,
the honourable, the conscientious, if he be all this,
not from a supernatural power—(I do not determine
whether this is likely to be the fact, but I am contrast-
ing views and principles)—not from a supernatural
power, but from mere natural virtue. Polished,
delicate - minded ladies, with little of temptation
around them, and no self-denial to practise, in spite
of their refinement and taste, if they be nothing more,
are objects of less interest to her, than many a poor
outcast who sins, repents, and is with difficulty kept
just within the territory of grace. Again, excess in
drinking is one of the world's most disgraceful offences
odious it ever is in the eyes of the Church, but if it
does not proceed to the loss of reason, she thinks it a
far less sin than one deliberate act of detraction,
though the matter of it be truth. And again, not
unfrequently does a priest hear a confession of thefts,
which he knows would sentence the penitent to trans-
portation, if brought into a court of justice, but which
he knows, too, in the judgment of the Church, might
be pardoned on the man's private contrition, without
any confession at all. Once more, the State has the
guardianship of property, as the Church is the guardian of the faith:—in the Middle Ages, as is often
objected, the Church put to death for heresy; well
but, on the other hand, even in our own times, the

State has put to death for forgery; nay, I suppose for sheep-stealing. How distinct must be the measure of crime in Church and in State, when so heterogeneous is the rule of punishment in the one and in the other!

My brethren, you may think it impolitic in me thus candidly to state what may be so strange in the eyes of the world;—but not so, my dear brethren, just the contrary. The world already knows quite enough of our difference of judgment from it on the whole; it knows that difference also in its results; but it does not know that it is based on principle; it taunts the Church with that difference, as if nothing could be said for her,—as if it were not, as it is, a mere question of a balance of evils,—as if the Church had nothing to show for herself, were simply ashamed of her evident helplessness, and pleaded guilty to the charge of her inferiority to the world in the moral effects of her teaching. The world points to the children of the Church, and asks if she acknowledges them as her own. It dreams not that this contrast arises out of a difference of principle, and that she claims to act upon a principle higher than the world's. Principle is always respectable; even a bad man is more respected, though he may be more hated, if he owns and justifies his actions, than if he is wicked by accident; now the Church professes to judge after the judgment of the Almighty; and it cannot be imprudent or impolitical to bring this out clearly and boldly. His judgment is not as man's: "I judge not according to the look of man," He says, "for man seeth those things which appear, but the Lord beholdeth the heart." The Church aims at realities, the world at decencies; she dispenses with a complete work, so she can but make a thorough one. Provided she can do for the soul what is necessary, if she can but pull the brands out of the burning, if she can but extract the poisonous root which is the death of the soul, and expel the disease, she is content, though she leaves in it lesser maladies, little as she sympathises with them.

7.

Now, were it to my present purpose to attack the principles and proceedings of the world, of course it would be obvious for me to retort upon the cold, cruel, selfish system, which this supreme worship of comfort, decency, and social order necessarily introduces; to show you how the many are sacrificed to the few, the poor to the wealthy, how an oligarchical monopoly of enjoyment is established far and wide, and the claims of want, and pain, and sorrow, and affliction, and guilt, and misery, are practically forgotten. But I will not have recourse to the common-places of controversy when I am on the defensive. All I would say to the world is, — Keep your theories to yourselves, do not inflict them upon the sons of Adam everywhere; do not measure heaven and earth by views which are in a great degree insular, and can never be philosophical and catholic. You do your work, perhaps, in a more business-like way, compared with ourselves, but we are immeasurably more tender, and gentle, and angelic than you. We come to poor human nature as the Angels of God, and you as police-men. Look at your poor-houses, hospitals, and prisons; how perfect are their externals! what skill and ingenuity appear in their structure, economy, and administration! they are as decent, and bright, and calm, as what our Lord seems to name them,— dead men's sepulchres. Yes! they have all the world can give, all but life; all but a heart. Yes! you can hammer up a coffin, you can plaster a tomb; you are nature's undertakers; you cannot build it a home. You cannot feed it or heal it; it lies, like Lazarus, at your gate, full of sores. You see it gasping and panting with privations and penalties; and you sing to it, you dance to it, you show it your picture-books, you let off your fireworks, you open your menageries. Shallow philosophers! is this mode of going on so winning and persuasive that we should imitate it?

Look at your conduct towards criminals, and honestly say, whether you expect a power which claims to be divine, to turn copyist of you? You have the power of life and death committed to you by Heaven; and some wretched being is sentenced to fall under it for

some deed of treachery and blood. It is a righteous
sentence, re-echoed by a whole people; and you have
a feeling that the criminal himself ought to concur in
it, and sentence himself. There is an universal feeling
that he ought to resign himself to your act, and, as it
were, take part in it; in other words, there is a sort of
instinct among you that he should make confession,
and you are not content without his doing so. So far
the Church goes along with you. So far, but no further.
To whom is he to confess? To me, says the Priest, for
he has injured the Almighty. To me, says the world,
for he has injured me. Forgetting that the power to
sentence is simply from God, and that the sentence,
if just, is God's sentence, the world is peremptory
that no confession shall be made by the criminal to
God, without itself being in the secret. It is right,
doubtless, that that criminal should make reparation
to man as well as to God; but it is not right that the
world should insist on having precedence of its Maker,
or should prescribe that its Maker should have no secrets
apart from itself, or that no divine ministration should
relieve a laden breast without its meddling in the act.
Yet the world rules it, that whatever is said to a minister
of religion in religious confidence is its own property.
It considers that a clergyman who attends upon the
culprit is its own servant, and by its boards of magistrates, and by its literary organs, it insists on his re-
vealing to its judgment-seat what was uttered before

the judgment-seat of God. What wonder, then, if
such forlorn wretches, when thus plainly told that
the world is their only god, and knowing that they
are quitting the presence of that high potentate for
ever, steel themselves with obduracy, encounter it
with defiance, baffle its curiosity, and inflict on its
impatience such poor revenge as is in its power?
They come forth into the light, and look up into the
face of day for the last time, and, amid the jests and
blasphemies of myriads, they pass from a world which
they hate into a world which they deny. Small mercies,
indeed, has this world shown them, and they make no
trial of the mercies of another!

8.

Oh, how contrary is the look, the bearing of the
Catholic Church to these poor outcasts of mankind!
There was a time, when one who denied his Lord was
brought to repentance by a glance; and such is the
method which His Church teaches to those nations
who acknowledge her authority and her sway. The
civil magistrate, stern of necessity in his function, and
inexorable in his resolve, at her bidding gladly puts on
a paternal countenance, and takes on him an office of
mercy towards the victim of his wrath. He infuses
the ministry of life into the ministry of death; he
afflicts the body for the good of the soul, and converts
the penalty of human law into an instrument of

everlasting bliss. It is good for human beings to die as infants, before they have known good or evil, if they have but received the baptism of the Church; but next to these, who are the happiest, who are the safest, for whose departure have we more cause to rejoice, and be thankful, than for theirs, who, if they live on, are so likely to relapse into old habits of sin, but who are taken out of this miserable world in the flower of their contrition and in the freshness of their preparation;— just at the very moment when they have perfected themselves in good dispositions, and from their heart have put off sin, and have come humbly for pardon, and have received the grace of absolution, and have been fed with the bread of Angels, and thus amid the prayers of all men have departed to their Maker and their Judge? I say, "the prayers of all:" for oh the difference, in this respect, in the execution of the extreme sentence of the law, between a Catholic State and another! We have all heard of the scene of im- piety and profaneness which attends on the execution of a criminal in England; so much so, that benevolent and thoughtful men are perplexed between the evil of privacy and the outrages which publicity occasions. Well, England surpasses Rome in ten thousand matters of this world, but never would the Holy City tolerate an enormity which powerful England cannot hinder. An arch-confraternity was instituted there at the close of the fifteenth century, under the invocation of San

Giovanni Decollato, that Holy Baptist, who lost his head by a king's sentence, though an unjust one; and it exercises its pious offices towards condemned criminals even now. When a culprit is to be executed, the night preceding the fatal day, two priests of the brotherhood, who sometimes happen to be Bishops or persons of high authority in the city, remain with him in prayer, attend him on the scaffold the next morning, and assist him through every step of the terrible ceremonial of which he is the subject. The Blessed Sacrament is exposed in all the churches all over the city, that the faithful may assist a sinner about to make a compulsory appearance before his Judge. The crowd about the scaffold is occupied in but one thought, whether he has shown signs of contrition. Various reports are in circulation, that he is obdurate, that he has yielded, that he is obdurate still. The women cry out that it is impossible; Jesus and Mary will see to it; they will not believe that it is so; they are sure that he will submit himself to his God before he enters into His presence. However, it is perhaps confirmed that the unhappy man is still wrestling with his pride and hardness of heart, and though he has that illumination of faith which a Catholic cannot but possess, yet he cannot bring himself to hate and abhor sins, which, except in their awful consequences, are, as far as their enjoyment, gone from him for ever. He cannot taste again the pleasure of revenge or of for-

R

bidden indulgence, yet he cannot get himself to give
it up, though the world is passing from him. The
excitement of the crowd is at its height: an hour
passes; the suspense is intolerable, when the news is
brought of a change; that before the Crucifix, in the
solitude of his cell, at length the—unhappy no longer
—the happy criminal has subdued himself; has prayed
with real self-abasement; has expressed, has felt a
charitable, a tender thought, towards those he has
hated; has resigned himself lovingly to his destiny;
has blessed the hand that smites him; has supplicated
pardon; has confessed with all his heart, and placed
himself at the disposal of his Priest, to make such
amends as he can make in his last hour to God and
man; has even desired to submit here to indignity, to
pain, to which he is not sentenced; has taken on
himself any length of purgatory hereafter, if thereby
he may now, through God's mercy, show his sincerity,
and his desire of pardon and of gaining the lowest
place in the kingdom of Heaven. The news comes;
it is communicated through the vast multitude all at
once; and, I have heard from those who have been
present, never shall they forget the instantaneous
shout of joy which burst forth from every tongue, and
formed itself into one concordant act of thanksgiving
in acknowledgment of the grace vouchsafed to one so
near eternity.

It is not wonderful then to find the holy men who,

from time to time, have done the pious office of pre-
paring such criminals for death, so confident of their
salvation. "So well convinced was Father Claver of
the eternal happiness of almost all whom he assisted,"
says this saintly missionary's biographer, "that, speaking once of some persons who had in a bad spirit
delivered a criminal into the hands of justice, he said,
'God forgive them; but they have secured the salvation
of this man at the probable risk of their own.' Most
of the criminals considered it a grace to die in the
hands of this holy man. As soon as he spoke to
them the most savage and indomitable became gentle
as lambs; and, in place of their ordinary imprecations
nothing was heard but sighs, and the sound of bloody
disciplines, which they took before leaving the prison
for execution."

But I must come to an end. I do not consider, my
brethren, I have said all that might be said in answer
to the difficulty which has come under our consideration; nor have I proposed to do so. Such an undertaking does not fall within the scope of these Lectures;
it would be an inquiry into facts. It is enough if I
have suggested to you one thought which may most
materially invalidate the objection. You tell me, that
the political and civil state of Catholic countries is
below that of Protestant: I answer, that, even though

you prove the fact, you have to prove something besides, if it is to be an argument for your purpose, viz., that the standard of civil prosperity and political aggrandisement is the truest test of grace and the largest measure of salvation.

LECTURE IX.

I CONSIDERED, in the preceding Lecture, the
objection brought in this day against the Catholic
Church, from the state of the countries which belong
to her. It is urged, that they are so far behind the
rest of the world in the arts and comforts of life, in
power of political combination, in civil economy, and
the social virtues, in a word, in all that tends to make
this world pleasant, and the loss of it painful, that their
religion cannot come from above. I answered, that,
before the argument could be made to tell against us,
proof must be furnished, not only that the fact was as
stated (and I think it should be very closely examined),
but especially that there is that essential connection in
the nature of things between true religion and temporal
prosperity, which the objection took for granted. That
there is a natural and ordinary connection between
them no one would deny; but it is one thing to say
that prosperity ought to follow from religion, quite
another to say that it must follow from it. Thus, health,

for instance, may be expected from a habit of regular
exercise; but no one would positively deny the fact
that exercise had been taken in a particular case,
merely because the patient gave signs of an infirm and
sickly state of the body. And, indeed, there may be
particular and most wise reasons in the scheme of
Divine Providence, whatever be the legitimate tendency of the Catholic faith, for its being left, from time
to time, without any striking manifestations of its
beneficial action upon the temporal interests of mankind, without the influence of wealth, learning, civil
talent, or political sagacity; nay, as in the days of
St. Cyprian and St. Augustine, with the actual reproach
of impairing the material resources and the social greatness of the nations which embrace it: viz., in order to
remind the Church, and to teach the world, that she
needs no temporal recommendations who has a heavenly
Protector, but can make her way (as they say) against
wind and tide.

This, then, was the subject I selected for my foregoing Lecture, and I said there were three reasons why
the world is no fit judge of the work, or the kind of
work, really done by the Church in any age:—first,
because the world's measure of good and scope of action
are so different from those of the Church, that it judges
as unfairly and as narrowly of the fruits of Catholicism
and their value, as the Caliph Omar might judge of the
use and the influence of literature, or rather indefinitely

more so. The Church, though she embraces all conceivable virtues in her teaching, and every kind of good, temporal as well as spiritual, in her exertions, does not survey them from the same point of view, or classify them in the same order as the world. She makes secondary what the world considers indispensable: she places first what the world does not even recognise, or undervalues, or dislikes, or thinks impossible; and not being able, taking mankind as it is found, to do everything, she is often obliged to give up altogether what she thinks of great indeed, but of only secondary moment, in a particular age or a particular country, instead of effecting at all risks that extirpation of social evils, which, in the world's eyes, is so necessary, that it thinks nothing really is done till it is secured. Her base of operations, from the difficulties of the season or the period, is sometimes not broad enough to enable her to advance against crime as well as against sin, and to destroy barbarism as well as irreligion. The world, in consequence, thinks, that because she has not done the world's work, she has not fulfilled her Master's purpose; and imputes to her the enormity of having put eternity before time.

And next, let it be observed that she has undertaken the more difficult work; it is difficult, certainly, to enlighten the savage, to make him peaceable, orderly, and self-denying; to persuade him to dress like a European, to make him prefer a feather-bed to the

heather or the cave, and to appreciate the comforts of
the fire-side and the tea-table: but it is indefinitely
more difficult, even with the supernatural powers given
to the Church, to make the most refined, accomplished,
amiable of men, chaste or humble; to bring, not only
his outward actions, but his thoughts, imaginations,
and aims, into conformity to a law which is naturally
distasteful to him. It is not wonderful, then, if the
Church does not do so much in the Church's way, as
the world does in the world's way. The world has
nature as an ally, and the Church, on the whole, and
as things are, has nature as an enemy.

And lastly, as I have implied, her best fruit is
necessarily secret: she fights with the heart of man;
her perpetual conflict is against the pride, the impurity,
the covetousness, the envy, the cruelty, which never
gets so far as to come to light; which she succeeds in
strangling in its birth. From the nature of the case,
she ever will do more in repressing evil than in creating
good; moreover, virtue and sanctity, even when realised,
are also in great measure secret gifts, known only to
God and good Angels; for these, then, and other
reasons, the powers and the triumphs of the Church
must be hid from the world, unless the doors of the
Confessional could be flung open, and its whispers
carried abroad on the voices of the winds. Nor indeed
would even such disclosures suffice for the due comparison of the Church with religions which aim at no

personal self-government, and disown on principle examination of conscience and confession of sin; but in order to our being able to do justice to that comparison, we must wait for the Day when the books shall be opened and the secrets of hearts shall be disclosed. For all these reasons, then, from the peculiarity, and the arduousness, and the secrecy of the mission entrusted to the Church, it comes to pass that the world is led, at particular periods, to think very slightly of the Church's influence on society, and vastly to prefer its own methods and its own achievements.

So much I have already suggested towards the consideration of a subject, to which justice could not really be done except in a very lengthened disquisition, and by an examination of matters which lie beyond the range of these Lectures. If then to-day I make a second remark upon it, I do so only with the object I have kept before me all along, of smoothing the way into the Catholic Church for those who are already very near the gate; who have reasons enough, taken by themselves, for believing her claims, but are perplexed and stopped by the counter-arguments which are urged against her, or at least against their joining her.

1.

To-day, then, I shall suppose an objector to reply to what I have said in the following manner: viz., I

shall suppose him to say, that "the reproach of
Catholicism is, not what it does not do, so much as
what it does; that its teaching and its training do
produce a certain very definite character on a nation
and on individuals; and that character, so far from
being too religious or too spiritual, is just the reverse,
very like the world's; that religion is a sacred, awful,
mysterious, solemn matter; that it should be ap-
proached with fear, and named, as it were, *sotto voce;*
whereas Catholics, whether in the North or the South,
in the Middle Ages or in modern times, exhibit the
combined and contrary faults of profaneness and superstition. There is a bold, shallow, hard, indelicate
way among them of speaking of even points of faith,
which is, to use studiously mild language, utterly out
of taste, and indescribably offensive to any person of
ordinary refinement. They are rude where they should
be reverent, jocose where they should be grave, and
loquacious where they should be silent. The most
sacred feelings, the most august doctrines, are glibly
enunciated in the shape of some short and smart theological formula; purgatory, hell, and the evil spirit,
are a sort of household words upon their tongue; the
most solemn duties, such as confession, or saying
office, whether as spoken of or as performed, have a
business-like air and a mechanical action about them,
quite inconsistent with their real nature. Religion is
made both free and easy, and yet is formal. Supersti-

tions and false miracles are at once preached, assented
to, and laughed at, till one really does not know what
is believed and what is not, or whether anything is
believed at all. The saints are lauded, yet affronted.
Take medieval England or France, or modern Belgium
or Italy, it is all the same; you have your Boy-bishop
at Salisbury, your Lord of Misrule at Rheims, and at
Sens your Feast of Asses. Whether in the South now,
or in the North formerly, you have the excesses of
your Carnival. Legends, such as that of St. Dunstan's
fight with the author of all evil at Glastonbury, are
popular in Germany, in Spain, in Scotland, and in
Italy; while in Naples or in Seville your populations
rise in periodical fury against the celestial patrons
whom they ordinarily worship. These are but single
instances of a widespread and momentous phenomenon,
to which you ought not to shut your eyes, and to
which we can never be reconciled;—a phenomenon in
which we see a plain providential indication, that, in
spite of our certainty,—first, that there *is* a Catholic
Church, next, that it is *not* the religious communion
dominant in England, or Russia, or Greece, or Prussia,
or Holland; in short, that it *can* be nothing else *but*
the communion of Rome,—still, that it is our bounden
duty to have nothing to do with the Pope, the Holy
See, or the Church of which it is the centre." Such is
the charge, my brethren, brought against the Catholic

Church, both by the Evangelical section of the Establishment, and by your own.

2.

Now I will, on the whole and in substance, admit the fact to be as you have stated it; and next I will grant, that to no national differences can be attributed a character of religion so specific and peculiar. It is too uniform, too universal, to be ascribed to anything short of the genius of Catholicism itself; that is, to its principles and influence acting upon human nature, such as human nature is everywhere found. I admit both your fact and your account of the fact; I accept it, I repeat, in general terms what you have said; but I would add to it, and turn a particular fact into a philosophical truth. I say, then, that such a hard, irreverent, extravagant tone in religion, as you consider it, is the very phenomenon which must necessarily result from a revelation of divine truth falling upon the human mind in its existing state of ignorance and moral feebleness.

The wonder and offence which Protestants feel arises, in no small measure, from the fact that they hold the opinions of Protestants. They have been taught a religion, and imbibed ideas and feelings, and are suffering under disadvantages, which create the difficulty of which they complain; and, to remove it, I shall be obliged, as on some former occasions, against my will, to explain a point of doctrine:—Protestants, then, consider that faith and love are inseparable; where there is faith, there, they think, are love and obedience; and in proportion to the strength and degree of the former, are the strength and degree of the latter. They do not think the inconsistency possible of really believing without obeying; and, where they see disobedience, they cannot imagine there the existence of real faith. Catholics, on the other hand, hold that faith and love, faith and obedience, faith and works, are simply separable, and ordinarily separated, in fact; that faith does not imply love, obedience, or works; that the firmest faith, so as to move mountains, may exist without love,—that is, real faith, as really faith in the strict sense of the word as the faith of a martyr or a doctor. In other words, when Catholics speak of faith they are contemplating the existence of a gift which Protestantism does not even imagine. Faith is a spiritual sight of the unseen; and since in matter of fact Protestantism does not impart this sight, does not see the unseen, has no experience of this habit, this act of the mind—therefore, since it retains the word "faith," it is obliged to find some other meaning for it; and its common, perhaps its commonest, idea is, that faith is substantially the same as obedience; at least, that it is the impulse, the motive of obedience, or the fervour and heartiness which attend good works. In a word, faith is hope or it is love, or it is a mixture of the two. Protestants define or determine faith, not by its nature or essence, but by its effects. When it succeeds in producing good works, they call it real faith; when it does not, they call it counterfeit—as though we should say, a house is a house when it is inhabited; but that a house to let is not a house. If we so spoke, it would be plain that we confused between house and home, and had no correct image before our minds of a house *per se.* And in like manner, when Protestants maintain that faith is not really faith, except it be fruitful, whether they are right or wrong in saying so, anyhow it is plain that the idea of faith, as a habit in itself, as a something substantive, is simply, from the nature of the case, foreign to their minds, and that is the particular point on which I am now insisting.

Now faith, in a Catholic's creed, is a certainty of things not seen but revealed; a certainty preceded indeed in many cases by particular exercises of the intellect, as conditions, by reflection, prayer, study, argument, or the like, and ordinarily, by the instrumental sacrament of Baptism, but caused directly by a supernatural influence on the mind from above. Thus it is a spiritual sight; and the nearest parallel by which it can be illustrated is the moral sense. As nature has impressed upon our mind a faculty of recognising certain moral truths, when they are presented to us from without, so that we are quite sure that veracity, for instance, benevolence, and purity, are right and good, and that their contraries involve guilt, in a somewhat similar way, grace impresses upon us inwardly that revelation which comes to us sensibly by the ear or eye; similarly, yet more vividly and distinctly, because the moral perception consists in sentiments, but the grace of faith carries the mind on to objects. This certainty, or spiritual sight, which is included in the idea of faith, is, according to Catholic teaching, perfectly distinct in its own nature from the desire, intention, and power of acting agreeably to it. As men may know perfectly well that they ought not to steal, and yet may deliberately take and appropriate what is not theirs; so may they be gifted with a simple, undoubting, cloudless belief, that, for instance, Christ is in the Blessed Sacrament, and yet commit the sacrilege of breaking open the tabernacle, and carrying off the consecrated particles for the sake of the precious vessel containing them. It is said in Scripture, that the evil spirits "believe and tremble;" and reckless men, in like manner, may, in the very sight of hell, deliberately sin for the sake of some temporary gratification. Under these circumstances, even though I did not assume the Catholic teaching on the subject of faith to be true (which in the present state of the argument I fairly may do, considering whom I am addressing), though I took it merely as an hypothesis probable and philosophical, but not proved, still I would beg you to consider whether, *as* an hypothesis, it does not serve and suffice to solve the difficulty which is created in your minds by the aspect of Catholic countries. This, too, at least I may say: if it shall turn out that the aspect which Catholic countries present to the looker-on is accounted for by Catholic doctrine, at least that aspect will be no difficulty to you when once you have joined the Catholic Church, for, in joining the Church, you will be, of course, accepting the doctrine. Walk forward, then, into the Catholic Church, and the difficulty, like a phantom, will, as a matter of necessity, disappear. And now, assuming the doctrine as an hypothesis, I am going to show its bearing upon the alleged difficulty.

3.

The case with most men is this: certainly it is the case of any such large and various masses of men as constitute a nation, that they grow up more or less in practical neglect of their Maker and their duties to Him. Nature tends to irreligion and vice, and in matter of fact that tendency is developed and fulfilled in any multitude of men, according to the saying of the old Greek, that "the many are bad," or according to the Scripture testimony, that the world is at enmity with its Creator. The state of the case is not altered, when a nation has been baptized; still, in matter of fact, nature gets the better of grace, and the population falls into a state of guilt and disadvantage, in one point of view worse than that from which it has been rescued. This is the matter of fact, as Scripture prophesied it should be: "Many are called, few are chosen;" "the kingdom of heaven is like unto a net gathering together of every kind." But still, this being granted, a Catholic people is far from being in the same state in all respects as one which is not Catholic, as theologians teach us. A soul which has received the grace of baptism receives with it the germ or faculty of all supernatural virtues whatever,—faith, hope, charity, meekness, patience, sobriety, and every other that can be named; and if it commits mortal sin, it falls out of grace, and forfeits these supernatural powers. It is no longer what it was, and is, so far, in the feeble and frightful condition of those who were never baptized. But there are certain remarkable limitations and alleviations in its punishment, and one is this: that the faculty or power of faith remains to it. Of course the soul may go on to resist and destroy this supernatural faculty also; it may, by an act of the will, rid itself of its faith, as it has stripped itself of grace and love; or it may gradually decay in its faith till it becomes simply infidel; but this is not the common state of a Catholic people. What commonly happens is this, that they fall under the temptations to vice or covetousness, which naturally and urgently beset them, but that faith is left to them. Thus the many are in a condition which is absolutely novel and

s

strange in the ideas of a Protestant; they have a vivid
perception, like sense, of things unseen, yet have no
desire at all, or affection, towards them; they have
knowledge without love. Such is the state of the many;
the Church at the same time is ever labouring with all
her might to bring them back again to their Maker;
and in fact is ever bringing back vast multitudes one
by one, though one by one they are ever relapsing from
her. The necessity of yearly confession, the Easter
communion, the stated seasons of indulgence, the high
festivals, Lent, days of obligation, with their Masses and
preaching,—these ordinary and routine observances
and the extraordinary methods of retreats, missions,
jubilees, and the like, are the means by which the
powers of the world unseen are ever acting upon
the corrupt mass, of which a nation is composed, and
breaking up and reversing the dreadful phenomenon
which fact and Scripture conspire to place before us.

Nor is this all: good and bad are mixed together,
and the good is ever influencing and mitigating the
bad. In the same family one or two holy souls may
shed a light around and raise the religious tone of the
rest. In large and profligate towns there will be
planted here and there communities of religious men
and women, whose example, whose appearance, whose
churches, whose ceremonies, whose devotions,—to say
nothing of their sacerdotal functions, or their charitable
ministrations,—will ever be counteracting the intensity

of the poison. Again, you will have vast multitudes neither good nor bad; you will have many scandals; you will have, it may be, particular monasteries in a state of relaxation; rich communities breaking their rule, and living in comfort and refinement, and individuals among them lapsing into sin; cathedrals sheltering a host of officials, many of whom are a dishonour to the sacred place; and in country districts, priests who set a bad example to their flock, and are the cause of anxiety and grief to their bishops. And besides, you will have all sorts of dispositions and intellects, as plentiful of course as in a Protestant land: there are the weak and the strong-minded, the sharp and the dull, the passionate and the phlegmatic, the generous and the selfish, the idle, the proud, the sceptical, the dry-minded, the scheming, the enthusiastic, the self-conceited, the strange, the eccentric; all of whom grace leaves more or less in their respective natural cast or tendency of mind. Thus we have before us a confused and motley scene, such as the world presents generally; good and evil mingled together in all conceivable measures of combination and varieties of result; a perpetual vicissitude; the prospect brightening and then overcast again; luminous spots, tracts of splendour, patches of darkness, twilight regions, and the glimmer of day; but in spite of this moral confusion, in one and all a clear intellectual apprehension of the truth.

Perhaps you will say that this conflict of good and

evil is to be seen in a Protestant country in just the
same way : that is not the point; but this,—that, in a
Catholic country, on the mixed multitude, and on each
of them, good or bad, is written, is stamped deep, this
same wonderful *knowledge.* Just as in England, the
whole community, whatever the moral state of the
individuals, *knows* about railroads and electric tele
graphs ; and about the Court, and men in power, and
proceedings in Parliament; and about religious controversies, and about foreign affairs, and about all that
is going on around and beyond them : so, in a Catholic
country, the ideas of heaven and hell, Christ and the
evil spirit, saints, angels, souls in purgatory, grace, the
Blessed Sacrament, the sacrifice of the Mass, absolution,
indulgences, the virtue of relics, of holy images, of holy
water, and of other holy things, are of the nature of
facts, which all men, good and bad, young and old, rich
and poor, take for granted. They are facts brought home
to them by faith ; substantially the same to all, though
coloured by their respective minds, according as they are
religious or not, and according to the degree of their
religion. Religious men use them well, the irreligious
use them ill, the inconsistent vary in their use of them,
but all use them. As the idea of God is before the
minds of all men in a community not Catholic, so, but
more vividly, these revealed ideas confront the minds of
a Catholic people, whatever be the moral state of that
people, taken one by one. They are facts attested by

each to all, and by all to each, common property, primary points of thought, and landmarks, as it were, upon the territory of knowledge.

4.

Now, it being considered, that a vast number of sacred truths are taken for granted as *facts* by a Catholic nation, in the same sense as the sun in the heavens is a fact, you will see how many things take place of necessity, which to Protestants seem shocking, and which could not be avoided, unless it had been promised that the Church should consist of none but the predestinate; nay, unless it consisted of none but the educated and refined. It is the spectacle of super-natural faith acting upon the multitudinous mind of a people; of a divine principle dwelling in that myriad of characters, good, bad, and intermediate, into which the old stock of Adam grafted into Christ has developed. If a man sins grossly in a Protestant country, he is at once exposed to the temptation of unbelief; and he is irritated when he is threatened with judgment to come. He is threatened, not with what to him is a fact, but with what to him is at best an opinion. He has power over that opinion; he holds it to-day, whether he shall hold it to-morrow he cannot exactly say; it depends on circumstances. And, being an opinion, no one has a right to assume that it is anything more, or to thrust it upon him, and to threaten him with it. This is what is to him so provoking and irritating. Protestants hold that there is a hell, as the conclusion of a syllogism; they prove it from Scripture; it is from first to last a point of controversy, and an opinion, and must not be taken for granted as immutable. A vicious man is angry with those who hold opinions condemnatory of himself, because those opinions are the creation of the holders, and seem to reflect personally upon him. Nothing is so irritating to others as my own private judgment. But men are not commonly irritated by facts; it would be irrational to be so, as it is in children who beat the ground when they fall down. A bad Catholic does not deny hell, for it is to him an incontestable fact, brought home to him by that supernatural faith, with which he assents to the Divine Word speaking through Holy Church; he is not angry with others for holding it, for it is no private decision of their own. He may indeed despair, and then he blasphemes; but, generally speaking, he will retain hope as well as faith, when he has lost charity. Accordingly, he neither complains of God nor of man. His thoughts will take a different turn; he seeks to evade the difficulty; he looks up to our Blessed Lady; he knows by supernatural faith her power and her goodness; he turns the truth to his own purpose, his bad purpose; and he makes her his patroness and protectress against the penalty of sins which he does not mean to abandon. Such, I say, is the natural effect of having faith and hope without the saving grace of divine love.

Hence, the strange stories of highwaymen and brigands devout to the Madonna. And, their wishes leading to the belief, they begin to circulate stories of her much-coveted compassion towards impenitent offenders; and these stories, fostered by the circumstances of the day, and confused with others similar but not impossible, for a time are in repute. Thus, the Blessed Virgin has been reported to deliver the reprobate from hell, and to transfer them to purgatory; and absolutely to secure from perdition all who are devout to her, repentance not being contemplated as the means. Or men have thought, by means of some sacred relic, to be secured from death in their perilous and guilty expeditions. So, in the middle ages, great men could not go out to hunt without hearing Mass, but were content that the priest should mutilate it and worse, to bring it within limits. Similar phenomena occur in the history of chivalry: the tournaments were held in defiance of the excommunications of the Church, yet were conducted with a show of devotion; ordeals, again, were even religious rites, yet in like manner undergone in the face of the Church's prohibition. We know the dissolute character of the medieval knights and of the troubadours; yet, that dissoluteness, which would lead Protestant poets and travellers to scoff at religion, led them, not to deny revealed truth, but to combine it with their own wild and extravagant profession. The knight swore before Almighty God, His Blessed Mother, and—

the ladies; the troubadour offered tapers, and paid for Masses, for his success in some lawless attachment; and the object of it, in turn, painted her votary under the figure of some saint. Just as a heathen phraseology is now in esteem, and "the altar of hymen" is spoken of, and the trump of fame, and the trident of Britannia, and a royal cradle is ornamented with figures of Nox and Somnus; so in a Catholic age or country, the Blessed Saints will be invoked by virtuous and vicious in every undertaking, and will have their place in every room, whether of palace or of cottage. Vice does not involve a neglect of the external duties of religion. The Crusaders had faith sufficient to bind them to a perilous pilgrimage and warfare; they kept the Friday's abstinence, and planted the tents of their mistresses within the shadow of the pavilion of the glorious St. Louis. There are other pilgrimages besides military ones, and other religious journeys besides the march on Jerusalem; but the character of all of them is pretty much the same, as St. Jerome and St. Gregory Nyssen bear witness in the first age of the Church. It is a mixed multitude, some members of it most holy, perhaps even saints; others penitent sinners; but others, again, a mixture of pilgrim and beggar, or pilgrim and robber, or half gipsy, or three-quarters boon companion, or at least, with nothing saintly, and little religious about them. They will let you wash their feet, and serve them at table, and the hosts have

more merit for their ministry than the guests for their
wayfaring. Yet, one and all, saints and sinners, have
faith in things invisible, which each uses in his own
way.

5.

Listen to their conversation; listen to the conversation of any multitude of them or any private party:
what strange oaths mingle with it! God's heart, and
God's eyes, and God's wounds, and God's blood: you
cry out, "How profane!" Doubtless; but do you
not see, that their special profaneness over Protestant
oaths, lies, not in the words, but simply in the speaker,
and is the necessary result of that insight into the
invisible world, which you have not? You use the
vague words "Providence," or "the Deity," or "good-
luck," or "nature:" you would use more sacred words
did you believe in the things denoted by them: Catholics, on the contrary, whether now or of old, realise
the Creator in His supernatural works and personal
manifestations, and speak of the "Sacred Heart," or of
"the Mother of mercies," or of "our Lady of Walsing-
ham," or of "St. George, for merry England," or of
loving "St. Francis," or of dear "St. Philip." Your
people would be as varied and fertile in their adjura-
tions and invocations as a Catholic populace, if they
had as rich a creed. Again, listen how freely the
name of the evil spirit issues from the mouth even of
the better sort of men. What is meant by this very

off-hand mention of the most horrible object in
creation, of one who, if allowed, could reduce us to
ashes by the very hideousness of his countenance, or
the odour of his breath? Well, I suppose they act
upon the advice of the great St. Anthony; he, in
the lonely wilderness, had conflicts enough with the
enemy, and he has given us the result of his long experience. In the sermon which his far-famed biographer puts into his mouth, he teaches his hearers that
the devil and his host are not to be feared by those
who are within the fold, for the Good Shepherd has
put the wolf to flight. Henceforth, the evil spirit
could do no more than frighten them with empty
noises (except by some particular permission of God),
and could only pretend to do what was now really
beyond his power. The experience of a saint, I suppose, is imprudently acted on by sinners; not as if
Satan's malice were not equal to any assault upon body
or soul; but faith accepts the word that his rule over
the earth is now broken, and that any child or peasant
may ordinarily make sport of him and put him to
ridiculous flight by the use of the "Hail Mary!" or
holy water, or the sign of the cross.

Once more, listen to the stories, songs, and ballads
of the populace; their rude and boisterous merriment
still runs upon the great invisible subjects which
possess their imagination. Their ideas, of whatever
sort, good, bad, and indifferent, rise out of the next

world. Hence, if they would have plays, the subjects
are sacred; if they would have games and sports, these
fall, as it were, into procession, and are formed upon
the model of sacred rites and sacred persons. If they
sing and jest, the Madonna and the Bambino, or St.
Joseph, or St. Peter, or some other saint, is introduced,
not for irreverence, but because these are the ideas
that absorb them. There is a festival in the streets;
you look about: what is it you see? What would be
impossible here in London. Set up a large Crucifix
at Charing Cross; the police would think you simply
insane. Insane, and truly: but why? why dare you
not do it? why must you not? Because you are
averse to the sacred sign? Not so; you have it in
your chamber, yet a Catholic would not dare to do so,
more than another. It is true that awful, touching,
winning Form has before now converted the very
savage who gazed upon it; he has wondered, has
asked what it meant, has broken into tears, and been
converted ere he knew that he believed. The mani-
festation of love has been the incentive to faith. I
cannot certainly predict what would take place, if a
saint appealed to the guilty consciences of those thousand passers-by, through the instrumentality of the
Divine Sign. But such occurrences are not of every
day; what you would too securely and confidently
foretell, my brethren, were such an exhibition made,
would be, that it would but excite the scorn, the rage,

the blasphemy, of the out-pouring flocking multitude,
a multitude who in their hearts are unbelievers. Alas!
there is no idea in the national mind, supernaturally implanted, which the Crucifix embodies. Let a
Catholic mob be as profligate in conduct as an English,
still it cannot withstand, it cannot disown, it can but
worship the Crucifix; it is the external representation
of a fact, of which one and all are conscious to themselves and to each other. And hence, I say, in their
fairs and places of amusement, in the booths, upon the
stalls, upon the doors of wine-shops, will be paintings
of the Blessed Virgin, or St. Michael, or the souls in
purgatory, or of some Scripture subject. Innocence,
guilt, and what is between the two, all range themselves under the same banners; for even the resorts of
sin will be made doubly frightful by the blasphemous
introduction of some sainted patron.

6.

You enter into one of the churches close upon the
scene of festivity, and you turn your eyes towards
a confessional. The penitents are crowding for admission, and they seem to have no shame, or solemnity,
or reserve about the errand on which they are come;
till at length, on a penitent's turning from the grate,
one tall woman, bolder than a score of men, darts
forward from a distance into the place he has vacated,
to the disappointment of the many who have waited

longer than she. You almost groan under the weight
of your imagination that such a soul, so selfish, so
unrecollected, must surely be in very ill dispositions
for so awful a sacrament. You look at the priest, and
he has on his face a look almost of impatience, or of
good-natured compassion, at the voluble and superfluous matter which is the staple of her confession.
The priests, you think, are no better than the people.
My dear brethren, be not so uncharitable, so unphiloso-
phical. Things we thoroughly believe, things we see,
things which occur to us every day, we treat as things
which *do* occur and *are* seen daily, be they of this
world, or be they of the next. Even Bishop Butler
should have taught you that "practical habits are
strengthened by repeated acts, and passive impres-
sions grow weaker by being repeated upon us." It is
not by frames of mind, it is not by emotions, that we
must judge of real religion; it is the having a will and
a heart set towards those things unseen; and though
impatience and rudeness are to be subdued, and are
faulty even in their minutest exhibitions, yet do not
argue from them the absence of faith, nor yet of
love, or of contrition. You turn away half satisfied,
and what do you see? There is a feeble old woman,
who first genuflects before the Blessed Sacrament,
and then steals her neighbour's handkerchief, or
prayer-book, who is intent on his devotions. Here
at last, you say, is a thing absolutely indefensible and

inexcusable. Doubtless; but what does it prove?
Does England bear no thieves? or do you think this
poor creature an unbeliever? or do you exclaim against
Catholicism, which has made her so profane? but
why? Faith is illuminative, not operative; it does not
force obedience, though it increases responsibility; it
heightens guilt, it does not prevent sin; the will is the
source of action, not an influence, though divine, which
Baptism has implanted, and which the devil has only
not eradicated. She worships and she sins; she kneels
because she believes, she steals because she does not
love; she may be out of God's grace, she is not altogether out of His sight.

You come out again and mix in the idle and dis-
sipated throng, and you fall in with a man in a
palmer's dress, selling false relics, and a credulous
circle of customers buying them as greedily as though
they were the supposed French laces and India silks
of a pedlar's basket. One simple soul has bought of
him a cure for the rheumatism or ague, the use of
which might form a case of conscience. It is said to
be a relic of St. Cuthbert, but only has virtue at sun-
rise, and when applied with three crosses to the head,
arms, and feet. You pass on, and encounter a rude
son of the Church, more like a showman than a
religious, recounting to the gaping multitude some tale
of a vision of the invisible world, seen by Brother
Augustine of the Friars Minors, or by a holy Jesuit

preacher who died in the odour of sanctity, and sending round his bag to collect pence for the souls in purgatory; or of some appearance of our Lady (the like of which has really been before and since), but on no authority except popular report, and in no shape but that which popular caprice has given it. You go forward, and you find preparations in progress for a great pageant or mystery; it is a high festival, and the incorporated trades have each undertaken their special religious celebration. The plumbers and glaziers are to play the Creation; the barbers, the Call of Abraham; and at night is to be the grandest performance of all, the Resurrection and Last Judgment, played by the carpenters, masons, and blacksmiths. Heaven and hell are represented,—saints, devils, and living men; and the *chef d'œuvre* of the exhibition is the display of fireworks to be let off as the *finale.* "How unutterably profane!" again you cry. Yes, profane to you, my dear brother—profane to a population which only half believes; not profane to those who, however coarse-minded, however sinful, believe wholly, who, one and all, have a vision within, which corresponds with what they see, which resolves itself into, or rather takes up into itself, the external pageant, whatever be the moral condition of each individual composing the mass. They gaze, and, in drinking in the exhibition with their eyes, they are making one continuous and intense act of faith.

You turn to go home, and, on your way, you pass through a retired quarter of the city. Look up at those sacred windows; they belong to the convent of the Perpetual Adoration, or to the poor Clares, or to the Carmelites of the reform of St. Theresa, or to the nuns of the Visitation. Seclusion, silence, watching, meditation, is their life day and night. The immaculate Lamb of God is ever before the eyes of the worshippers; or at least the invisible mysteries of faith ever stand out, as if in bodily shape, before their mental gaze. Where will you find such a realised heaven upon earth? Yet that very sight has acted otherwise on the mind of a weak sister; and the very keenness of her faith and wild desire of approaching the Object of it, has led her to fancy or to feign that she has received that singular favour vouchsafed only to a few elect souls; and she points to God's wounds, as imprinted on her hands, and feet, and side, though she herself has been instrumental in their formation.

7.

In these and a thousand other ways it may be shown, that that special character of a Catholic country, which offends you, my brethren, so much, that mixture of seriousness and levity, that familiar handling of sacred things, in word and deed, by good and bad, that publication of religious thoughts and practices, so far as it is found, is the necessary con-

sequence of its being Catholic. It is the consequence
of mixed multitudes all having faith; for faith impresses the mind with supernatural truths, as if it
were sight, and the faith of this man, and the faith of
that, is one and the same, and creates one and the
same impression. The truths of religion, then, stand in
the place of facts, and public ones. Sin does not obli-
terate the impression; and did it begin to do so in
particular cases, the consistent testimony of all around
would bring back the mind to itself, and prevent
the incipient evil. Ordinarily speaking, once faith,
always faith. Eyes once opened to good, as to evil,
are not closed again; and, if men. reject the truth, it
is, in most cases, a question whether they have ever
possessed it. It is just the reverse among a Protestant
people; private judgment does but create opinions,
and nothing more; and these opinions are peculiar to
each individual, and different from those of any one
else. Hence it leads men to keep their feelings to
themselves, because the avowal of them only causes in
others irritation or ridicule. Since, too, they have no
certainty of the doctrines they profess, they do but
feel that they *ought* to believe them, and they try to
believe them, and they nurse the offspring of their
reason, as a sickly child, bringing it out of doors only
on fine days. They feel very clear and quite satisfied,
while they are very still; but if they turn about their
head, or change their posture ever so little, the vision

T

of the Unseen, like a mirage, is gone from them. So they keep the exhibition of their faith for high days and great occasions, when it comes forth with sufficient pomp and gravity of language, and ceremonial of manner. Truths slowly totter out with Scripture texts at their elbow, as unable to walk alone. Moreover, Protestants know, if such and such things *be* true, what *ought* to be the voice, the tone, the gesture, and the carriage attendant upon them; thus reason, which is the substance of their faith, supplies also the rubrics, as I may call them, of their behaviour. This some of you, my brethren, call reverence; though I am obliged to say it is as much a mannerism, and an unpleasant mannerism, as that of the Evangelical party, which they have hitherto condemned. They condemn Catholics, because, however religious they may be, they are natural, unaffected, easy, and cheerful, in their mention of sacred things; and they think themselves never so real as when they are especially solemn.

8.

And now, my brethren, I will only observe, in conclusion, how merciful a providence it has been, that faith and love are separable, as the Catholic creed teaches. I suppose it might have been, as Luther said it is, had God so willed it—faith and love might have been so intimately one, that the abandonment of the latter was the forfeiture of the former. Now, did sin not only throw the soul out of God's favour, but at once empty it of every supernatural principle, we should see in Catholics, what is, alas! so common among Protestants, souls brought back to a sense of guilt, frightened at their state, yet having no resource, and nothing to build upon. Again and again it happens, that, after committing some offence greater than usual, or being roused after a course of sin, or frightened by sickness, a Protestant wishes to repent; but what is he to fall back upon? whither is he to go? what is he to do? He has to dig and plant his foundation. Every step is to be learned, and all is in the dark; he is to search and labour, and after all for an opinion. And then, supposing him to have made some progress, perhaps he is overcome again by temptation; he falls, and all is undone again. His doctrinal views vanish, and it can hardly be said that he believes anything. But the Catholic knows just where he is and what he has to do; no time is lost when compunction comes upon him; but, while his feelings are fresh and keen, he can betake himself to the appointed means of cure. He may be ever falling, but his faith is a continual invitation and persuasive to repent. The poor Protestant adds sin to sin, and his best aspirations come to nothing; the Catholic wipes off his guilt again and again; and thus, even if his repentance does not endure, and he has not strength to persevere, in a

certain sense he is never getting worse, but ever beginning afresh. Nor does the apparent easiness of
pardon operate as an encouragement to sin, unless,
indeed, repentance be easy, and the grace of repentance
to be expected, when it has already been quenched, or
unless we come to consider past repentance to avail,
when it is not persevered in.

And, above all, let death come suddenly upon him,
and let him have the preparation of a poor hour; what
is the Protestant to do? He has nothing but sights
of this world around him; wife, and children, and
friends, and worldly interests; the Catholic has these
also, but the Protestant has nought but these. He
may, indeed, in particular cases, have got firm hold of his
party's view of justification or regeneration; or it may
be, he has a real apprehension of our Lord's divinity,
which comes from divine grace. But I am speaking,
not of the more serious portion of the community,
but of the popular religion; and I wish you to take a
man at random in one of our vast towns, and tell me,
has he any supernatural idea before his mind at all?
The minutes hasten on; and, having to learn everything, supposing him desirous of learning, he can
practise nothing. His thoughts rise up in some vague
desire of mercy, which neither he nor the bystanders
can analyze. He asks for some chapter of the Bible to
be read to him, but rather as the expression of his
horror and bewilderment, than as the token of his

faith; and then his intellect becomes clouded, and he dies.

How different is it with the Catholic! He has within him almost a principle of recovery, certainly an instrument of it. He may have spoken lightly of the Almighty, but he has ever believed in Him; he has sung jocose songs about the Blessed Virgin and Saints, and told good stories about the evil spirit, but in levity, not in contempt; he has been angry with his heavenly Patrons when things went ill with him, but with the waywardness of a child who is cross with his parents. Those heavenly Patrons were ever before him, even when he was in the mire of mortal sin and in the wrath of the Almighty, as lights burning in the firmament of his intellect, though he had no part with them, as he perfectly knew. He has absented himself from his Easter duties years out of number, but he never denied he was a Catholic. He has laughed at priests, and formed rash judgments of them, and slandered them to others, but not as doubting the divinity of their function and the virtue of their ministrations. He has attended Mass carelessly and heartlessly, but he was ever aware what really was before him, under the veil of material symbols, in that august and adorable action. So, when the news comes to him that he is to die, and he cannot get a priest, and the ray of God's grace pierces his heart, and he yearns after Him whom he has neglected, it is with no inarticulate, confused emotion, which does but oppress him, and which has no means of relief. His thoughts at once take shape and order; they mount up, each in its due place, to the great Objects of faith, which are as surely in his mind as they are in heaven. He addresses himself to his Crucifix; He invokes the Precious Blood or the Five Wounds of his Redeemer; he interests the Blessed Virgin in his behalf; he betakes himself to his patron Saints; he calls his good Angel to his side; he professes his desire of that sacramental absolution, which from circumstances he cannot obtain; he exercises himself in acts of faith, hope, charity, contrition, resignation, and other virtues suitable to his extremity. True, he is going into the unseen world; but true also, that that unseen world has already been with him here. True, he is going to a foreign, but not to a strange place; judgment and purgatory are familiar ideas to him, more fully realised within him even than death. He has had a much deeper perception of purgatory, though it be a supernatural object, than of death, though a natural one. The enemy rushes on him, to overthrow the faith on which he is built; but the whole tenor of his past life, his very jesting, and his very oaths, have been overruled, to create in him a habit of faith, girding round and protecting the supernatural principle. And thus, even one who has been a bad Catholic may have a hope in his death, to which the most virtuous of Protestants, nay, my brethren, the most correct and most thoughtful among yourselves, however able, or learned, or sagacious—if you have lived not by faith but by private judgment—are necessarily strangers.

٭

LECTURE X.

DIFFERENCES AMONG CATHOLICS NO PREJUDICE TO THE UNITY OF THE CHURCH.

I AM going to-day to take notice of an objection to the claims of that great Communion, into which, my brethren, I am inviting you, which to me sounds so feeble and unworthy, that I am loth to take it for my subject; for an answer, if corresponding to it, must be trifling and uninteresting also, and if careful and exact, will be but a waste of effort. I, therefore, do not know what to do with it: treat it with respect I cannot; yet since it is frequently, nay, triumphantly, urged by those who wish to make the most of such difficulties as they can bring together against our claims, I do not like to pass it over. Bear with me then, my brethren, nay, I may say, sympathize with me, if you find that the subject is not one which is very fertile in profitable reflection.

I.

When, then, the variations of Protestantism, or the divisions in the Establishment, are urged as a reason for your distrusting the Communion in which they are

found, it is answered, that divisions as serious and as
decided are to be found in the Catholic Church. It is
a well-known point in controversy, to say that the
Catholic Church has not any real unity more than
Protestantism; for, if Lutherans are divided in creed
from Calvinists, and both from Anglicans, and the
various denominations of Dissenters each has its own
doctrine and its own interpretation, yet Dominicans
and Franciscans, Jesuits and Jansenists, have had their
quarrels too. Nay, that at this moment the greatest
alienation, rivalry, and difference of opinion exist
among the members of the Catholic priesthood, so that
the Church is but nominally one, and her pretended
unity resolves itself into nothing more specious than
an awkward and imperfect uniformity. This is what
is said: and, I repeat, my answer to it cannot contain
anything either new or important, or even satisfactory
to myself. However, since I must enter upon the
subject, I must make the best of it; so let me begin
with an extract from Jewel's Apology, in which the
objection is to be found.

"Who are these," he says, "that find fault with
dissensions among us? Are they all agreed among
themselves? Hath every one of them determined, to
his own satisfaction, what he should follow? Have
there been no differences, no disputes among them?
Then why do not the Scotists and the Thomists come
to a more perfect agreement touching the merit of con-

gruity and condignity, touching original sin in the
Blessed Virgin, and the obligations of simple and
solemn vows? Why do the Canonists affirm auricular
confession to be of human and positive, and the Schoolmen, on the contrary, maintain that it is of divine
right? Why does Albertus Pighius differ from Caje-
tan, Thomas Aquinas from Peter Lombard, Scotus from
Thomas Aquinas, Occham from Scotus, Peter D'Ailly
from Occham, the Nominalists from the Realists?
And, not to mention the infinite dissensions of the
friars and monks (how some of them place their
holiness in the eating of fish, others in herbs; some in
wearing of shoes, others in sandals; some in linen
garments, others in woollen; some go in white, some in
black; some are shaven broader, some narrower; some
shod, some barefoot; some girded, others ungirded),
they should remember that some of their own adherents say, that the body of Christ is in the Lord's
supper naturally; that others again, of their own party,
teach the very reverse: that there are some who affirm
that the body of Christ in the Holy Communion is
torn and ground with our teeth; others again there are
who deny it: that there are some who say that the
body of Christ in the Eucharist hath quantity; and
others again deny it: that there are some who say
that Christ consecrated the bread and wine by the
especial putting forth of His divine power; others,
that He consecrated in the benediction: some, by the

conceiving the five words in His mind; others, by His uttering them: others there are who, in these five words, refer the demonstrative pronoun 'this' to the wheaten bread; others to what they call an *individuum vagum:* some there are who affirm that dogs and mice can verily and truly eat the body of Christ; others there are who do not hesitate to deny it; some there are who say that the very accidents of the bread and wine give nourishment; others, that the substance of bread and wine returns after consecration. And why should we bring forward more? It would be only tedious and burdensome to enumerate them all; so *unsettled and disputed* is yet the *whole form* of these men's religion and doctrine even among themselves, from whom it sprang and proceeded. For scarcely ever are they agreed together, unless, as of old, the Pharisees and Sadducees were, or Herod and Pilate, against Christ."

It is equally common to insist upon the breaches of charity which are to be found among the members of the Catholic Church. For instance, Leslie says, "If you have not unity in faith, nor in those principles and practices which are no less necessary to salvation, nor in that love and charity which Christ has made the characteristic of Christians, and without which no man can know who are His disciples; but, instead of that, if you have envyings and strife among you, among your several religious orders, betwixt National

and National Church, concerning the infallibility and
supremacy of the Pope, and of his power to depose
princes, upon which the peace and unity of the world
and our eternal salvation does depend; and, in short,
if you have no unity concerning your rule of faith
itself, or of your practice, what will the unity of
communion do, upon which you lay the whole
stress?"[1]

Such is the retort, by which Protestants would
divert our attack upon their own mutual differences
and variations in matters of faith. They answer, that
differences of religious opinion and that party dissensions are found within the Catholic Church.

2.

Now, in beginning my remarks upon this objection,
I would have you observe, my brethren, that the very
idea of the Catholic Church, as an instrument of supernatural grace, is that of an institution which innovates
upon, or rather superadds to nature. She does something for nature above or beyond nature. When, then,
it is said that she makes her members one, this implies
that by nature they are not one, and would not become
one. Viewed in themselves, the children of the Church
are not of a different nature from the Protestants
around them; they are of the very same nature.
What Protestants are, such would they be, but for the

[1] Works, 1832, vol. iii. p. 171.

Church, which brings them together forcibly, though persuasively, "fortiter et suaviter," and binds them into one by her authority. Left to himself, each Catholic likes and would maintain his own opinion and his private judgment just as much as a Protestant; and he has it, and he maintains it, just so far as the Church does not, by the authority of Revelation, supersede it. The very moment the Church ceases to speak, at the very point at which she, that is, God who speaks by her, circumscribes her range of teaching, there private judgment of necessity starts up; there is nothing to hinder it. The intellect of man is active and independent: he forms opinions about everything; he feels no deference for another's opinion, except in proportion as he thinks that that other is more likely than he to be right; and he never absolutely sacrifices his own opinion, except when he is sure that that other knows for certain. He *is* sure that God knows; therefore, if he is a Catholic, he sacrifices his opinion to the Word of God, speaking through His Church. But, from the nature of the case, there is nothing to hinder his having his own opinion, and expressing it, whenever, and so far as, the Church, the oracle of Revelation, does not speak.

But again, human nature likes, not only its own opinion, but its own way, and will have it whenever it can, except when hindered by physical or moral restraint. So far forth, then, as the Church does not compel her children to do one and the same thing (as, for instance, to abstain from work on Sunday, and from flesh on Friday), they will do different things: and still more so, when she actually allows or commissions them to act for themselves, gives to certain persons or bodies privileges and immunities, and recognizes them as centres of combination, under her authority, and within her pale.

And further still, in all subjects and respects whatever, whether in that range of opinion and of action which the Church has claimed to herself, and where she has superseded what is private and individual, or, on the other hand, in those larger regions of thought and of conduct, as to which she has not spoken, though she might speak, the natural tendency of the children of the Church, as men, is to resist her authority. Each mind naturally is self-willed, self-dependent, self-satisfied; and except so far as grace has subdued it, its first impulse is to rebel. Now this tendency, through the influence of grace, is not often exhibited in matters of faith; for it would be incipient heresy, and would be contrary, if knowingly indulged, to the first element of Catholic duty; but in matters of conduct, of ritual, of discipline, of politics, of social life, in the ten thousand questions which the Church has not formally answered, even though she may have intimated her judgment, there is a constant rising of the human mind against the authority of the Church.

and of superiors, and that, in proportion as each individual is removed from perfection. For all these reasons, there ever has been, and ever will be, a vast exercise and a realized product, partly praiseworthy, partly barely lawful, of private judgment within the Catholic Church. The freedom of the human mind is " in possession " (as it is called), and it meddles with every question, and wanders over heaven and earth, except so far as the authority of the Divine Word, as a superincumbent weight, presses it down, and restrains it within limits.

3.

The most obvious instance of this liberty or licence within the Church is that of nationality; and I do not understand why it has not been urged in the controversy more prominently than the mere rivalry and party-spirit of monastic bodies. What a vast assemblage of private attachments and feelings, judgments, tastes, and traditions, goes to make up the idea of nationality! yet, there it exists in the Church, because the Church has not been divinely instructed to forbid it, and it fights against the Church and the Church's objects, except where the Church authoritatively repels it. The Church is a preacher of peace, and nationality is the fruitful cause of quarrels, far more sinful and destructive than the paper wars, and rivalry of customs or precedents, which alone can possibly exist between religious bodies. The Church grants to the magistrate the power of the sword, and the right of making war in a lawful quarrel, and nations abuse this prerogative to break up that unity of love which ought to exist in the baptized servants of a common Master, and to put to death by wholesale those whom they pray to live with for ever in heaven. This, I say, might be urged in controversy against Catholicism, as an extreme instance of the want of unity in the Church; and yet, when properly considered, it is rather a special instance, I do not say of her unity, but of her uniting power. She fights the battle of unity against nationality, and she wins. Look through her history, and you cannot deny but she is the one great principle of unity and concord which the world has seen. In this day, I grant, scientific unions, free trade, railroads, and industrial exhibitions are put forward as a substitute for her influence, with what success posterity will be able to judge; but, as far as the course of history has yet proceeded, the Church is the only power that has wrestled, as with the concupiscence, so with the pride, irritability, selfishness, and self-love of human nature. Her annals present a series of victories over that human nature, which is the subject-matter of her operations; and to object to her that she has an enemy to overcome, surely would be a most perverse view of the case, and a most sophistical argument in controversy. The barbarian invaders of the empire were the enemies of the human race and of each other;

and to subdue and unite them, and to harness them, as it were, to her triumphal chariot by her look and by her voice, was an exploit of moral power, such as the world has never seen elsewhere. Such, too, was her continual arbitration between the fierce feudal monarchs of the Middle Ages, which, though not always successful to the extent of her desire, exhibits her most signally in that her great and heavenly character of peacemaker, and vindicates for her the attribute, given her in the Creed, and envied her by her enemies, of being One.

And here I cannot but allude to the subject which employed our attention yesterday; for, be it for good or for evil, it then seemed a truth beyond contradiction, that one and the same character was to be found in all Catholic nations, in north and south, in the middle age and in the present. I repeat, I am not assuming now, any more than then, that this common character is admirable and beautiful, or denying (as far as this argument goes) that it is despicable and offensive; I only remind you that its identity everywhere was in yesterday's Lecture taken for granted; and what was granted by me to our own prejudice then, must be conceded to me in our favour now. Considering the wide differences in nations and in times, it surely is very remarkable that the religious character, which the Catholic Church forms in her populations, is so identical as it is found to be. Can,

U

indeed, there be a more marvellous, or even awful, instance of her real internal unity, than that a modern Naples should be like medieval England? and if we do not see the same character more than partially developed in Ireland at this moment, is not this the plain reason, that the Irish people has been worn down by oppression, not allowed to be joyous, not allowed to be natural, as little capable of exhibiting human nature in a Catholic medium, as primitive Christianity while it lived in the Catacombs?

4.

After considerations such as these, I own I can scarcely treat seriously the earnestness with which Protestant controversialists would call me back to contemplate the quarrels and jealousies of seculars and regulars, among themselves, or with each other; as if the human mind were not at all times, so far as it is left to itself, selfish and exclusive, and especially in the various circumstances under which it is found in a far-spreading polity or association. When Catholics in any country are poor or few, each religious body, each college, each priest, is tempted to do his utmost for himself, at the expense of every one else. I do not mean for his temporal interests, for he has not the temptation, but for the interests of his own mission and place, and of his own people. He has to build his chapel, to support his school, to feed his poor; and if his next-door neighbour gets the start of him, no means will be left for himself. Or if he is of a mendicant order, he feels he has a claim on the support of the faithful, prior to a religious body which lives on endowments or has other property; but the latter has lately come to the country, and thinks it very fair, on its first start, once for all to make a general appeal, without which it never will be able to get afloat. All parties, then, are naturally led to look out for themselves in the first instance; and this state of mind may easily degenerate into a jealousy of the good fortune or prosperity of others. And then again, some men, or races of men, are more sudden in their tempers than others, or individuals may be deficient in moral training or refinement, and strangers may mistake for a real dissension what is nothing more than momentary and transitory collision.

Or again, let the country be Catholic, and the Church rich; then, what so natural, so inevitable, taking men as they are, as that large, and widely-spread, and powerful congregations or orders, high in repute, commanding in station, famous in historical memories, rich in saints, proud of their doctors, and of schools founded on their tradition, should be exposed to the various infirmities of party spirit, adhere sensitively and obstinately to the privileges they possess, or to the doctrines which have been their watchwords, disparage others and wish to overbear them, and provoke the

interposition of authority to put an end to the disputes
which they have excited? I should be curious to
know whether there ever was a case when two Protestant
sects or parties found any umpire at all, in a question
of opinion between them, except indeed the strong arm
of the law. And, in saying all this, I am not determining the fact of such quarrels among Catholics, nor
the degree to which they proceed; for, as in former
Lectures, I am not specially concerned with the investigation of facts; I am taking for granted what is
alleged by our opponents, and is antecedently probable,
taking human nature as it is. But, in truth, you
might far better refer to the *esprit de corps* of separate
regiments in her Majesty's service, in order to prove
that the tribes of Red Indians may be fairly said to
live in peace together,—or point to the rivalries and
party politics of separate colleges in the national seats
of learning as a proof that those bodies are mutual
belligerents, and assert that the university is not one,
and does not act as one, because its colleges differ
among themselves,—than assert the like of any of
those religious bodies, established and sanctioned by
the Catholic Church. The very same parties, who have
their domestic feuds with one another, will defend, as
Catholics, their common faith, or common Mother,
against an external foe; but when did the Bishops of
the Establishment ever stand by the Friends or by the
Independents, or the Wesleyans by the Baptists, on

any one point of doctrine, with a unity of opinion, intelligent, positive, and exact?

You recollect the popular story, which is intended to exemplify the supremacy of the instinct of benevolence over religious opinion. It is supposed to be one o'clock on Sunday, and a number of congregations are pouring out, their devotions being over, from their respective chapels and meeting-houses, when a woman is taken ill in the street. The sight of this physical calamity is represented as sufficient to supersede all other considerations in the minds of the beholders, and to bind together for the moment the most bitter opponents in the common work of Christian charity. This argument of course is based upon the assumption, and a very reasonable one, that the differences which exist between man and man in religious matters, far from disproving, do but illustrate and confirm the fact of the participation of all men in the natural sentiment of compassion; and surely the case is the same in the Catholic Church, as regards the differences and the unanimity of her religious bodies. Augustinians, Dominicans, Franciscans, Jesuits, and Carmelites have indeed their respective homes and schools; but they have, in spite of all that, a common school and a common home in their Mother's voice and their Mother's bosom; "omnes omnium caritates patria una complexa est;" but Protestants can but "agree to differ." Quarrels, stopping short of division, do but

prove the strength of the principle of combination;
they are a token not of the languor, but of the vigour,
of its life.   Surely this is what we see and say daily as
regards the working of the British constitution.

5.

But we have not yet got to the real point of the
question which lies between us : you allege these
differences in the Catholic Church, my brethren, as a
reason for your not submitting to her authority.   Now,
in order to ascertain their force in this point of view,
let it be considered that the primary question, with
every serious inquirer, is the question of salvation.   I
am speaking to those who feel this to be so; not to
those who make religion a sort of literature or philosophy, but to those who desire, both in their creed and
in their conduct, to approve themselves to their Maker,
and to save their souls.   This being taken for granted,
it immediately follows to ask, " What must I *do* to be
saved ?" and " who is to *teach* me ?" and next, can
Protestantism, can the National Church, teach me ?
No, is the answer of common sense, for this simple
reason, because of the variations and discordances in
teaching of both the one and the other.   The National
Church is no guide into the truth, because no one
knows what it holds, and what it commands : one party
says this, and a second party says that, and a third
party says neither this nor that.   I must seek the truth

then elsewhere; and then the question follows, Shall I seek it in the Communion of Rome? In answer, this objection is instantly made, "You cannot find the truth in Rome, for there are as many divisions there as in the national Communion." Who would not suppose the objection to mean, that these divisions were such as to make it difficult or impossible to ascertain what it was that the Roman Communion taught? Who would not suppose it to mean that there was within the Communion of Rome a difference of creed and of dogmatic teaching; whereas the state of the case is just the reverse? No one can pretend that the quarrels in the Catholic Church are questions of faith, or have tended in any way to obscure or impair what she declares to be such, and what is acknowledged to be such by the very parties in those quarrels. That Dominicans and Franciscans have been zealous respectively for certain doctrinal views, which they declare at the same time to be beyond and in advance of the promulgated faith of the Church, throws no doubt upon that faith itself; how does it follow that they differ in questions of faith, because they differ in questions not of faith? Rather, I would say, if a number of parties distinct from each other give the same testimony on certain points, their differences on other points do but strengthen the evidence for the truth of those matters in which they all are agreed; and the greater the difference, the more remarkable is the unanimity. The question is, " *Where* can I be taught, who cannot be taught by the national communion, because it does *not* teach?" and the Protestant warning runs, "Not in the Catholic Church, because she, in spite of differences on subordinate points amongst her members, *does* teach."

In truth, she not only teaches in spite of those differences, but she has ever taught by means of them. Those very differences of Catholics on further points have themselves implied and brought out their absolute faith in the doctrines which are previous to them. The doctrines of faith are the common basis of the combatants, the ground on which they contend, their ultimate authority, and their arbitrating rule. They are assumed, and introduced, and commented on, and enforced, in every stage of the alternate disputation; and I will venture to say, that, if you wish to get a good view of the unity, consistency, solidity, and reality of Catholic teaching, your best way is to get up the controversy on grace, or on the Immaculate Conception. No one can do so without acquiring a mass of theological knowledge, and sinking in his intellect a foundation of dogmatic truth, which is simply antecedent and common to the rival schools, and which they do but exhibit and elucidate. To suppose that they perplex an inquirer or a convert, is to fancy that litigation destroys the principles and the science of law, or that spelling out words of five syllables makes a child forget his alphabet. On the other hand, place your unfortunate

inquirer between Luther and Calvin, if the Holy
Eucharist is his subject; or, if he is determining the
rule of faith, between Bramhall and Chillingworth,
Bull and Hoadley, and what residuum will be left, when
you have eliminated their contrarieties?

6.

It is imprudent in opponents of the Catholic Religion
to choose for their attack the very point in which it
is strong. As truth is tried by error, virtue by temptation, courage by opposition, so is individuality and life
tried by disturbance and disorder; and its trial is its
evidence. The long history of Catholicism is but a co-
ordinate proof of its essential unity. I suppose, then,
that Protestants must be considered as turning to bay
upon their pursuers, when they would retort upon us
the argument available against themselves from their
religious variations. "The Romanist must admit," it
has been urged, "that the state, whether of the Church
Catholic or of the Roman Church, at periods before or
during the Middle Ages, was such as to bear a very
strong resemblance to the picture he draws of our own.
I do not speak of corruptions in life and morals merely,
or of errors of individuals, however highly exalted, but
of the general disorganized and schismatical state of
the Church, her practical abandonment of her spiritual
pretensions, the tyranny exercised over her by the civil
power, and the intimate adherence of the worst pas-

sions and of circumstantial irregularities to those acts which are vital portions of her system."[1] Such is the imputation; but yet, to tell the truth, I do not know any passages in her history which supply so awful an evidence of her unity and self-dependence, or so luminous a contrast to Anglicanism or other Protestantism, as these very anomalies in the rule and tenor of her course as I have already observed, and shall presently show by examples.

Two years back, when European society was shaken to its basis, the question which came before us was, not whether this or that nation was great and powerful, and able, in case of necessity, to go to war with vigour and effect, but even whether it could hold together, whether it possessed that internal consistency, reality, and life, which made it one. This was the question asked even about England; it was a problem, debated before it could be tried, settled distinctly in the affirmative, when a trial was granted. Much as we might have confided in the steadiness of character, good sense, reverence for law, contentment and political discipline of our people, we shall, I suppose, admit that there was an evidence laid before the world of our national stability, after April 1848, to which no mere anticipation was equivalent. No one can deny, that, fully as we may be impressed with the security of Russia, still we have not, as regards Russia, such a

vivid impression on our mind, almost on our senses, of
the fact, as was created by the threat and the failure of
a political rising in England at the date I have mentioned. And sometimes the longer is the trial, and the
more critical the contest (as in the instance of the civil
discords of ancient Rome), the greater vigour and the
more obstinate life is exhibited by the nation and state,
when once it is undeniably victorious over its internal
disorders. As external enemies do not prove a state to
be weak till they prevail over it, so rebellions from
within may but prove its strength, if they are smitten
down and extinguished. Now, the disorders which have
afflicted the Church have just had this office assigned
them in the designs of Providence, and teach us this
lesson. They have but assayed what may be called the
unitive and integrating virtue of the See of St. Peter,
in contrast to such counterfeits as the Anglican Church,
which, set up in unconditional surrender to the nation,
has never been able to resist the tyranny or caprice of
the national will. The Establishment, having no internal principle of individuality, except what it borrows
from the nation, can neither expel what is foreign to
itself, nor heal its own wounds; the Church, a living
body, when she becomes the seat of a malady or
disorder, tends from the first to its eradication, which
is but a matter of time. This great fact continually
occurring in her history, I will briefly illustrate by two
examples, which will be the fairest to take, from the

extraordinary obstinacy of the evil, and its occasional
promise of victory:—the history of the heresies concerning the Incarnation, and the history of Jansenism.
Each controversy had a reference to a great mystery of
the faith; in each every inch of the ground was contested, and the enemy retired step by step, or at least
from post to post. The former of the two lasted for
between four and five hundred years, and the latter
nearly two hundred.

7.

First, as to the doctrine of the Incarnation, the mind
of man is naturally impatient of whatever it cannot
reduce to the system of order and of causation to which
it subjects all its knowledge; that is, of whatever is
mysterious and incomprehensible; no wonder, then,
that it was discontented with a doctrine so utterly impossible to fathom as that of the Almighty and Eternal
becoming man. As private judgment is ever rising
up against Revelation, as the irascible principle in our
nature is ever insurgent against reason, so there was
a most determined effort and (to use a familiar word)
set against this capital and vital article of faith, age
after age, on the part of various schools of opinion all
over Christendom. They differed, and indeed were
almost indifferent, *how* the mystery was to be disposed
of; they took up opposite theories against it; they were
antagonists of each other; but go it must. The attack

came upon the Church, not on this side or that, but from all quarters, at once or successively, whether in the wide field of speculation, or within the territory of the Church, and circled round the Holy See, rallying and forming again and again in very various positions, though beaten back for a time, and apparently brought under. It was a very stubborn fight; and till the end appeared, which was not till after many generations, it would have been easy to indulge misgivings whether it would ever have an ending. Let us fancy an erudite Nestorian of the day living in Seleucia, beyond the limits of the Roman Empire, and looking out over the Euphrates upon the battle which was waging between the See of St. Peter and the subtle heresy of the Monophysites, through so protracted a period; and let him write a defence of his own Communion for the use of theological students. Doubtless he would have used that long contest as a decisive argument against the unity and purity of the Catholic Church, and might have adopted, by anticipation, the triumphant words of a learned Anglican divine, rashly uttered in 1838, and prudently recalled in 1842, with reference to that Jansenistic controversy, which I reserve for my second example. "This very [Monophysite] heresy," he would have said, "has, in opposition to all these anathemas and condemnations, and in spite of the persecution of the temporal powers, continued to exist for nearly [300] years; and, what is more, it has existed all along in the

very heart of the Roman Church itself. Yet, it has
perpetuated itself in all parts of that Church, sometimes
covertly, sometimes openly, exciting uneasiness, tumults,
innovations, reforms, persecution, schisms, but always
adhering to the Roman communion with invincible
tenacity. It is in vain that, sensible of so great an
evil, the Roman Church struggles and resorts to every
expedient to free her from its presence; the loathed
and abhorred heresy perpetuates itself in her vitals,
and infects her bishops, her priests, her monks, her
universities; and, depressed for a time by the arm of
civil power, gains the ascendancy at length, influences
the councils of kings, . . . produces religious innovations of the most extraordinary character, and inflicts
infinite and permanent injury and disgrace on the cause
of the Roman Church."[1]

Such is the phenomenon which Monophysitism distinctly presents to us more than a thousand years before the rise of a heresy, which this author seems to
have fancied the first instance of such an anomaly.
The controversy began amid the flourishing schools of
Syria, the most learned quarter of Christendom; it
extended along Asia Minor to Greece and Constantinople; and then there was a pause. Suddenly it
broke out in an apparently dissimilar shape, and with
a new beginning, in the imperial city; summoned its
adherents, confederates, and partisans from North to

[1] Palmer's Essay on the Church, vol. i. p. 320.

South, came into collision with the Holy See, and con-
vulsed the Catholic world. Subdued for a while, it
returned to what was very like its original form and
features, and reared its head in Egypt with a far more
plausible phraseology, and in a far more promising
position. There, and in Syria, and thence through the
whole of the East, supported by the emperors, and afterwards by the Mahometans, it sustained itself with great
ingenuity, inventing evasion after evasion, and throwing
itself into more and more subtle formulas, for the space
of near three hundred years. Lastly, it suddenly
appeared in a new shape, and in a final effort, four
hundred years from the time of its first rise, in the
extreme West of Europe, among the theologians of
Spain; and formed matter of controversy for our own
Alcuin, the scholar of St. Bede, for the interposition
of Charlemagne, and the labours of the great Council
of Frankfort.

It is impossible, I am sure, for any one patiently to
read the history of this series of controversies, whatever may be his personal opinions, without being
intimately convinced of the oneness or identity of the
mind, which lived in the Catholic Church through
that long period; which baffled the artifices and
sophistries of the subtlest intellects, was proof against
human infirmity and secular expedience, and succeeded
in establishing irrevocably and for ever those points
of faith with which she started in the contest. "Any

one false step would have thrown the whole theory of the doctrine into irretrievable confusion; but it was as if some individual and perspicacious intellect, to speak humanly, ruled the theological discussion from first to last. That in the long course of centuries, and in spite of the failure, in points of detail, of the most gifted fathers and saints, the Church thus wrought out the one and only consistent theory which can be formed on the great doctrine in dispute, proves how clear, simple, and exact her vision of that doctrine was."[1] Now I leave the retrospect of this long struggle with two remarks—first, that it was never doubtful to the world for any long time *what* was the decision of authority on each successive question as each came into consideration; next, that the series of doctrinal errors which was evolved tended from the first to an utter overthrow of the heresy, each decision of authority being a new and further victory over it, which was never undone. It was all along in visible course of expulsion from the Catholic fold. Contrast this with the denial of baptismal grace, viewed as a heresy within the Anglican Church; has the sentiment of authority against it always been unquestionable? Has there been a series of victories over it? Is it in visible course of expulsion? Is it ever tending to be expelled? Are the influence and prospects of the heresy less formidable now than in the age of Wesley, or of

[1] Essay on Doctrinal Development, p. 438.

Calamy, or of Baxter, or of Abbot, or of Cartwright, or
of the Reformers?

8.

The second controversy which I shall mention is one
not so remarkable in itself, not so wide in its field of
conflict, nor so terrible in its events, but more interesting perhaps to us, as relating almost to our own times,
and because it is used as an argument against the
Church's unity and power of enforcing her decisions,
by such writers as the theologian, of whose words I
just now availed myself. For the better part of two
centuries Jansenism has troubled the greater part of
Catholic Europe, has had great successes, and has
expected greater still; yet, somehow or other, such is
the fact, as a looker-on would be obliged to say, whatever be the internal reasons for it, of which he would
not be a judge, at the end of the time you look for it
and it is gone. As fire among the stubble threatens
great things, but suddenly is quenched in the very
fulness of its blaze, so has it been with the heresy
in question. One might have thought that an age like
this would have been especially favourable for the
development of many of its peculiarities; one never
should be surprised even now, if it developed them
again. The heresy almost rose with Protestantism,
and kept pace with it; it extended and flourished in
those Catholic countries on which Protestantism had

X

made its greatest inroads, and it grew by the side of
Protestantism ; when now suddenly we find it dead in
France, and it is receiving its death-blow in Austria,
in the very generation, at the very hour, when Protestantism is at length getting acknowledged possession of
the far-famed communion of Laud and Hammond.

There was a time when nearly all that was most
gifted, learned, and earnest in France seemed corrupted
by the heresy ; which, though condemned again and
again by the Holy See, discovered new subterfuges,
and gained to itself fresh patrons and protectors, to
shelter it from the Apostolic ban.   What circle of
names can be produced, comparable in their times
for the combination of ability and virtue, of depth of
thought, of controversial dexterity, of poetical talent,
of extensive learning, and of religious reputation, with
those of Launoy, Pascal, Nicole, Arnauld, Racine,
Tillemont, Quesnel, and their co-religionists, admirable
in every point, but in their deficiency in the primary
grace of a creature, humility ?   What shall we say to
the prospects of a school of opinion, which was influencing so many of the most distinguished Congregations
of the day; and which, though nobly withstood by
the Society of Jesus and the Sulpicians, yet at length
found an entrance among the learned Benedictines of
St. Maur, and had already sapped the faith of various
members of another body, as erudite and as gifted
as they ?   For fifteen years a Cardinal Archbishop of

Paris was its protector and leader, and this at a distance of sixty years after its formal condemnation. First, the book itself of Jansenius had been condemned; and then, in consequence of an evasion, the sense of the book; and then a controversy arose whether the Church could decide such a matter of fact as that a book *had* a particular sense. And then the further question came into discussion whether the sense of the book was to be condemned with the mere intention of an external obedience, or with an internal assent. Eleven bishops of France interposed with the Pope to prevent the condemnation; there were four who required nothing more of their clergy than a respectful silence on the subject in controversy; and nineteen wrote to the Pope in favour of these four. Before these difficulties had been settled, a fresh preacher of the same doctrines appeared in the person of Quesnel; and on the Pope's condemning his opinions in the famous bull *Unigenitus*, six bishops refused to publish it, and fourteen formally opposed it; and then sixteen suspended the effects of it. Three universities took part with them, and the parliaments of various towns banished their Archbishops, Bishops, or Priests, and confiscated their goods, either for taking part against the Jansenists or for refusing them the Sacraments.[1]

As time went on, the evil spread wider and grew

---

[1] Vide Mémoires pour servir, &c., and Palmer on the Church.

more intense, instead of being relieved. In the middle
of last century, a hundred years after the condemnation
of the heresy at Rome, it was embodied in the person
of a far more efficacious disputant than Jansenius or
Quesnel. The Emperor Joseph developed the apparently
harmless theories of a theological school in the practical
form of Erastianism. He prohibited the reception of
the famous bull *Unigenitus* in his dominions; subjected
all bulls, rescripts, and briefs from Rome to an imperial
supervision; forbade religious orders to obey foreign
superiors; "suppressed confraternities, abolished the
processions, retrenched festivals, prescribed the order of
offices, regulated the ceremonies, the number of masses,
the manner of giving benediction, nay the number of
waxlights."[1] He seized the revenues of the Bishops,
destroyed their sees, and even for a time forbade them
to confer orders. He permitted divorce in certain
cases, and removed images from the churches. The new
Reformation reached as far as Belgium on the one
hand, and down to Naples on the other. The whole of
the Empire and its alliances were apparently on the
point of disowning their dependence on the Apostolic
See. The worship of the saints, auricular confession,
indulgences, and other Catholic doctrines, were openly
written against or disputed by bishops and professors.
The Archduke of Tuscany, imitating the Emperor, sent
catechisms to the bishops, and instructed them by his

---

[1] Mémoires pour servir. &c.

circulars or charges; while a Neapolitan prelate, instead
of his ordinary title of "Bishop by the grace of the
Holy Apostolic See," styled himself "Bishop by the
grace of the King." Who would not have thought that
Henry of England had risen from his place, and was at
once in Vienna, Belgium, Tuscany, and Naples? The
reforming views had spread into Portugal; and, to
complete the crisis, the great antagonist of Protestantism, which was born with it in one day, and had ever
since been the best champion of the Holy See, the
Society of Jesus itself, by the inscrutable fiat of
Providence, was, in that hour of need, to avoid worse
evils, by that very See suppressed. Surely the Holy
Roman Church is at length in the agonies of dis-
solution. The Catholic powers, Germany, France,
Portugal, and Naples, all have turned against her.
Who is to defend her? The mystery of Protestantism
is unravelled; the day of Luther is come; the Catholics
send up a cry, and their enemies a shout of joy.

9.

Noli æmulari. Is it not written in the book of truth,
that the ungodly shall spread abroad like a green bay-
tree, and then shall wither? that the adversary reaches
out his hand towards his prey, in order that he may be
more emphatically smitten? "Yet a little while, and
the wicked shall not be: I passed by, and lo! he was not;
I sought him, and his place was not found. Better is

a little to the just than the great riches of the wicked; for the arms of the wicked shall be broken, but the Lord strengtheneth the just." So was it with the great Arian heresy, which the civil power would fain have forced upon the Church; but it fell to pieces, and the Church remained One. So was it with Nestorius, with Eutyches, with the Image-breakers, with Manichees, with Lollards, with Protestants, into whom the State would put life, but who, one and all, refuse to live. So is it with the communion of Cranmer and Parker, which is kept together only by the heavy hand of the State, and cannot aspire to be free without ceasing to be one. One power alone on earth has the gift and destiny of ever being one. It has been so of old time; surely so will it be now. Man's necessity is God's opportunity. *Noli æmulari,* "Be not jealous of the evil-doers." . . .

It is towards the end of the century: what shall be, ere that end arrive? . . . Suddenly there is heard a rushing noise, borne north and south upon the wings of the wind. Is it a deluge to sweep over the earth, and to bear up the ark of God upon its bosom? or is it the fire which is ravaging to and fro, to try every man's work what it is, and to discriminate between what is of earth and what is of heaven? Now we shall see what can live and what must die; now shall we have the proof of Jansenism; now shall we see whether the Catholic Church has that eternal individuality which is of the essence of life, or whether it be an external thing, a birth of the four elements, a being of chance and circumstance, made up of parts, but with no integrity or immaterial principle informing it. The breath of the Lord hath gone forth far and wide upon the face of the earth; the very foundations of society are melting in the fiery flood which it has kindled; and we shall see whether the Three Children will be able to walk in the midst of the furnace, and will come forth with their hair unsinged, their garments whole, and their skin untainted by the smell of fire.

So closed the last century upon the wondering world; and for years it wondered on; wondered what should be the issue of the awful portant which it witnessed, and what new state of things was to rise out of the old. The Church disappeared before its eyes as by a yawning earthquake, and men said it was a fulfilment of the prophecies, and they sang a hymn, and went to their long sleep, content and with a *Nunc Dimittis* in their mouths; for now at length had an old superstition been wiped off from the earth, and the Pope had gone his way. And other powers, kings, and the like, disappeared too, and nothing was to be seen.

Fifty years have passed away since the time of those wonders, and we, my brethren, behold in our degree the issue of what our fathers could but imagine. Great changes surely have been wrought, but not those which they anticipated. The German Emperor has ceased to be: he persecuted the Church, and he has lost his place of pre-eminence. The Gallican Church, too, with its much-prized liberties, and its fostered heresy, was also swept away, and its time-honoured establishment dissolved. Jansenism is no more. The Church lives, the Apostolic See rules. That See has greater acknowledged power in Christendom than ever before, and that Church has a wider liberty than she has had since the days of the Apostles. The faith is extending in the great Anglo-Saxon race, its recent enemy, the lord of the world, with a steadiness and energy, which that proud people fears, yet cannot resist. Out of the ashes of the ancient Church of France has sprung a new hierarchy, worthy of the name and the history of that great nation, as fervent as their St. Bernard, as tender as their St. Francis, as enterprising as their St. Louis, as loyal to the Holy See as their Charlemagne. The Empire has rescinded the impious regulations of the Emperor Joseph, and has commenced the emancipation of the Church. The idea and the genius of Catholicism has triumphed within its own pale with a power and a completeness which the world has never seen before. Never was the whole body of the faithful so united to each other and to their head. Never was there a time when there was less of error, heresy, and schismatical perverseness among them. Of course the time will never be in this world, when trials and persecutions shall be at an end: and doubtless such are to come, even though they be below the horizon. But we may be thankful and joyful for what is already granted us; and nothing which is to be can destroy the mercies which have been.

"So let all Thy enemies perish, O Lord; but let them that love Thee shine, as the sun shineth in his rising!"

LECTURE XI.

HERETICAL AND SCHISMATICAL BODIES NÒ PREJU-DICE TO THE CATHOLICITY OF THE CHURCH.

I.

THERE is no objection made at this time to the claims of the Catholic Church more imposing to the imagination, yet less tenable in the judgment of reason, than that which is grounded on there being at present so many nations and races, which have kept the name of Christian, yet given up Catholicism. If fecundity has ever been considered one of the formal notes or tokens of the Mother of souls, it is fair to look out for it now; and if it has told in favour of the communion of Rome in former times, so now surely it may be plausibly made to tell against it. It would seem as if in this age of the world the whole number of anti-Catholics were nearly equal to the number of Catholics, at least so our opponents say; and I am willing, for argument's sake, to grant it. Let it be so, or, in other words, let it be assumed that scarcely more than half of Christendom subjects itself to the Catholic Church. "Is it not preposterous, then," it is asked of ns, "to claim to be the whole, when you are but a moiety? And with what countenance can you demand that we should unhesitatingly and without delay leave our own Communion for yours, when there is so little to show at first sight that you have more pretensions to the Christian name than we have?"

This is the argument, put in its broadest, simplest shape; and you, my brethren, would like to avail yourselves of it just as I have stated it, if you could. But you cannot; for it puts together all creeds and opinions, all communions, whatever their origin and history, and adds up the number of their members in rivalry of that of the Church's children. You would do so if you could, as your forefathers did before you; two centuries ago Archbishop Bramhall did so, and you have every good wish to copy him, as in his other representations, so in this. "We hold communion," he says, speaking of the Church of England in contrast with those whom he would call Romanists, "with thrice so many Catholic Christians as they do; that is, the eastern, southern, and northern Christians, besides Protestants."[1] "Divide Christendom into five parts, and in four of them they have very little or nothing to do. Perhaps they have here a monastery, or there a small handful of proselytes; but what are five or six persons to so many millions of Christian souls, that *they* should be Catholics, and not all the others?"[2] This being the case, as he

[1] Vol. i. p. 628. Ed. 1842.   [2] Ibid. p. 258.

views the matter, it of course follows that we are but
successors of the ancient Donatists, a mere fraction
of the Church excommunicating all the rest. "The
Donatists," he says, "separated the whole Church from
their Communion, and substituted themselves, being
but a small part of the Christian world, in the place of
the Catholic Church, just as the Romanists do at this
day."[1]

This, certainly, was turning the tables against his
opponents, who had been accustomed to consider that
the Church of England, granting it was a Church, was
in the very position of the followers of Donatus, a
fragment of Christendom claiming for itself immaculate
purity; but let us observe what he is forced to do to
make his argument good. First, of course, he throws
himself into communion, whether they will have him
or not, not only with the Greek Church, but with the
various heretical bodies all over the East; the Nestorians of Chaldæa, the Copts of Egypt, the Jacobites
of Syria, and the Eutychians of Armenia, whose heresy
in consequence he finds it most expedient to doubt.
"Those Churches," he says, speaking of the East, "do
agree better, both among themselves and with other
Churches, than the Roman Church itself, both in profession of faith (for they and we do generally acknowledge the same ancient Creeds, and no other) and in
inferior questions, being free from the intricate and

[1] Ibid p. 106.

perplexed difficulties of the Roman schools. . . . How
are they 'heretical' Churches? Some of them are
called Nestorians, but most injuriously, who have nothing of Nestorius but the name. Others have been
suspected of Eutychianism, and yet in truth orthodox
enough. . . . It is no new thing for great quarrels to
arise from mere mistakes."[1] Elsewhere he says: "It
is true that some few Eastern Christians, in comparison of those innumerable multitudes, are called
Nestorians; and some others, by reason of some un-
usual expression, suspected of Eutychianism, but both
most wrongfully. Is this the requital that he," that is,
his Catholic opponent, "makes to so many of these poor
Christians, for maintaining their religion inviolated so
many ages under Mahometan princes?"[2]

Admitting, as he does, these ancient and distant
sectaries to have a portion in the Catholic faith and
communion, it is not surprising that he extends a like
privilege to the recently formed Protestant communities
in his own neighbourhood. "Because I esteem these
Churches not completely formed," he says, "do I therefore exclude them from all hope of salvation? or esteem
them aliens and strangers from the commonwealth of
Israel? or account them formal schismatics? No such
thing."[3] "I know no reason why we should not
admit Greeks and Lutherans to our communion; and,
if he" (that is, his opponent) "had added them,

[1] Ibid. p. 260.   [2] Ibid. p. 328.   [3] Ibid. p. 70.

Armenians, Abyssenes, Muscovites.[1] . . . For the Lutherans, he does them egregious wrong. Throughout the kingdoms of Denmark and Sweden they have their bishops, name and thing; and throughout Germany they have their superintendents." [2]

Such was the line of argument which the defenders of the National Church adopted two centuries back; and, of course, it was much stronger in the way of argument than anything which is attempted now. Now, the Protestants are given up; we hear little or nothing of "Churches not completely formed;" not much account is taken of the "superintendents" of Germany; and as to the episcopacy of Denmark and Sweden, the thing, if not the name, is simply gone. Nor would any adherent of the theological party whom I am addressing, think with much respect either of the Nestorians or of the Monophysites of Asia and Egypt. The anti-Catholic bodies, which are made the present basis of the argument against us, are mainly or solely the Greek and the Anglican communities; and, as the antiquity, prescriptive authority, orders, and doctrine of Anglicanism, are the very subject in dispute, it is usual to simplify the argument by resting it upon

---

[1] He adds: "And all those who do profess the Apostolical Creed, as it is expounded in the first four general councils under the primitive discipline." These words are not quoted above, because they are certainly ambiguous. Bramhall does not say, "All those who do profess the decrees of the first four general councils."

[2] Ibid. p. 564.

grounds which it is supposed we cannot deny; viz., the pretensions of the Greek Church, whose apostolical descent is unquestionable, and whose faith almost unquestioned.

2.

The argument, then, which I have to consider, is an appeal to the imagination of the following kind: The Russian Church, according to the statistical tables of 1835, includes 39,862,473 souls within its pale;[1] the Byzantine, or what is commonly called the Greek Church, is said to number about three millions;[2] so that, excluding the heretical bodies of the East, we may place the whole Greek communion, from north to south, at about forty-three millions,[3] with such increase of population as in the last fifteen years it has gained. On the other hand, the whole number of Catholics, which has been placed by some as low as one hundred and sixteen millions, is considered by Catholics at present to reach two hundred. But, whatever be the proportion between the Greeks and ourselves, anyhow so vast a communion as one of forty-three million souls is a difficulty, it is said, too positive for us to overcome. It seems incredible that we can have exclusive claims to be Christ's heritage, if those claims issue in the exclusion of such immense populations from it; it is

---

[1] Theiner, L'Eglise Russe, 1846.   [2] Conder, View of Religions.

[3] In controversial writings, the numbers of the Greek orthodox communion are put at seventy or even ninety millions; it does not appear on what data. Conder puts them at fifty millions.

incredible that we should be the Catholic Church, if we have not the power to take them up into our system, but let them lie in their own place. "If the Greeks are separate from the See of Rome," it is argued, "as we see they are, we too may without hazard be separate also. They are too powerful, too numerous for you to consider them as the subjects of a schism; they are too large a limb to admit of your amputation; they enter into the Church's life and essence; in ejecting them from her bosom, she would be tearing out herself; in excommunicating them, you rather excommunicate yourselves; you are affording us a plain *reductio ad absurdum* of your Catholicity. And there is a second consideration which urges us, and that is, the frightful cruelty of denying to such multitudes of men, and to so great an extent of territory, a place in the Church, claiming it as they do from generation to generation, and fully believing their own possession of it. Charity, still more than the necessities of controversy, obliges you to acknowledge them as a portion of the fold of Christ."

This is the objection which I am to examine, and you will observe that I am to examine it only *as* an objection; that is to say, I am supposing that there is sufficient proof on other grounds that the Communion of Rome is the Catholic Church, for to this the movement of 1833 has already been supposed to lead; and then, with this fact sufficiently proved, an objection is brought as an obstacle to our surrendering ourselves to the conviction which follows upon the proof of the fact. What I have to do, then, is to show that the proof already brought home to us of the Catholicity of the Roman Communion, is not affected by the phenomenon in question; or that there are ways of accounting for it, if we do but assume, which I claim to do, that the Church of Rome and Catholicism are synonymous terms.

3.

I observe, then, that this phenomenon is but one instance of a great and broad fact, which has ever been seen on the earth, viz., that truth is opposed not only by direct contradictions which are unequivocal, but also by such pretences as are of a character to deceive men at first sight, and to confuse the evidence of what alone is divine and trustworthy. Thus, if I must begin from the very beginning, the enemy of man did not overcome him in Paradise, except by pretending to be a prophet, and, as it were, preaching against his Maker. "Ye shall not die the death," he said; "ye shall be as gods, knowing good and evil." Again, when Moses displayed his miracles before Pharaoh, Jannes and Mambres were allowed to imitate them; in order, so to speak, to give the king a pretext, if he was perverse enough to take it, for rejecting the divine message. When the same great prophet had led out the chosen people towards the promised land, their enemies made the attempt to set up a rival prophet in Balaam, though

Y

it was overruled, as in other cases, by their Almighty Protector. When a prophet denounced the schism of Jeroboam, there was an old deceiver who seduced him by the claim, "I also am a prophet like unto thee." The Temple had not long been built before a rival shrine arose on Mount Gerizim, as if with the very object of perplexing the inquirer. "Our fathers adored in this mountain," says the Samaritan woman to our Lord, "and ye say that at Jerusalem is the place where men must adore." And He Himself warns us of false Christs and Antichrists, who were to mislead the many with the imitation of His claims; and His Apostles were resisted, and in a manner thwarted, by Simon Magus, and others who set up against them. They themselves distinctly prophesied that such delusions were to be after them, and apparently to endure till the end of all things; so much so, that were such imposing phenomena as the Greek Church taken out of the way, it would be difficult to say how the actual state of Christendom corresponded to the apostolic anticipations of it; nor should we have any cause to be surprised though the effect of such phenomena in time to come were more practically urgent and visibly influential than it has been hitherto. "After my departure," says St. Paul, "ravenous wolves will enter in among you, not sparing the flock. And of your own selves will rise up men speaking perverse things to draw away disciples after them." And in his parting words he warns us

that "in the last days shall come dangerous times,
for men shall be lovers of themselves . . . having an
appearance indeed of piety," that is, of orthodoxy, "but
denying the power thereof." "Evil men and seducers
shall grow worse and worse, erring, and driving into
error." And "there shall be a time when they will
not bear sound doctrine, but according to their own
desires they will heap to themselves teachers having
itching ears." I need not remind you that St. John and
St. Jude bear a similar testimony, which the event in
no long time fulfilled.

If you would ask me for the most remarkable fulfilment of their warning, I should point to Mahometanism, which is a far more subtle contrivance of the
enemy than we are apt to consider. In the first place,
it perplexes the evidence of Christianity just in that
point in which it is most original and striking: I mean,
it professes the propagation of a religion through the
world, which I suppose was quite a new idea when
Christianity appeared. In the event, indeed, it did but
illustrate the divinity of Christianity by the contrast;
for while the Catholic Church is a proselytizing power,
as her enemies confess, even at the end of eighteen
centuries, Mahometanism soon got tired of its own
undertaking, and, when the novelty and excitement of
conversion were over, it relapsed into a sort of conservative, local, national religion, such as the Greek and
Latin polytheisms before it, and Protestantism since.

And next, it acted over again, as if in mockery, the part which Christianity had taken towards Judaism, viz., it professed to be an improvement on the Gospel, as the Gospel had been upon the law; and just as Christianity dealt with Judaism, so it pointed to the Christian prophecies themselves in evidence of its claims, which it affected to interpret better than Christians themselves. Moreover, it swept away a considerable portion of the Christian heritage; and there it remains to this day in the countries which it seized upon, lying over against us, and for this reason only not interfering with the arguments of our opponents for the divine origin of Christianity, that England lies north and Islamism is in the south.

Then again, I cannot help thinking that Judaism is somewhat of a difficulty of the same kind; not as if any one were likely to prefer it, any more than Mahometanism, to Christianity; that is another matter altogether; nor, in like manner, do I think that any of you, my brethren, would turn Greek rather than become Catholic: but I mean, that, as the fact of the Greek Church impairs the simplicity of the Catholic argument, by its rival pretensions, so does the existence of Judaism interfere with Christianity; for, compared with it, Christianity is a novelty; and it may be said to Christians, Do not stand midway, but either go on to some newer novelty, such as first Montanus, then Manes, and then Mahomet introduced, and others since, or else go back to the mother of all religions, the Jewish Law, which, as yourselves allow, once at least was a prophet of God. On the other hand, even if we became Jews, as considering Judaism to be the permanent religion which God had given, still this would not get rid of the difficulty I am describing, for the proper claims of Christianity would remain; then, as before, you would have two rival prophets, one true, and one not true, though you would have changed your mind, as to which was true and which was false. Looking, then, at the world as it is, taking facts as they are, you cannot rid yourselves of those difficulties in the evidence of religion, which arise from the existence of bold, plausible, imposing counter-claims on the part of error, such as the Greek communion makes against Catholicism; and you must reconcile yourselves to them, unless you are content to believe nothing, and give up the pretension of faith altogether.

But we need not go to Judaism or Mahometanism for parallels to the Greek communion; look at the history of the Christian Church herself, and you will find precedents in former times of the present difficulty, more exact and apposite than those which can be adduced from the existence of Jew or Mussulman. It may be observed that the Apostle, in the passage already quoted, speaks of the sects and persuasions, which by implication he condemns, not merely as collateral and independent creations, but as born in the Catholic body, and going out from it. "Of your own selves shall men arise," he says; and St. John says, "They went out from us, but they were not of us; for, if they had been of us, they would no doubt have continued with us." If this was not fulfilled in the very days of the Apostles on the extensive scale on which it was afterwards, this was simply because large national conversions and serious schisms are not the growth of a day; but, as far as it could exist in the first ages, it has existed from the very first, though far more strikingly in the succeeding centuries of the Church. From the first, the Church was but one Communion among many which bore the name of Christian, some of them more learned, and others affecting a greater strictness than herself; till at length her note of Catholicity was for a while gathered up and fulfilled simply in the name of Catholic, rather than was a property visibly peculiar to herself and none but her. Hence the famous advice of the Fathers, that if one of the faithful went to a strange city, he should not ask for the "Church," for there were so many churches belonging to different denominations that he would be sure to be perplexed and to mistake, but for the Catholic Church. "If ever thou art sojourning in any city," says St. Cyril, "inquire not simply where the Lord's House is, for the sects also make an attempt to call their own conventicles houses of the Lord, nor merely where the Church is, but where is the Catholic

Church." St. Cyril wrote in Palestine; but St. Austin, in Africa, and St. Pacian in Spain say the same thing. The present Greek Church is at best but a local form of religion, and does not pretend to occupy the earth; whereas some of the early heretical bodies might almost have disputed with the See of St. Peter the prerogative of Catholicity. The stern discipline of the Novatians extended from Rome to Scythia, to Asia Minor, to Alexandria, to Africa, and to Spain; while, at an earlier date, the families of Gnosticism had gone forth over the face of the world from Italy to Persia and Egypt on the east, to Africa on the south, to Spain on the west, and to Gaul on the north.

4.

But you will say, there were, in those times, no *national* heresies or schism, and these alone can be considered parallel to the case of the Greek Church, supposing it schismatical;—turn then to the history of the Gothic race. This great people, in all its separate tribes, received Christianity from Arian preachers; and, before it took possession of the Empire, Mæsogoths, Visigoths, Ostrogoths, Alani, Suevi, Vandals, and Burgundians, had all learned to deny the divinity of Christ. Suddenly France, Spain, Portugal, Africa, and Italy, found themselves buried under the weight of heretical establishments and populations. This state of things lasted for eighty years in France,

for a hundred in Italy and Africa, and for a hundred
and eighty in Spain, extending through a space of two
centuries.   It should be added that these Gothic hordes,
which took possession of the Empire, had little of the
character of barbarism, except that they were cruel;
they were chaste, temperate, just, and devout, and
some of their princes were men of ability and patrons
of learning.   Did you live in that day, my brethren,
you would, perhaps, be looking with admiration at
these Arians, as now you look at the Greeks;—not from
love of their heresy, but, your imagination being
affected by their number, power, and nobleness, you
would try to make out that they really did hold the
orthodox faith, or at least that it was not at all certain that they did not, though they did deny, to be
sure, the Nicene Creed, against which they had been
unhappily prejudiced, and anathematized Athanasius
from defective knowledge of history.   You would have
used the words of Bramhall, quoted above, when speaking of later families of heretics:—" How are they
heretical Churches ? some of them are *called* Arians;
but most injuriously, who have nothing of Arius, but
the name; others have been *suspected* of Macedonianism,
and yet in truth *orthodox enough*.   It is no new thing
for great quarrels to arise from mere mistakes."   Bulk,
not symmetry; vastness, not order; show, not principle
—I fear I must say it, my dear brethren—these are
your tests of truth.   A century earlier than the Goths,

you would have been enlarging on the importance of
the Donatists. "Four hundred sees!" you would
have said; "a whole four hundred! why, it is a fifth
of the Episcopate of Christendom. Unchurch them!
impossible; we shall excommunicate ourselves in the
attempt."

5.

Still, it may be said, I have produced nothing yet
to match the venerable antiquity and the authoritative
traditions of the Greek Church, which is coeval with
the Apostles, and for near a thousand years has been
in its present theological position, and which, since
its separation from the Holy See, has been able, as is
alleged, to expand itself in a vast heathen country,
which it has converted to the faith. Such is the objection; and, as to the facts on which it is built, I will
take them for granted, as before, for argument's sake,
for anyhow they are not sufficient to make the objection sound. For in truth, whether the facts be as
represented or not, you will find them all, and more
than them all, in the remarkable history of the
Nestorians. The tenet on which these religionists
separated from the See of Rome is traceable to
Antioch, the very birthplace of the Christian name;
and it was taken up and maintained by Churches
which were among the oldest in Christendom. Driven
by the Roman power over the boundaries of the Empire,
it placed itself, as early as the fifth century, under the

protection of Persia, and laid the foundations of a schismatical communion, the most wonderful that the world has seen. It propagated itself, both among Christians and pagans, from Cyprus to China; it was the Christianity of Bactrians, Huns, Medes, and Indians, of the coast of Malabar and Ceylon on the south, and of Tartary on the north. This ecclesiastical dominion lasted for eight centuries and more, into the depth of the middle ages—beyond the Pontificate of Innocent III. It was administered by as many as twenty-five archbishoprics; and, though there is perhaps no record of the number of its people, yet it is said, that they and the opposite sect of the Monophysites, in Syria and Egypt, taken together, at one time surpassed in populousness the whole Catholic Church, in its Greek and Latin divisions. And it is to be observed, which is much to the purpose, that it occupied a portion of the world, with which, as far as I am aware, the Catholic Church, during those many centuries, interfered very little. It had the further Asia all to itself, from Mesopotamia to China; far more so than the Greek Church has at this time possession of Russia and Greece.

With this prominent example before our eyes, during so large a portion of the history of Christianity, I do not see how the present existence of the Greek Church can form any valid objection to the Catholicity which we claim for the Communion of Rome. Nestorianism came from Antioch, the original

Apostolic see; Photianism, as it has been called, from Constantinople, a younger metropolis. Nestorianism had its Apostolical Succession, as Photianism has, and a formed hierarchy. If its principal seat was new and foreign, in Chaldæa, not at Antioch, so the principal seat of Photianism is foreign too, being Russia; if from Russia it has sent out missions and made conversions, so, and much more so, did Nestorianism from Chaldæa. You will, perhaps, object that Nestorianism was a heresy;—therein lies the force of my argument, viz., that large, organized, flourishing, imposing communions, which strike the imagination as necessary portions of the heritage of Christ, may, nevertheless' in fact be implicated in some heresy, which, in the judgment of reason, invalidates their claim. If the Nestorian communion, enormous as it was, was yet external to the Church, why must the Greek communion be within it, merely because, supposing the fact to be so, it has some portion of the activity and success which were so conspicuous in the Nestorian missioners? Do not, then, think to overcome us with descriptions of the multitude, antiquity, and continuance of the Greek Churches; dismiss the vision of their rites, their processions, or their vestments; spare yourselves the recital of the splendour of their churches, or the venerable aspect of their bishops; Nestorianism had then all:—the question lies deeper.

6.

It lies, for what we know, and to all appearance, in the very constitution of the human mind; corruptions of the Gospel being as necessary and ordinary a phenomenon, taking men as they are, as its rejection. Why do you not bring against us the vast unreclaimed populations of paganism, or the political power of the British Colonial Empire, in proof that we are not the Catholic Church? Is misbelief a greater marvel than unbelief? or do not the same intellectual and moral principles, which lead men to accept nothing, lead them also to accept half of revealed truth? Both effects are simple manifestations of private judgment in the bad sense of the phrase, that is, of the use of one's own reason against the authority of God. If He has made it a duty to submit to the supreme authority of the Holy See (and of this I am all along assuming there is fair proof), and if there is a constant rising of the human mind against authority, as such, however legitimate, the necessary consequence will be the very state of things we see before our eyes,—not merely individuals casting off the Roman Supremacy (for individuals, as being of less account, have less temptation, or even opportunity, to rebel, than collections of men), but, much more, the powerful and the great, the wealthy and the flourishing, kings and states, cities and races, falling back upon their own resources and their own

connections, making their home their castle, and refusing any longer to be dependent on a distant centre, or
to regulate their internal affairs by a foreign tribunal.
Assuming then that there is a supreme See, divinely
appointed, in the midst of Christendom, to which all
ought to submit and be united, such phenomena, as the
Greek Church presents at this day, and the Nestorian
in the middle ages, are its infallible correlatives, as
human nature is constituted; it would require a miracle
to make it otherwise. It is but an exemplification of
the words of the Apostle, " The law entered in, that sin
might abound;" and again, "There must be heresies,
that they also who are proved may be made manifest
among you." A command is both the occasion of
transgression, and the test of obedience. All depends
on the fact of the Supremacy of Rome; I assume this
fact; I admit the contrary fact of the Arian, Nestorian,
and the Greek Communions; and strong in the one,
I feel no difficulty in the other. Neither Arian, nor
Nestorian, nor Greek insubordination is any true objection to the fact of such supremacy, unless the divine
foresight of such a necessary result can be supposed
to have dissuaded the Divine Wisdom from giving
occasion to it.

7.

But another remark is in place here. Nothing is
more likely to characterize large populations of Christians, if left to themselves, than a material instead of

a formal faith. By a material faith, I mean that sort of habitual belief which persons possess in consequence of having heard things said in this or that way from their childhood, being thoroughly familiar with them, and never having had difficulty suggested to them from without or within. Such is the sort of belief which many Protestants have in the Bible; which they accept without a doubt, till objections occur to them. Such as this becomes the faith of nations in process of time, where a clergy is negligent; it becomes simply national and hereditary, the truth being received, but not on the authority of God. That is, their faith is but material not formal, and really has neither the character nor the reward of that grace-implanted, grace-sustained principle, which believes, not merely because it was so taught in the nursery, but because God has spoken; not because there is no temptation to doubt, but because there is a duty to believe. And thus it may easily happen, in the case of individuals, that even the restless mind of a Protestant, who sets the Divine Will before him in his thoughts and actions, and wishes to be taught and wishes to believe, may have more of grace in it, and be more acceptable in the divine sight, than his, who only believes passively, and not as assenting to a divine oracle; just as one who is ever fighting successfully with temptations against purity has, so far, a claim of merit, which they do not share, who from natural temperament have not the trial. Now, the faultiness of this passive state of mind is detected, whenever a new definition of doctrine is promulgated by the competent authority. Its immediate tendency, as exhibited in a population, will be to resist it, simply because it is new, while they on the other hand are disposed to recognise nothing but what is familiar to them; whereas a ready and easy acceptance of the apparent novelty, and a cordial acquiescence in its promulgation, may be the very evidence of a mind, which has lived, not merely in certain doctrines, but in those doctrines as revealed,—not simply in a Creed, but in its Giver,— or, in other words, which has lived by real faith.

As, then, heathens are tried by the original preaching of the Word, so are Christians tested by recurring declarations of it; and the same habit of mind, which makes one man an infidel, when he was before merely a pagan, makes another a heretic, who before was but an hereditary or national Christian. And surely we can fancy without difficulty the circumstances, in which a people, and their priesthood, who ought to hinder it, may gradually fall into those heavy and sluggish habits of mind, in which faith is but material and obedience mechanical, and religion has become a superstition instead of a reasonable service; and then it is as certain that they will become schismatics or heretics, should trial come, as that heathen cities, which have no heart for the truth, when it is for the first time preached to them, will harden into direct infidelity. It is much to

be feared, from what travellers tell us of the Greek
priesthood and their flocks, that both in Russia and in
Greece Proper, they are more or less in this state,—
which may be called the proper disposition towards
heresy and schism; I mean, that they rely on things
more than on persons, and go through a round of duties
in one and the same way, because they are used to
them, and because in consequence they are attached to
them, not as having any intelligent faith in a divine
oracle which has ordered them; and that in consequence
they would start in irritation, as they have started,
from such indications of that oracle's existence as is
necessarily implied in the promulgation of a new
definition of faith.

8.

I am speaking of the mass of the population; and, at
first sight, it is a very serious question, whether the
population can be said to be simply gifted with divine
faith, any more than our own Protestant people; yet I
would as little dare to deny or to limit exceptions to
this remark, as I would deny them or limit them among
ourselves. Let there be as many exceptions, as there
can be found tokens of their being; and the more they
are, to God the greater praise! In this point of view it
is, that we are able to take comfort even from the contemplation of a country which is given up whether to
heresy or schism. Such a country is far from being
in the miserable state of a heathen population: it has

portions of the truth remaining in it, it has some supernatural channels of grace; and the results are such as
can never be known till we have all passed out of this
visible scene of things, and the accounts of the world
are finally made up for the last tremendous day.
While, then, I think it plain that the existence of large
Anti-Catholic bodies professing Christianity are as inevitable, from the nature of the case, as infidel races or
states, except under some extraordinary dispensation of
divine grace, while there must ever be in the world
false prophets and Antichrists, standing over against
the Catholic Church, yet it is consolatory to reflect how
the schism or heresy, which the self-will of a monarch
or of a generation has caused, does not suffice altogether
to destroy the work for which in some distant age
Evangelists have left their homes, and Martyrs have
shed their blood. Thus, the blessing is inestimable to
England, so far as among us the Sacrament of Baptism
is validly administered to any portion of the population.
In Greece, where a far greater attention is paid to
ritual exactness, the whole population may be considered regenerate; half the children born into the
world pass through baptism from a schismatical Church
to heaven, and in many of the rest the same Sacrament
may be the foundation of a supernatural life, which is
gifted with perseverance in the hour of death. There
may be many too, who, being in invincible ignorance
on those particular points of religion on which their

z

Communion is wrong, may still have the divine and unclouded illumination of faith on those numerous points on which it is right. And further, if we consider that there is a true priesthood in certain countries, and a true sacrifice, the benefits of Mass to those who never had the means of knowing better, may be almost the same as they are in the Catholic Church. Humble souls who come in faith and love to the heavenly rite, under whatever disadvantages they lie, from the faulty discipline of their Communion, may obtain, as well as we, remission of such sins as the Sacrifice directly effects, and that supernatural charity which wipes out greater ones. Moreover, when the Blessed Sacrament is lifted up, they adore, as well as we, the true Immaculate Lamb of God; and when they communicate, it is the True Bread of Life, and nothing short of it, which they receive for the eternal health of their souls.

And in like manner, I suppose, as regards this country, as well as Greece and Russia, we may entertain most reasonable hopes, that vast multitudes are in a state of invincible ignorance; so that those among them who are living a life really religious and conscientious, may be looked upon with interest and even pleasure, though a mournful pleasure, in the midst of the pain which a Catholic feels at their ignorant prejudices against what he knows to be true. Amongst the most bitter railers against the Church in this country, may be found those who are influenced by divine grace, and are at present travelling towards heaven, whatever be their ultimate destiny. Among the most irritable disputants against the Sacrifice of the Mass or Transubstantiation, or the most impatient listeners to the glories of Mary, there may be those for whom she is saying to her Son, what He said on the cross to His Father, "Forgive them, for they know not what they do." Nay, while such persons think as at present, they are bound to act accordingly, and only so far to connect themselves with us as their conscience allows. "When persons who have been brought up in heresy," says a Catholic theologian, "are persuaded from their childhood that we are the enemies of God's word, are idolaters, pestilent deceivers, and therefore, as pests, to be avoided, they cannot, while this persuasion lasts, hear us with a safe conscience, and they labour under invincible ignorance, inasmuch as they doubt not that they are in a good way."[1]

Nor does it suffice, in order to throw them out of this irresponsible state, and to make them guilty of their ignorance, that there are means actually in their power of getting rid of it. For instance, say they have no conscientious feeling against frequenting Catholic chapels, conversing with Catholics, or reading their books; and say they are thrown into the neighbourhood of the one or the company of the other, and do not avail themselves of their opportunities; still these

---

[1] Busembaum, vol. i. p. 54.

persons do not become responsible for their present
ignorance till such time as they actually feel it, till a
doubt crosses them upon the subject, and the thought
comes upon them, that inquiry is a duty. And thus
Protestants may be living in the midst of Catholic
light, and labouring under the densest and most stupid
prejudices; and yet we may be able to view them with
hope, though with anxiety—with the hope that the
question has never occurred to them, strange as it may
seem, whether we are not right and they wrong. Nay,
I will say something further still; they may be so circumstanced that it is quite certain that, in course of
time, this ignorance will be removed, and doubt will be
suggested to them, and the necessity of inquiry consequently imposed; and according to our best judgment,
fallible of course as it is, we may be quite certain too,
that, when that time comes, they will refuse to inquire,
and will quench the doubt; yet should it so happen
that they are cut off by death before that time has
arrived (I am putting an hypothetical case), we may
have as much hope of their salvation as if we had had
no such foreboding about them on our mind; for there
is nothing to show that they were not taken away on
purpose, in order that their ignorance might be their
excuse.

As to the prospect of those countless multitudes of a
country like this, who apparently have no supernatural
vision of the next world at all, and die without fear

because they die without thought, with these, alas! I
am not here concerned. But the remarks I have been
making suggest much of comfort, when we look out
into what is called the religious world in all its varieties,
whether it be the High Church section, or the Evangelical, whether it be in the Establishment, or in
Methodism, or in Dissent, so far as there seems to be
real earnestness and invincible prejudice. One cannot
but hope that that written Word of God, for which they
desire to be jealous, though exhibited to them in a
mutilated form and in a translation unsanctioned by
Holy Church, is of incalculable blessing to their souls,
and may be, through God's grace, the divine instrument
of bringing many to contrition and to a happy death
who have received no sacrament since they were
baptized in their infancy. One cannot hope but that the
Anglican Prayer Book, with its Psalter and Catholic
prayers, even though these, in the translation, have
passed through heretical intellects, may retain so much
of its old virtue as to co-operate with divine grace in
the instruction and salvation of a large remnant. In
these and many other ways, even in England, and much
more in Greece, the difficulty is softened which is presented to the imagination by the view of such large
populations, who, though called Christian, are not
Catholic or orthodox in creed.

9.

There is but one set of persons, indeed, who inspire
the Catholic with special anxiety, as much so as the
open sinner, who is not peculiar to any Communion,
Catholic or schismatic, and who does not come into the
present question. There is one set of persons in whom
every Catholic must feel intense interest, about whom
he must feel the gravest apprehensions; viz., those who
have some rays of light vouchsafed to them as to their
heresy or as to their schism, and who seem to be
closing their eyes upon it; or those who have actually
gained a clear view of the nothingness of their own
Communion, and the reality and divinity of the Catholic
Church, yet delay to act upon their knowledge. You,
my dear brethren, if such are here present, are in a very
different state from those around you. You are called
by the inscrutable grace of God to the possession of a
great benefit, and to refuse the benefit is to lose the
grace. You cannot be as others: they pursue their
own way, they walk over this wide earth, and see
nothing wonderful or glorious in the sun, moon, and stars
of the spiritual heavens; or they have an intellectual
sense of their beauty, but no feeling of duty or of love
towards them; or they wish to love them, but think
they ought not, lest they should get a distaste for that
mire and foulness which is their present portion. They
have not yet had the call to inquire, and to seek, and
to pray for further guidance, infused into their hearts

by the gracious Spirit of God; and they will be judged according to what is given them, not by what is not. But on you the thought has dawned, that possibly Catholicism may be true; you have doubted the safety of your present position, and the present pardon of your sins, and the completeness of your present faith. You, by means of that very system in which you find yourselves, have been led to doubt that system. If the Mosaic law, given from above, was a schoolmaster to lead souls to Christ, much more is it true that an heretical creed, when properly understood, warns us against itself, and frightens us from it, and is forced against its will to open for us with its own hands its prison gates, and to show us the way to a better country. So has it been with you. You set out in simplicity and earnestness intending to serve it, and your very serving taught you to serve another. You began to use its prayers and act upon its rules, and they did but witness against it, and made you love it, not more but less, and carried off your affections to one whom you had not loved. The more you gazed upon your own communion the more unlike it you grew; the more you tried to be good Anglicans, the more you found yourselves drawn in heart and spirit to the Catholic Church. It was the destiny of the false prophetess that she could not keep the little ones who devoted themselves to her; and the more simply they gave up their private judgment to her, the more sure they were of being thrown off by her, against their will, into the current

of attraction which led straight to the true Mother of
their souls. So month has gone on after month, and
year after year; and you have again and again vowed
obedience to your own Church, and you have protested
against those who left her, and you have thought you
found in them what you liked not, and you have prophesied evil about them and good about yourselves;
and your plans seemed prospering and your influence
extending, and great things were to be; and yet, strange
to say, at the end of the time you have found yourselves steadily advanced in the direction which you
feared, and never were nearer to the promised land
than you are now.

Oh, look well to your footing that you slip not; be
very much afraid lest the world should detain you;
dare not in anything to fall short of God's grace, or to
lag behind when that grace goes forward. Walk with
it, co-operate with it, and I know how it will end. You
are not the first persons who have trodden that path;
yet a little time, and, please God, the bitter shall be
sweet, and the sweet bitter, and you will have undergone the agony, and will be lodged safely in the true
home of your souls and the valley of peace. Yet but
a little while, and you will look out from your resting-
place upon the wanderers outside; and will wonder
why they do not see that way which is now so plain to
you, and will be impatient with them that they do not
come on faster. And, whereas you now are so perplexed in mind that you seem to yourselves to believe

nothing, then you will be so full of faith, that you will almost see invisible mysteries, and will touch the threshold of eternity. And you will be so full of joy that you will wish all around you to be partakers of it, as if for your own relief; and you will suddenly be filled with yearnings deep and passionate, for the salvation of those dear friends whom you have out-stripped; and you will not mind their coolness, or stiffness, or distance, or constrained gravity, for the love you bear to their souls. And, though *they* will not hear you, you will address yourselves to those who will; I mean, you will weary heaven with your novenas for them, and you will be ever getting Masses for their conversion, and you will go to communion for them, and you will not rest till the bright morning comes, and they are yours once again. Oh, is it possible that there is a resurrection even upon earth! O wonderful grace, that there should be a joyful meeting, after part-ing, before we get to heaven! It was a weary time, that long suspense, when with aching hearts we stood on the brink of a change, and it was like death both to witness and to undergo, when first one and then another disappeared from the eyes of their fellows. And then friends stood on different sides of a gulf, and for years knew nothing of each other or of their welfare. And then they fancied of each other what was not, and there were misunderstandings and jealousies; and each saw the other, as if his ghost, only in imagination and in memory; and all was sickness and anxiety, and hope delayed, and ill-requited care. But now it is all over; the morning is come; the severed shall unite. I see them as if in sight of me. Look at us, my brethren, from our glorious land; look on us radiant with the light cast upon us by the Saints and Angels who stand over us; gaze on us as you approach, and kindle as you gaze. We died, you thought us dead: we live; we cannot return to you, you must come to us,—and you are coming. Do not your hearts beat as you approach us? Do you not long for the hour which makes us one? Do not tears come into your eyes at the thought of the superabundant mercy of your God?

"Sion is the city of our strength, a saviour; a wall, and a bulwark shall be set therein. Open ye the gates, and let the just Nation that keepeth the truth enter in. The old error is passed away; Thou wilt keep peace, peace because we have hoped in Thee. In the way of Thy judgments, O Lord, have we waited for Thee; Thy Name and Thy remembrance are the desire of our soul. O Lord, our God, other lords beside Thee have had possession of us; but in Thee only may we have remembrance of Thy Name. The dying, let them not live; the giants let them not rise again; therefore Thou hast visited and crushed them, and hast destroyed all their memory."

LECTURE XII.

ECCLESIASTICAL HISTORY NO PREJUDICE TO THE APOSTOLICITY OF THE CHURCH.

I.

FEELING, my dear brethren, I should be encroaching on your patience, if I extended this course of Lectures beyond the length which it is now reaching, I have been obliged, in order to give a character of completeness to the whole, to omit the discussion of subjects which I would fain have introduced, and to anticipate others which I would rather have viewed in another connection. This must be my apology, if in their number and selection I shall in any respect disappoint those who have formed their expectations of what I was to do in these Lectures, upon the profession contained in their general title. I have done what my limits allowed me : if I have not done more, it is not, I assure you, from having nothing to say,—for there are many questions upon which I have been anxious to enter,—but because I could neither expect you, my brethren, to give me more of your time, nor could command my own.

As, then, I have already considered certain popular

objections which are made respectively to the Sanctity, Unity, and Catholicity of the Church, now let me, as far as I can do it in a single Lecture, direct your attention to a difficulty felt, not indeed by the world at large, but by many of you in particular, in admitting her Apostolical pretensions.

I say, "a difficulty not felt by the world at large;" for the world at large has no such view of any contrariety between the Catholic Church of to-day and the Catholic Church of fifteen hundred years ago, as to be disposed on that account to deny our Apostolical claims; rather, it is the fashion of the mass of Protestants, whenever they think on the subject, to accuse the Church of the Fathers of what they call Popish superstition and intolerance; and some have even gone so far as to say, that in these respects that early Church was more Popish than the Papists themselves. But when, leaving this first look of the subject, and the broad outline, and the general impression, we come to inspect matters more narrowly, and compare them exactly, point by point, together, certainly it is not difficult to find various instances of discrepancy, apparent or real, important or trivial, between the modern and the ancient Church; and though no candid person who has fairly examined the state of the case can doubt, that, if we differ from the Fathers in some things, Protestants differ from them in all, and if we vary from them in accidentals, Protestants contradict them in

essentials, still, since attack is much easier and plea-
santer than defence, it has been the way with certain
disputants, especially with the Anglican school, instead
of accounting for their own serious departure in so many
respects from the primitive doctrine and ritual, to call
upon us to show why we differ at all from our first
Fathers, though partially and intelligibly, in matters
of discipline and in the tone of our opinions. Thus
it is that Jewel tries to throw dust in the eyes of the
world and does his best to make an attack upon the
Papacy and its claims pass for an Apology for the
Church of England; and more writers have followed
his example than it is worth while, or indeed possible,
to enumerate. And they have been answered again
and again; and the so-called novelties of modern
Catholicism have been explained, if not so as to silence
all opponents (which could not be expected), yet at the
very lowest so far as this (which is all that is incumbent
on us in controversy), so far as to show that we have a
case in our favour. I say, even though we have not
done enough for our proof, we have done enough for
our argument, as the world will allow; for on our
assailants, not on us, lies the *"onus probandi,"* and
they have done nothing till they have actually made
their charges good, and destroyed the very tenableness of our position and even the mere probability of
our representations. However, into the consideration,
whether of these objections or of their answers, I shall

not be expected to enter; and especially, because
each would form a separate subject in itself, and fur-
nish matter for a separate Lecture. How, for instance,
would it be possible in the course of an hour, and with
such an exercise of attention as might fairly be exacted
of you, to embrace subjects as distinct from each other
as the primitive faith concerning the Blessed Virgin,
and the Apostolic See, and the Holy Eucharist, and
the worship of images? You would not expect such
an effort of me, nor promise it for yourselves; and the
less so, because, as you know, my profession all along
has been to confine myself, as far as I can, to general
considerations, and to appeal, in proof of what I assert,
rather to common sense and truths before our eyes than
to theology and history.

2.

In thus opening the subject, my brethren, I have
been both explaining and apologizing for what I am
proposing to do. For, if I am to say something, not
directly in answer to the particular objections in detail,
brought from Antiquity against the doctrine and discipline of the present Catholic Church, but by way of
appeasing and allaying that general misgiving and
perplexity which these objections excite, what can I do
better than appeal to a fact,—though I cannot do so
without some indulgence on the part of my hearers,—
a fact connected with myself? And it is the less unfair

to do so, because, as regards the history of the early
Church and the writings of the Fathers, so many must
go by the testimony of others, and so few have opportunity to use their own experience. I say, then, that
the writings of the Fathers, so far from prejudicing at
least one man against the modern Catholic Church,
have been simply and solely the one intellectual cause
of his having renounced the religion in which he was
born and submitted himself to her. What other causes
there may be, not intellectual, unknown, unsuspected
by himself, though freely imputed on mere conjecture
by those who would invalidate his testimony, it would
be unbecoming and impertinent to discuss; for himself,
if he is asked why he became a Catholic, he can only
give that answer which experience and consciousness
bring home to him as the true one, viz., that he joined
the Catholic Church simply because he believed it, and
it only, to be the Church of the Fathers; because he
believed that there was a Church upon earth till the end
of time, and one only; and because, unless it was the
Communion of Rome, and it only, there was none;—
because, to use language purposely guarded, because it
was the language of controversy, "all parties will agree
that, of all existing systems, the present Communion
of Rome is the nearest approximation in fact to the
Church of the Fathers; possible though some may
think it, to be still nearer to it on paper;"—because,
"did St. Athanasius or St. Ambrose come suddenly to

life, it cannot be doubted what communion they would mistake," that is, would recognize, "for their own;"—because "all will agree that these Fathers, with whatever differences of opinion, whatever protests if you will, would find themselves more at home with such men as St. Bernard or St. Ignatius Loyola, or with the lonely priest in his lodgings, or the holy sisterhood of charity, or the unlettered crowd before the altar, than with the rulers or the members of any other religious community."[1]

This is the great, manifest, historical phenomenon which converted me,—to which all particular inquiries converged. Christianity is not a matter of opinion, but an external fact, entering into, carried out in, indivisible from, the history of the world. It has a bodily occupation of the world; it is one continuous fact or thing, the same from first to last, distinct from everything else: to be a Christian is to partake of, to submit to, this thing; and the simple question was, Where, what is this thing in this age, which in the first age was the Catholic Church? The answer was undeniable; the Church called Catholic now, is that very same thing in hereditary descent, in organization, in principles, in position, in external relations, which was called the Catholic Church then; name and thing have ever gone together, by an uninterrupted connection and succession, from then till now. Whether it had

[1] Essay on Doctrinal Development, p. 138.

been corrupted in its teaching was, at best, a matter of
opinion. It was indefinitely more evident a fact, that
it stood on the ground and in the place of the ancient
Church, as its heir and representative, than that certain
peculiarities in its teaching were really innovations and
corruptions. Say there is no Church at all, if you will,
and at least I shall understand you; but do not meddle
with a fact attested by mankind. I am almost ashamed
to insist upon so plain a point, which in many respects
is axiomatically true, except that there are persons
who wish to deny it. Of course, there are and have
been such persons, and men of deep learning; but their
adverse opinion does not interfere with my present use
of what I think so plain. Observe, I am not insisting
on it as an axiom, though that is my own view of the
matter; nor proving it as a conclusion, nor forcing it on
your acceptance as *your* reason for joining the Catholic
Church, as it was mine. Let every one have his own
reason for becoming a Catholic; for reasons are in
plenty, and there are enough for you all, and moreover
all of them are good ones and consistent with each
other. I am not assigning reasons why you should be
Catholics; you have them already: from first to last I
am doing nothing more than removing difficulties in
your path, which obstruct the legitimate effect of those
reasons which have, as I am assuming, already convinced you. And to-day I am answering the objection,
so powerfully urged upon those who have no means of

examining it for themselves, that, as a matter of fact, the modern Church has departed from the teaching of the ancient. Now even one man's contrary testimony obscures the certainty of this supposed matter of fact, though it is not sufficient to establish any opposite matter of fact of his own. I say, then, the Catholicism of to-day is not likely to be really very different from the Catholicism of Antiquity, if its agreement, or rather its identity, with Antiquity forms the very reason on which even one educated and reflecting person was induced, much against every natural inducement, to submit to its claims. Ancient Catholicity cannot supply a very conclusive argument against modern Catholicity, if the ancient has furnished even one such person with a conclusive argument in favour of the modern. Let us grant that the argument against the modern Church drawn from Antiquity, is not altogether destroyed by this antagonistic argument in her behalf, drawn from the same Antiquity; yet surely that argument adverse to her will be too much damaged and enfeebled by the collision to do much towards resisting such direct independent reasons, personal to yourselves, as are already leading you to her.

3.

My testimony, then, is as follows. Even when I was a boy, my thoughts were turned to the early Church, and especially to the early Fathers, by the perusal of the Calvinist John Milner's Church History, and I have never lost, I never have suffered a suspension of the impression, deep and most pleasurable, which his sketches of St. Ambrose and St. Augustine left on my mind. From that time the vision of the Fathers was always, to my imagination, I may say, a paradise of delight to the contemplation of which I directed my thoughts from time to time, whenever I was free from the engagements proper to my time of life. When years afterwards (1828) I first began to read their works with attention and on system, I busied myself much in analysing them, and in cataloguing their doctrines and principles; but, when I had thus proceeded very carefully and minutely for some space of time, I found, on looking back on what I had done, that I had scarcely done anything at all; I found that I had gained very little from them, and I came to the conclusion that the Fathers I had been reading, which were exclusively those of the ante-Nicene period, had very little in them. At the time I did not discover the reason of this result, though, on the retrospect, it was plain enough: I had read them simply on Protestant ideas, analysed and catalogued them on Protestant principles of division, and hunted for Protestant doctrines and usages in them. My headings ran, "Justification by faith only," "Sanctification," and the like. I knew not what to look for in them; I sought what was not there, I missed what was there; I laboured through the night and caught nothing. But I should make one important exception: I rose from their perusal with a vivid perception of the divine institution, the prerogatives, and the gifts of the Episcopate; that is, with an implicit aversion to the Erastian principle.

Some years afterwards (1831) I took up the study of them again, when I had occasion to employ myself on the history of Arianism. I read them with Bull's *Defensio*, as their key, as far as his subject extended; but I am not aware that I made any other special doctrinal use of them at that time.

After this I set myself to the study of them, with the view of pursuing the series of controversies connected with our Lord's Person; and to the examination of these controversies I devoted two summers, with the interval of several years between them (1835 and 1839). And now at length I was reading them for myself; for no Anglican writer had specially and minutely treated the subjects on which I was engaged. On my first introduction to them I had read them as a Protestant; and next, I had read them pretty much as an Anglican, though it is observable that, whatever I gained on either reading, over and above the theory or system with which I started, was in a Catholic direction. In the former of the two summers above mentioned (1835), my reading was almost entirely confined to strictly doctrinal subjects, to the exclusion of history, and I believe it left me pretty much where I was on the question of the Catholic Church; but in the latter of them (1839) it was principally occupied with the history of the Monophysite controversy, and the circumstances and transactions of the Council of Chalcedon, in the fifth century, and at once and irrevocably I found my faith in the tenableness of the fundamental principle of Anglicanism disappear, and a doubt of it implanted in my mind which never was eradicated. I thought I saw in the controversy I have named, and in the Ecumenical Council connected with it, a clear interpretation of the present state of Christendom, and a key to the different parties and personages who have figured on the Catholic or the Protestant side at and since the era of the Reformation. During the autumn of the same year, a paper I fell in witl upon the schism of the Donatists,[1] deepened the impression which the history of the Monophysites had made; and I felt dazzled and excited by the new view of things which was thus opened upon me. Distrusting my judgment, and that I might be a better judge of the subject, I determined for a time to put it away from my mind; nor did I return to it till I gave myself to the translation of the doctrinal Treatises of St. Athanasius, at the end of 1841. This occupation brought up again before me the whole question of the Arian controversy and the Nicene Council; and now I clearly saw in that history, what I had not perceived on the first study of it, the same phenomenon which had already startled me in the history of St. Leo and the Monophysites. From that time, what delayed my

[1] By Dr. Wiseman.

conviction of the claims of the Catholic Church upon me, was not any confidence in Anglicanism as a system of doctrine, but particular objections which as yet I saw no way of reducing, such as may at present weigh with you, and the fear that, since I found my friends strongly opposed to my view of the matter, I might, in some way or other, be involved in a delusion.

4.

And now you will ask me, what it is I saw in the history of primitive controversies and Councils which was so fatal to the pretensions of the Anglican Church ? I saw that the general theory and position of Anglicanism was no novelty in ancient history, but had a distinct place in it, and a series of prototypes, and that these prototypes had ever been heretics or the patrons of heresy. The very badge of Anglicanism, as a system, is that it is a *Via Media;* this is its life; it is this, or it is nothing; deny this, and it forthwith dissolves into Catholicism or Protestantism. This constitutes its only claim to be recognized as a distinct form of Christianity ; it is its recommendation to the world at large, and its simple measuring-line for the whole field of theology. The *Via Media* appeals to the good sense of mankind; it says that the human mind is naturally prone to excess, and that theological combatants in particular are certain to run into extremes. Truth, as virtue, lies in a mean ; whatever, then, is true, whatever is not true, extremes certainly are false. And, whereas truth is in a mean, for that very reason it is very moderate and liberal; it can tolerate either extreme with great patience, because it views neither with that keenness of contrariety with which one extreme regards the other. For the same reason, it is comprehensive; because, being in a certain sense in the centre of all errors, though having no part in any of them, it may be said to rule and to temper them, to bring them together, and to make them, as it were, converge and conspire together in one under its own meek and gracious sway. Dispassionateness, forbearance, indulgence, toleration, and comprehension are thus all of them attributes of the *Via Media.* It is obvious, moreover, that a doctrine like this will find especial acceptance with the civil magistrate. Religion he needs as an instrument of government; yet in religious opinion he sees nothing else but the fertile cause of discord and confusion. Joyfully then does he welcome a form of theology, whose very mission it is to temper the violence of polemics, to soften and to accommodate differences, and to direct the energies of churchmen to the attainment of tangible good instead of the discussion of mysteries.

This sentiment I expressed in the following passage, in the year 1837, which I quote with shame and sorrow; the more so, because it is certainly inconsistent with my own general teaching, from the very time I began to write, except for a short interval in 1825 and 1826 which need not be noticed here. However, it is an accurate exponent of the Anglican theory of religion. "Though it is not likely," I said, "that Romanism should ever again become formidable in England, yet it may be in a position to make its voice heard; and, in proportion as it is able to do so, the *Via Media* will do important service of the following kind. In the controversy which will ensue, Rome will not fail to preach, far and wide, the tenet which it never conceals, that there is no salvation external to its own communion. On the other hand, Protestantism, as it exists, will not be behind-hand in consigning to eternal ruin all who are adherents of Roman doctrine. What a prospect is this! two widely-spread and powerful parties dealing forth solemn anathemas upon each other, in the Name of the Lord! Indifference and scepticism must be, in such a case, the ordinary refuge of men of mild and peaceable minds, who revolt from such presumption, and are deficient in clear views of the truth. I cannot well exaggerate the misery of such a state of things. Here the English theology would come in with its characteristic calmness and caution, clear and decided in its view, giving no encouragement to lukewarmness and liberalism, but withholding all absolute anathemas on errors of opinion, except where the primitive Church sanctions the use of them." [1]

Such, then, is the Anglican Church and its *Via Media,*

[1] Proph. Off. p. 26.

and such the practical application of it; it is an inter-position or arbitration between the extreme doctrines of Protestantism on the one hand, and the faith of Rome which Protestantism contradicts on the other. At the same time, though it may be unwilling to allow it, it is, from the nature of the case, but a particular form of Protestantism. I do not say that in secondary principles it may not agree with the Catholic Church; but, its essential idea being that she has gone into error, whereas the essential idea of Catholicism is the Church's infal-libility, the *Via Media* is really nothing else than Protestant. Not to submit to the Church is to oppose her, and to side with the heretical party; for medium there is none. The *Via Media* assumes that Protestant-ism is right in its protest against Catholic doctrine, only that that protest needs correcting, limiting, perfecting. This surely is but a matter of fact; for the *Via Media* has adopted all the great Protestant doctrines, as its most strenuous upholder and the highest of Anglo-Catholics will be obliged to allow; the mutilated canon, the defective Rule of Faith, justification by faith only, putative righteousness, the infection of nature in the regenerate, the denial of the five Sacraments, the relation of faith to the Sacramental Presence, and the like; its aim being nothing else than to moderate, with Melanc-thon, the extreme statements of Luther, to keep them from shocking the feelings of human nature, to protect them from the criticism of common sense, and from the

pressure and urgency of controversial attack. Thus we
have three parties on the historical stage; the See and
Communion of Rome; the original pure Protestant,
violent, daring, offensive, fanatical in his doctrines; and
a cautious middle party, quite as heretical in principle
and in doctrinal elements as Protestantism itself, but
having an eye to the necessities of controversy, sensible
in its ideas, sober in its tastes, safe in its statements,
conservative in its aims, and practical in its measures.
Such a *Via Media* has been represented by the line of
Archbishops of Canterbury from Tillotson downwards,
as by Cranmer before them. Such in their theology,
though not in their persons or their histories, were Laud
and Bull, Taylor and Hammond, and I may say nearly
all the great authorities of the Established Church.
This distinctive character has often been noticed,
especially by Mr. Alexander Knox, and much might be
said upon it; and, as I have already observed, it ever
receives the special countenance of the civil magistrate,
who, if he could, would take up with a religion without
any doctrines whatever, as Warburton well understands,
but who, in the case of a necessary evil, admires the
sobriety of Tillotson, and the piety of Patrick, and the
elegance of Jortin, and the biblical accomplishments of
Lowth, and the shrewd sense of Paley.

5.

Now this sketch of the relative positions of the See

of Rome, Protestantism, the *Via Media*, and the State, which we see in the history of the last three centuries, is, I repeat, no novelty in history; it is almost its rule, certainly its rule during the long period when relations existed between the Byzantine Court and the Holy See; and it is impossible to resist the conclusion, which the actual inspection of the history in detail forces upon us, that what the See of Rome was then such is it now; that what Arius, Nestorius, or Eutyches were then, such are Luther and Calvin now; what the Eusebians or Monophysites then, such the Anglican hierarchy now; what the Byzantine Court then, such is now the Government of England, and such would have been many a Catholic Court, had it had its way. That ancient history is not dead, it lives; it prophesies of what passes before our eyes; it is founded in the nature of things; we see ourselves in it, as in a glass, and if the *Via Media* was heretical then, it is heretical now.

I do not know how to convey this to others in one or two paragraphs; it is the living picture which history presents to us, which is the evidence of the fact; and to attempt a mere outline of it, or to detach one or two groups from the finished composition, is to do injustice to its luminousness. Take, for instance, the history of Arianism. Arius stood almost by himself; bold, keen, stern, and violent, he took his stand on two or three axiomatic statements, as he considered them, appealed to Scripture, despised authority and tradition, and carried out his heretical doctrine to its furthest limits. He absolutely maintained, without any reserve, that our Lord was a creature, and had a beginning. Next, he was one of a number of able and distinguished men, scattered over the East, united together by the bond of a common master and a common school, who might have been expected to stand by him on his appealing to them; but who left him to his fate, or at least but circuitously and indirectly served his cause. High in station, ecclesiastical and civil, they found it more consistent with their duties towards themselves to fall back upon a more cautious phraseology than his, and upon less assailable principles, to evade inquiry, to explain away tests, and to profess a submission to the voice of their forefathers and of the Catholic world; and they developed their formidable party in that form of heresy which is commonly called Semi-Arianism or Eusebianism. They preached peace, professed to agree with neither St. Athanasius nor Arius, excited the jealousies of the Eastern world against the West, were strong enough to insult the Pope, and dexterous enough to gain the favour of Constantine and the devoted attachment of his son Constantius. The name of Eusebians they received from their leader, the able and unscrupulous Bishop of Nicomedia, with whom was associated another Eusebius, better known to posterity as the learned historian of the Church, and one of the most accomplished and able of the Fathers. It will be to my purpose to

quote one or two sentences in description of the character
of this celebrated man, written by me at a time when
the subject of the *Via Media* had not as yet been mooted
in the controversy, nor the bearing of the Arian history
upon it been suggested to my mind.

" He seems," I said, speaking of Eusebius of Cæsarea,
"to have had the faults and the virtues of the mere
man of letters; strongly excited neither to good nor
to evil, and careless at once of the cause of truth and
the prizes of secular greatness, in comparison of the
comforts and decencies of literary ease. In his writings,
numerous as they are, there is very little which fixes
on Eusebius any charge, beyond that of an attachment
to the Platonic phraseology. Had he not connected
himself with the Arian party, it would have been unjust
to have suspected him of heresy. But his acts are his
confession. He openly sided with those whose blasphemies a true Christian would have abhorred; and
he sanctioned and shared their deeds of violence and
injustice perpetrated on the Catholics. . . . The grave
accusation under which he lies is not that of Arian-
ising,[1] but of corrupting the simplicity of the Gospel
with an Eclectic spirit. While he held out the ambiguous language of the schools as a refuge, and the
Alexandrian imitation of it as an argument, against
the pursuit of the orthodox, his conduct gave coun-

---

[1] The author has now still less favourable views of Eusebius' theology
than he had when he wrote this in 1832.

tenance to the secular maxim, that difference in creeds
is a matter of inferior moment, and that, provided we
confess as far as the very terms of Scripture, we may
speculate as philosophers and live as the world. . . .
The remark has been made, that throughout his Ecclesiastical History no instance occurs of his expressing
abhorrence of the superstitions of paganism; and that
his custom is either to praise, or not to blame, such
heretical writers as fall under his notice."[1]   Much
more might be added in illustration of the resemblance
of this eminent writer to the divines of the Anglican
Via Media.

The Emperor Constantine has already been named;
and looking at him in his ecclesiastical character we
find him committed to two remarkable steps; one that
he frankly surrendered himself to the intimate friend-
ship of this latitudinarian theologian; the other, that,
at the very first rumour of the Arian dissensions, he
promptly, and with the precision of an instinct, interfered in the quarrel, and in a politician's way pronounced it to be a logomachy, or at least a matter
of mere speculation, and bade bishops and heretics
embrace and make it up with each other at once.   This
did he in a question no less solemn than that of the
divinity of our Lord, which, if any question, could not
be other than most influential, one would think, in a

[1] Arians of the Fourth Century, p. 281. [p. 269 ed. 1871.]

Christian's creed. But Constantine was not a Christian
as yet; and this, while it partly explains the extravagance of his conduct, illustrates the external and utili-
tarian character of a statesman's religion.

I will present to you portions of the celebrated letter
which he addressed to the Bishop of Alexandria and
to Arius, as quoted in the history to which I have
already referred. "He professes therein two motives as
impelling him in his public conduct; first, the desire
of effecting the reception, throughout his dominions, of
some one definite and complete form of religious worship; next, that of settling and invigorating the civil
institutions of the empire. Desirous of securing a unity
of sentiment among all the believers in the Deity, he
first directed his attention to the religious dissensions
of Africa, which he had hoped, with the aid of the
Oriental Christians, to terminate. 'But glorious and
Divine Providence!' he continues, 'how fatally were my
ears, or rather, was my heart wounded, by the report
of a rising schism among you far more acrimonious
than the African dissensions. . . . On investigation, I
find that the reasons for this quarrel are insignificant
and worthless. . . . As I understand it, you, Alexander,
were asking the separate opinions of your clergy on
some passage of your law, or rather were inquiring
about some idle question, when you, Arius, inconsider-
ately committed yourself to statements, which should
either never have come into your mind, or have been

at once repressed. On this a difference ensued, Christian intercourse was suspended, the sacred flock was divided into two, and the harmonious unity of the Church broken. . . . Listen to the advice of me your fellow-servant ; — neither ask nor answer questions which are not any injunction of your law, but are the altercation of barren leisure; at best, keep them to yourselves, and do not publish them. . . . Your contention is not about any capital commandment of your law, neither of you is introducing any novel scheme of divine worship, you are of one and the same way of thinking, so that it is in your power to unite in one communion. Even the philosophers can agree together one and all, though differing in particulars. . . . Is it right for brothers to oppose brothers, for the sake of trifles ? . . . Such conduct might be expected from the multitude or from the recklessness of boyhood, but is little in keeping with your sacred profession and with your personal wisdom. . . . Give me back my days of calm, my nights of security ; that I may experience henceforth the comfort of the clear light and the cheerfulness of tranquillity. Otherwise I shall sigh and be dissolved in tears. . . . So great is my grief, that I put off my journey to the East on the news of your dissension. . . . Open for me that path towards you, which your contentions have closed up. Let me see you and all other cities in happiness, that I may offer due thanksgivings to God above for the unanimity and free intercourse which is seen among you.'"[1]

Such was the position which the Christian civil power assumed in the very first days of its nativity. The very moment the State enters into the Church, it shows its nature and its propensities, and takes up a position which it has never changed, and never will. Kings and statesmen may be, and have been, saints; but, in being such, they have acted against the interests and traditions of kingcraft and statesmanship. Constantine died, but his line of policy continued. His son, Constantius, embraced the *Via Media* of Eusebianism on conviction as well as from expediency. He sternly set himself against both extremes, as he considered them, banished the fanatical successors of Arius, and tortured and put to death the adherents to the Nicene Creed and the cause of St. Athanasius. Thus the *Via Media* party was in the ascendancy for about thirty years, till the death of the generation by whom it had been formed and protected;—with quarrels and defections among themselves, restless attempts at stability in faith, violent efforts after a definite creed, fruitless projects of comprehension,—when, towards the end of their domination, a phenomenon showed itself, which claims our particular attention, as not without parallel in ecclesiastical history, and as reminding us of what is going on, in an humbler way

---

[1] Arians of the Fourth Century, p. 267. [p. 255.]

and on a narrower stage, before our eyes. In various districts, especially of Asia Minor, a considerable party had gradually been forming, and had exercised a considerable influence in the ecclesiastical transactions of the period, who, though called Semi-Arians and professing their symbols, had no sympathies with the Eusebians, and indeed were ultimately disowned by them. There seems to have been about a hundred bishops who belonged to this party, and their leaders were men of religious habits and unblemished repute, and approximated so nearly to orthodoxy in their language, that Saints appear among the number of their friends, or have issued from their school. Things could not stand as they were : every year brought its event; Constantius died; parties were broken up,—and this among the rest. It divided into two; as many as fifty-nine of its bishops subscribed the orthodox formula, and submitted themselves to the Holy See. A body of thirty-four persisted in their separation from it, and afterwards formed a new heresy of their own.

These are but a few of the main features of the history of Arianism; yet they may be sufficient to illustrate the line of argument which Antiquity furnishes against the theories, on which alone the movement of 1833 had claim on the attention of Protestants. Those theories claimed to represent the theological and the ecclesiastical teaching of the Fathers; and the Fathers, when interrogated, did but pronounce them to be the offspring of eclecticism, and the exponent of a State Church. It could not maintain itself in its position without allying itself historically with that very Erastianism, as seen in Antiquity, of which it had so intense a hatred. What has been sketched from the Arian history might be shown still more strikingly in the Monophysite.[1]

6.

Nor was it solely the conspicuous parallel which I have been describing in outline, which, viewed in its details, was so fatal a note of error against the Anglican position. I soon found it to follow, that the grounds on which alone Anglicanism was defensible formed an impregnable stronghold for the primitive heresies, and that the justification of the Primitive Councils was as cogent an apology for the Council of Trent. It was difficult to make out how the Eutychians or Monophysites were heretics, unless Protestants and Anglicans were heretics also; difficult to find arguments against the Tridentine Fathers which did not tell against the Fathers of Chalcedon; difficult to condemn the Popes of the sixteenth century, without condemning the Popes of the fifth. The drama of religion and the combat of truth and error were ever one and the same. The principles and proceedings of the Church now were those of the Church then; the principles and proceedings of heretics then were those of Protestants now. I found it so—almost fearfully; there was an awful similitude,

---

[1] Vid. Essay on Doctrinal Development, chap. v. sec. 3.

more awful, because so silent and unimpassioned,
between the dead records of the past and the feverish
chronicle of the present. The shadow of the fifth century was on the sixteenth. It was like a spirit rising
from the troubled waters of the Old World with the
shape and lineaments of the new. The Church then,
as now, might be called peremptory and stern, resolute,
overbearing, and relentless; and heretics were shifting,
changeable, reserved, and deceitful, ever courting the
civil power, and never agreeing together, except by its
aid; and the civil power was ever aiming at comprehen-
sions, trying to put the invisible out of view, and to
substitute expediency for faith. What was the use of
continuing the controversy, or defending my position,
if, after all, I was but forging arguments for Arius or
Eutyches, and turning devil's advocate against the
much-enduring Athanasius and the majestic Leo? Be
my soul with the Saints! and shall I lift up my hand
against them? Sooner may my right hand forget her
cunning, and wither outright, as his who once stretched
it out against a prophet of God,—perish sooner a whole
tribe of Cranmers, Ridleys, Latimers, and Jewels,—
perish the names of Bramhall, Ussher, Taylor, Stillingfleet, and Barrow, from the face of the earth,—ere I
should do aught but fall at their feet in love and in
worship, whose image was continually before my eyes,
and whose musical words were ever in my ears and on
my tongue!

This, too, is an observable fact, that the more learned Anglican writers seem aware of the state of the case, and are obliged, by the necessities of their position, to speak kindly of the heretical communities of ancient history, and at least obliquely to censure the Councils, which, nevertheless, they profess to receive. Thus Bramhall, as we saw yesterday, strives to fraternize with the sectaries now existing in the East; nor could he consistently do otherwise, with the Council of Trent and the Protestants in the field of controversy; it being difficult indeed to show that the Eastern Churches in question are to be accounted heretical on any principles which a Protestant is able to put forward. It is not wonderful, then, that other great authorities in the Established Church are of the same way of thinking. "Jewel, Ussher, and Laud," says an Anglican divine of this day, "are apparently of this opinion, and Field expressly maintains it."[1]

Jeremy Taylor goes further still, that is, is still more consistent; for he not merely acquits of heresy the existing communities of the East who dissent from the third and fourth Councils, but he is bold enough to attack the first Council of all, the Nicene. He places the right of private judgment, or what he calls "the liberty of prophesying," above all Councils whatever. As to the Nicene, he says, "*I* am much pleased with the enlarging of the Creed which the Council of Nice

[1] Palmer on the Church, vol. i. p. 418.

made, because they enlarged it in *my* sense; but I am
not sure that others were satisfied with it."[1] "That
faith is best which hath greatest simplicity; and . . .
it is better, in all cases, humbly to submit, than
curiously to inquire, and pry into the mystery under
the cloud, and to hazard our faith by improving our
knowledge. If the Nicene Fathers had done so too,
possibly the Church would never have repented it."[2]
"If the article had been with more simplicity and less
nicety determined, charity would have gained more,
and faith would have lost nothing."[3] And he not only
calls Eusebius, whom it is hard to acquit of heresy,
"the wisest of them all,"[4] but actually praises the
letter of Constantine, which I have already cited, as
most true in its view and most pertinent to the occasion.
"The Epistle of Constantine to Alexander and Arius,"
he says, "tells the truth, and chides them both for com-
mencing the question; Alexander for broaching it,
Arius for taking it up. And although this be true,
that it had been better for the Church it never had
begun, yet, being begun, what is to be done in it? Of
this also, in that admirable epistle, we have the Emperor's judgment . . . for, first, he calls it a certain
vain piece of a question, ill begun and more unadvisedly
published, ... a fruitless contention, the product of
idle brains, a matter so nice, so obscure, so intricate,

---

[1] Vol. vii. p. 481, ed. 1828. [2] Jeremy Taylor, ibid. p. 485.
[3] Ibid. [4] Ibid.

that it was neither to be explicated by the clergy, nor understood by the people; a dispute of words. . . . . It concerned not the substance of faith, or the worship of God, nor any chief commandment of Scripture . . . the matter being of no great importance, but vain, and a toy, in respect of the excellent blessings of peace and charity."[1] When we recollect that the question confessedly in dispute was whether our Lord is the Eternal God or a creature, and that the Nicene symbol against which Taylor writes was confessedly the sole test adequate to the definition of his divinity, it is scarcely conceivable that a writer should really believe that divinity and thus express himself.

Taylor is no accident in the history of the *Via Media;* he does but speak plainer than Field and Bramhall; and soon others began to speak plainer than he. The school of Laud gave birth to the latitudinarians; Hales and Chillingworth, their first masters, were personal friends of the Archbishop, whose indignation with them only proves his involuntary sense of the tottering state of his own theological position. Lord Falkland, again, who thinks that before the Nicene Council "the generality of Christians had not been always taught the contrary to Arius's doctrine, but some one way, others the other, most neither,"[2] was the admired friend of Hammond; and Grotius, whose subsequent influence upon the national divines has been so serious, was

---

[1] P. 482.   [2] Hammond's Works, vol. ii. p. 655.

introduced to their notice by Hammond and Bramhall.

Such has been the issue of the *Via Media;* its tendency in theory is towards latitudinarianism; its position historically is one of heresy; in the National Church it has fulfilled both its theoretical tendency and its historical position. As this simple truth was brought home to me, I felt that, if continuance in the National Church was defensible, it must be on other grounds than those of the *Via Media*.

7.

Yet this was but one head of argument, which the history of the early Church afforded against the National Establishment, and in favour of the Roman See. I have already alluded to the light which the schism of the African Donatists casts on the question between the two parties in the controversy; it is clear, strong, and decisive, but perfectly distinct from the proof derivable from the Arian, Nestorian, and Monophysite histories.[1]

Then again, after drawing out from Antiquity the outlines of the ecclesiastical structure, and its relations to bodies and powers external to it, when we go on, as it were, to colour it with the thousand tints which are to be found in the same ancient records, when we consider the ritual of the Church, the ceremonial of religion,

---

[1] Vide *Dublin Review*, August 1839, Art. "Anglican Claim."

the devotions of private Christians, the opinions generally received, and the popular modes of acting, what do we find but a third and most striking proof of the identity between primitive Christianity and modern Catholicism ?[1] No other form of Christianity but this present Catholic Communion, has a pretence to resemble, even in the faintest shadow, the Christianity of Antiquity, viewed as a living religion on the stage of the world. This has ever attached me to such works as Fleury's Church History; because, whatever may be its incidental defects or mistakes, it brings before the reader so vividly the Church of the Fathers, as a fact and a reality, instead of speculating, after the manner of most histories, on the principles, or of making views upon the facts, or cataloguing the heresies, rites, or writers, of those ancient times. You may make ten thousand extracts from the Fathers, and not get deeper into the state of their times than the paper you write upon; to imbibe into the intellect the Ancient Church as a fact, is either to be a Catholic or an infidel.

Recollect, my brethren, I am going into these details, not as if I thought of convincing you on the spot by a view of history which convinced me after careful consideration, nor as if I called on you to be convinced by what convinced me at all (for the methods of conviction are numberless, and one man approaches

---

[1] *Dublin Review*, Dec. 1843, Art. "A Voice from Rome."

the Church by this road, another by that), but merely
in order to show you how it was that Antiquity,
instead of leading me from the Holy See as it leads
many, on the contrary drew me on to submit to its
claims. But, even had I worked out for you these
various arguments ever so fully, I should have brought
before you but a secondary portion of the testimony
which the Ancient Church seemed to me to supply
to its own identity with the modern. What was far
more striking to me than the ecclesiastical phenomena
which I have been drawing out, remarkable as they
are, is a subject of investigation which is not of a
nature to introduce into a popular lecture; I mean
the history of the doctrinal definitions of the Church.
It is well known that, though the creed of the Church
has been one and the same from the beginning, yet
it has been so deeply lodged in her bosom as to be
held by individuals more or less implicitly, instead
of being delivered from the first in those special statements, or what are called definitions, under which it
is now presented to us, and which preclude mistake
or ignorance. These definitions, which are but the
expression of portions of the one dogma which has
ever been received by the Church, are the work of
time; they have grown to their present shape and
number in the course of eighteen centuries, under the
exigency of successive events, such as heresies and the
like, and they may of course receive still further addi-

tions as time goes on. Now this process of doctrinal development, as you might suppose, is not of an accidental or random character; it is conducted upon laws, as everything else which comes from God; and the study of its laws and of its exhibition, or, in other words, the science and history of the formation of theology, was a subject which had interested me more than anything else from the time I first began to read the Fathers, and which had engaged my attention in a special way. Now it was gradually brought home to me, in the course of my reading, so gradually, that I cannot trace the steps of my conviction, that the decrees of later Councils, or what Anglicans call the Roman corruptions, were but instances of that very same doctrinal law which was to be found in the history of the early Church; and that in the sense in which the dogmatic truth of the prerogatives of the Blessed Virgin may be said, in the lapse of centuries, to have grown upon the consciousness of the faithful, in that same sense did, in the first age, the mystery of the Blessed Trinity also gradually shine out and manifest itself more and more completely before their minds. Here was at once an answer to the objections urged by Anglicans against the present teaching of Rome; and not only an answer to objections, but a positive argument in its favour; for the immutability and uninterrupted action of the laws in question throughout the course of Church history is a plain note of identity between the Catholic Church of the first ages and that which now goes by that name;—just as the argument from the analogy of natural and revealed religion is at once an answer to difficulties in the latter, and a direct proof that Christianity has the same Author as the physical and moral world. But the force of this, to me ineffably cogent argument, I cannot hope to convey to another.

8.

And now, my dear brethren, what fit excuse can I make to you for the many words I have used about myself, and not in this Lecture only, but in others before it? This alone I can say, that it was the apprehension, or rather the certainty that this would be the case, which, among other reasons, made me as unwilling as I was to begin this course of Lectures at all. I foresaw that I could not address you on the subjects which I proposed, without introducing myself into the discussion; I could not refer to the past without alluding to matters in which I had a part; I could not show that interest in your state of mind and course of thought which I really feel, without showing that I therefore understood it, because I had before now experienced it myself; and I anticipated, what I fear has been the case, that in putting before you the events of former years, and the motives of past transactions, and the operation of common principles, and the complexion

of old habits and opinions, I should be in no slight degree constructing, what I have ever avoided, a defence
of myself.

But I have had another apprehension, both before
and since beginning these Lectures, viz., lest it was (to
say the least) an impolitic proceeding to contemplate
them at all. Things were proceeding in that course in
which I knew they must proceed; I could not foretell
indeed that a decision would issue from the Committee
of Privy Council on the subject of Baptism; I could
not anticipate that this or that external event would
suddenly undo men's confidence in the National Church;
but it required no gift of prophecy to feel that falsehood, and pretence, and unreality could not for ever
enslave honest minds sincerely seeking the truth. It
needed no prophetical gift to be sure that others must
take ultimately the course which I had taken, though
I could not foretell the time or the occasion; no gift
to foresee, that those who did not choose to plunge into
the gulf of scepticism must at length fall back upon
the Catholic Church. Nor did it require in me much
faith in you, my dear brethren, much love for you, to
be sure that, though there were close around you men
who look like you, but are not, that you, the children
of the movement, were too conscientious, too much in
earnest, not to be destined by that God, who made you
what you are, to greater things. Others have scoffed
at you, but I never; others may have made light of

your principles, or your sincerity, but never I; others may have predicted evil of you, I have only felt vexed at the prediction. I have laughed, indeed, I have scorned, and scorn and laugh I must, when men set up an outside instead of the inside of religion—when they affect more than they can sustain—when they indulge in pomp or in minutiæ, which only then are becoming when there is something to be proud of, something to be anxious for. If I have been excessive here, if I have confused what is defective with what is hollow, or have mistaken aspiration for pretence, or have been severe upon infirmities of which self-know-ledge would have made me tender, I wish it otherwise. Still, whatever my faults in this matter, I have ever been trustful in that true Catholic spirit which has lived in the movement of which you are partakers. I have been steady in my confidence in that supernatural influence among you, which made me what I am,—which, in its good time, shall make you what you shall be. You are born to be Catholics; refuse not the unmerited grace of your bountiful God; throw off for good and all the illusions of your intellect, the bondage of your affections, and stand upright in that freedom which is your true inheritance.

And my confidence that you will do so at last, and that the sophistries of this world will not hold you for ever, is what has caused the hesitation to which I have referred, whether I have done wisely in deciding on addressing you at all. I have in truth had anxious misgivings whether I should not do better to let you alone, my own experience teaching me, that even the most charitable attempts are apt to fail, when their end is the conviction of the intellect. It is no work of a day to convince the intellect of an Englishman that Catholicism is true. And even when the intellect is convinced, a thousand subtle influences interpose in arrest of what should follow, carrying, as it were, an appeal into a higher court, and claiming to have the matter settled before some tribunal more sacred, and by pleadings more recondite, than the operations and the decision of the reason. The Eternal God deals with us one by one, each in his own way; and bystanders may pity and compassionate the long throes of our travail, but they cannot aid us except by their prayers. If, then, I have erred in entering upon the subjects I have brought before you, pardon me; pardon me if I have rudely taken on myself to thrust you forward, and to anticipate by artificial means a divine growth. If it be so, I will only hope that, though I may have done you no good, yet my attempt may be blessed in some other way; that I may have thrown light on the general subject which I have discussed, have contributed to map out the field of thought on which I have been engaged, and to ascertain its lie and its characteristics, and have furnished materials for what, in time to come, may be the science and received principles of the whole controversy, though I have failed in that which was my immediate object.

9.

At all events, my dear brethren, I hope I may be at least considered to be showing my good-will and kindness towards you, if nothing else, and my desire to be of use to you. All is vanity but what is done to the glory of God. It glitters and it fades away; it makes a noise and is gone. If I shall not do you or others good, I have done nothing. Yet a little while and the end will come, and all will be made manifest, and error will fail, and truth will prevail. Yet a little while, and "the fire shall try every man's work of what sort it is." May you and I live in this prospect; and may the Eternal God, Father, Son, and Spirit, Three in One, may His Ever-blessed Mother, may St. Philip, my dear father and master, the great Saints Athanasius and Ambrose, and St. Leo, pope and confessor, who have brought me thus far, be the hope, and help, and reward of you and me, all through this weary life, and in the day of account, and in glory everlasting!

A SELECT LIST

OF

THEOLOGICAL BOOKS

(MAINLY ROMAN CATHOLIC)

PUBLISHED BY

LONGMANS, GREEN, & CO.

LONDON, NEW YORK, AND BOMBAY.

MESSRS. LONGMANS, GREEN, & CO.

Issue the undermentioned Catalogues and Lists of their Publications, any of which may be had post free on application :—

1. MONTHLY LIST OF NEW BOOKS AND NEW EDITIONS.
2. QUARTERLY LIST OF ANNOUNCEMENTS AND NEW BOOKS.
3. NOTES ON BOOKS: BEING AN ANALYSIS OF THE WORKS PUBLISHED BY MESSRS. LONGMANS, GREEN & CO. DURING EACH QUARTER.
4. SCIENTIFIC AND TECHNICAL BOOKS.
5. MEDICAL AND SURGICAL BOOKS.
6. EDUCATIONAL AND SCHOOL BOOKS.
7. EDUCATIONAL BOOKS RECENTLY PUBLISHED.
8. BOOKS FOR ELEMENTARY SCHOOLS AND PUPIL TEACHERS.
9. BOOKS FOR SCHOOL PRIZES.
10. BOOKS FOR CHRISTMAS AND NEW YEAR PRESENTS.
11. THEOLOGICAL BOOKS (CHURCH OF ENGLAND).
12. THEOLOGICAL BOOKS (MAINLY ROMAN CATHOLIC).
13. BOOKS IN GENERAL LITERATURE AND GENERAL THEOLOGY.
14. A CLASSIFIED CATALOGUE (GENERAL LITERATURE, SCIENCE, THEOLOGY, EDUCATION).

CARDINAL NEWMAN'S WORKS.

Letters and Correspondence of John Henry Newman during his Life in the English Church. With a brief Autobiography. Edited, at Cardinal Newman's request, by ANNE MOZLEY. 2 vols. Cr. 8vo. 7s.

Parochial and Plain Sermons. Edited by REV. W. J. COPELAND, B.D. late Rector of Farnham, Essex. 8 vols. Sold separately. Crown 8vo. Cabinet Edition, 5s. each; Popular Edition, 3s. 6d. each.

CONTENTS OF VOL. I.:—Holiness necessary for Future Blessedness—The Immortality of the Soul—Knowledge of God's Will without Obedience—Secret Faults—Self-Denial the Test of Religious Earnestness—The Spiritual Mind—Sins of Ignorance and Weakness—God's Commandments not Grievous—The Religious Use of Excited Feelings—Profession without Practice—Profession without Hypocrisy—Profession without Ostentation—Promising without Doing—Religious Emotion—Religious Faith Rational—The Christian Mysteries—The Self-Wise Inquirer—Obedience the Remedy for Religious Perplexity—Times of Private Prayer—Forms of Private Prayer—The Resurrection of the Body—Witnesses of the Resurrection—Christian Reverence—The Religion of the Day—Scripture a Record of Human Sorrow—Christian Manhood.

CONTENTS OF VOL. II.:—The World's Benefactors—Faith without Sight—The Incarnation—Martyrdom—Love of Relations and Friends—The Mind of Little Children—Ceremonies of the Church—The Glory of the Christian Church—St. Paul's Conversion viewed in Reference to his Office—Secrecy and Suddenness of Divine Visitations—Divine Decrees—The Reverence Due to the Blessed Virgin Mary—Christ, a Quickening Spirit—Saving Knowledge—Self-Contemplation—Religious Cowardice—The Gospel Witnesses—Mysteries in Religion—The Indwelling Spirit—The Kingdom of the Saints—The Gospel, a Trust Committed to us—Tolerance of Religious Error—Rebuking Sin—The Christian Ministry—Human Responsibility—Guilelessness—The Danger of Riches—The Powers o Nature—The Danger of Accomplishments—Christian Zeal—Use of Saints' Days.

CARDINAL NEWMAN'S WORKS.

Parochial and Plain Sermons.—*Continued.*

CONTENTS OF VOL. III.:—Abraham and Lot—Wilfulness of Israel in Rejecting Samuel—Saul—Early Years of David—Jeroboam—Faith and Obedience—Christian Repentance—Contracted Views in Religion—A Particular Providence as revealed in the Gospel—Tears of Christ at the Grave of Lazarus—Bodily Suffering—The Humiliation of the Eternal Son—Jewish Zeal a Pattern to Christians—Submission to Church Authority—Contest between Truth and Falsehood in the Church—The Church Visible and Invisible—The Visible Church and Encouragement to Faith—The Gift of the Spirit—Regenerating Baptism—Infant Baptism—The Daily Service—The Good Part of Mary—Religious Worship a Remedy for Excitements—Intercession—The Intermediate State.

CONTENTS OF VOL IV.:—The Strictness of the Law of Christ—Obedience without Love, as instanced in the Character of Balaam—Moral Consequences of Single Sins—Acceptance of Religious Privileges Compulsory—Reliance on Religious Observances—The Individuality of the Soul—Chastisement amid Mercy—Peace and Joy amid Chastisement—The State of Grace—The Visible Church for the Sake of the Elect—The Communion of Saints—The Church a Home for the Lonely—The Invisible World—The Greatness and Littleness of Human Life—Moral Effects of Communion with God—Christ Hidden from the World—Christ Manifested in Remembrance—The Gainsaying of Korah—The Mysteriousness of our Present Being—The Ventures of Faith—Faith and Love—Watching—Keeping Fast and Festival.

CONTENTS OF VOL. V.:—Worship, a Preparation for Christ's Coming—Reverence, a Belief in God's Presence—Unreal Words—Shrinking from Christ's Coming—Equanimity—Remembrance of Past Mercies—The Mystery of Godliness—The State of Innocence—Christian Sympathy—Righteousness not of us, but in us—The Law of the Spirit—The New Works of the Gospel—The State of Salvation—Transgressions and Infirmities—Sins of Infirmity—Sincerity and Hypocrisy—The Testimony of Conscience—Many called, Few chosen—Present Blessings—Endurance, the Christian's Portion—Affliction, a School of Comfort—The Thought of God, the Stay of the Soul—Love, the One Thing Needful—The Power of the Will.

CONTENTS OF VOL. VI.:—Fasting, a Source of Trial—Life, the Season of Repentance—Apostolic Abstinence, a Pattern for Christians—Christ's Privations, a Meditation for Christians—Christ the Son of God made Man—The Incarnate Son, a Sufferer and Sacrifice—The Cross of Christ the Measure of the World—Difficulty of realising Sacred Privileges—The Gospel Sign Addressed to Faith—The Spiritual Presence of Christ in the Church—The Eucharistic Presence—Faith the Title for Justification—Judaism of the Present Day—The Fellowship of the Apostles—Rising with Christ—Warfare the Condition of Victory—Waiting for Christ—Subjection of the Reason and Feelings to the Revealed Word—The Gospel Palaces—The Visible Temple—Offerings for the Sanctuary—The Weapons of Saints—Faith Without Demonstration—The Mystery of the Holy Trinity—Peace in Believing.

CONTENTS OF VOL. VII.:—The Lapse of Time—Religion, a Weariness to the Natural Man—The World our Enemy—The Praise of Men—Temporal Advantages—The Season of Epiphany—The Duty of Self-Denial—The Yoke of Christ—Moses the Type of Christ—The Crucifixion—Attendance on Holy Communion—The Gospel Feast—Love of Religion, a new Nature—Religion Pleasant to the Religious—Mental Prayer—Infant Baptism—The Unity of the Church—Steadfastness in the Old Paths.

CONTENTS OF VOL. VIII.:—Reverence in Worship—Divine Calls—The Trial of Saul—The Call of David—Curiosity, a Temptation to Sin—Miracles no Remedy for Unbelief—Josiah, a Pattern for the Ignorant—Inward Witness to the Truth of the Gospel—Jeremiah, a Lesson for the Disappointed—Endurance of the World's Censure—Doing Glory to God in Pursuits of the World—Vanity of Human Glory—Truth Hidden when not Sought after—Obedience to God the Way to Faith in Christ—Sudden Conversions—The Shepherd of our Souls—Religious Joy—Ignorance of Evil.

Sermons Preached on Various Occasions. Crown 8vo. Cabinet Edition, 6s.; Popular Edition, 3s. 6d.

CONTENTS:—Intellect the Instrument of Religious Training—The Religion of the Pharisee and the Religion of Mankind—Waiting for Christ—The Secret Power of Divine Grace—Dispositions for Faith—Omnipotence in Bonds—St. Paul's Characteristic Gift—St. Paul's Gift of Sympathy—Christ upon the Waters—The Second Spring—Order, the Witness and Instrument of Unity—The Mission of St. Philip Neri—The Tree beside the Waters—In the World but not of the World—The Pope and the Revolution.

CARDINAL NEWMAN'S WORKS.

Selection, Adapted to the Seasons of the Ecclesiastical Year,
from the 'Parochial and Plain Sermons.' Edited by the REV. W. J. COPELAND, B.D. Crown 8vo. Cabinet Edition, 5s.; Popular Edition, 3s. 6d.

CONTENTS:—*Advent:* Self-Denial the Test of Religious Earnestness—Divine Calls—The Ventures of Faith—Watching. *Christmas Day:* Religious Joy, *New Year's Sunday:* The Lapse of Time. *Epiphany:* Remembrance of Past Mercies — Equanimity—The Immortality of the Soul — Christian Manhood — Sincerity and Hypocrisy — Christian Sympathy. *Septuagesima:* Present Blessings. *Sexagesima:* Endurance, the Christian's Portion. *Quinquagesima:* Love, the One Thing Needful. *Lent:* The Individuality of the Soul—Life, the Season of Repentance—Bodily Suffering—Tears of Christ at the Grave of Lazarus—Christ's Privations, a Meditation for Christians—The Cross of Christ the Measure of the World. *Good Friday:* The Crucifixion. *Easter Day:* Keeping Fast and Festval. *Easter Tide:* Witnesses of the Resurrection—A Particular Providence as revealed in the Gospel—Christ Manifested in Remembrance—The Invisible World—Waiting for Christ. *Ascension:* Warfare the Condition of Victory. *Snnday after Ascension:* Rising with Christ. *Whitsun Day:* The Weapons of Saints. *Trinity Sunday:* The Mysteriousness of our Present Being. *Sundays after Trinity:* Holiness Necessary for|Future Blessedness—The Religious Use of Excited Feelings—The Self-Wise Inquirer—Scripture a Record of Human Sorrow—The Danger of Riches—Obedience without Love, as instanced in the Character of Balaam—Moral Consequences of Single Sins—The Greatness and Littleness of Human Life—Moral Effects of Communion with God—The Thought of God the Stay of the Soul—The Power of the Will—The Gospel Palaces—Religion a Weariness to the Natural Man—The World our Enemy—The Praise of Men—Religion Pleasant to the Religious—Mental Prayer—Curiosity a Temptation to Sin—Miracles no Remedy for Unbelief—Jeremiah, a Lesson for the Disappointed—The Shepherd of our Souls—Doing Glory to God in Pursuits of the World.

Sermons Bearing upon Subjects of the Day. Edited by the REV.
W. J. COPELAND, B.D., late Rector of Farnham, Essex. Crown 8vo. Cabinet Edition, 5s.; Popular Edition, 3s. 6d.

CONTENTS:—The Work of the Christian—Saintliness not Forfeited by the Penitent—Our Lord's Last Supper and His First—Dangers to the Penitent—The Three Offices of Christ—Faith and Experience—Faith unto the World—The Church and the World—Indulgence in Religious Privileges—Connection between Personal and Public Improvement—Christian Nobleness—Joshua a Type of Christ and His Followers—Elisha a Type of Christ and His Followers—The Christian Church a Continuation of the Jewish—The Principles of Contiuuity between the Jewish and Christian Churches—The Christian Church an Imperial Power—Sanctity the Token of the Christian Empire—Condition of the Members of the Christian Empire—The Apostolic Christian—Wisdom and Innocence—Invisible Presence of Christ—Outward and Inward Notes of the Church—Grounds for Steadfastness in our Religious Profession—Elijah the Prophet of the Latter Days—Feasting in Captivity—The Parting of Friends.

Fifteen Sermons Preached before the University of Oxford,
between A.D. 1826 and 1843. Crown 8vo. Cabinet Edition, 5s.; Popular Edition, 3s. 6d.

CONTENTS:—The Philosophical Temper, first enjoined by the Gospel—The Influence of Natural and Revealed Religion respectively—Evangelical Sanctity the Perfection of Natural Virtue—The Usurpations of Reason—Personal Influence, the Means of Propagating the Truth—On Justice as a Principle of Divine Governance—Contest between Faith and Sight—Human Responsibility, as independent of Circumstances—Wilfulness, the Sin of Saul—Faith and Reason, contrasted as Habits of Mind—The Nature of Faith in Relation to Reason—Love, the Safeguard of Faith against Superstition—Implicit and Explicit Reason—Wisdom, as contrasted with Faith and with Bigotry—The Theory of Developments in Religious Doctrine.

CARDINAL NEWMAN'S WORKS.

Apologia pro Vita Sua. Crown 8vo. Cabinet Edition, 6s.; Popular Edition, 3s. 6d.

Verses on Various Occasions. Crown 8vo. Cabinet Edition, 6s.; Popular Edition, 3s. 6d.

Discourses Addressed to Mixed Congregations. Crown 8vo. Cabinet Edition, 6s.; Popular Edition, 3s. 6d.

CONTENTS:—The Salvation of the Hearer the Motive of the Preacher—Neglect of Divine Calls and Warnings—Men not Angels—The Priests of the Gospel—Purity and Love—Saintliness the Standard of Christian Principle—God's Will the End of Life—Perseverance in Grace—Nature and Grace—Illuminating Grace—Faith and Private Judgment—Faith and Doubt—Prospects of the Catholic Missioner—Mysteries of Nature and of Grace—The Mystery of Divine Condescension—The Infinitude of Divine Attributes—Mental Sufferings of our Lord in His Passion—The Glories of Mary for the Sake of Her Son—On the Fitness of the Glories of Mary.

Lectures on the Doctrine of Justification. Crown 8vo. Cabinet Edition, 5s.; Popular Edition, 3s. 6d.

CONTENTS:—Faith considered as the Instrumental Cause of Justification—Love considered as the Formal Cause of Justification—Primary Sense of the term 'justification'—Secondary Senses of the term 'Justification'—Misuse of the term 'Just' or 'Righteous'—The Gift of Righteousness—The Characteristics of the Gift of Righteousness—Righteousness viewed as a Gift and as a Quality—Righteousness the Fruit of our Lord's Resurrection—The Office of Justifying Faith—The Nature of Justifying Faith—Faith viewed relatively to Rites and Works—On Preaching the Gospel—Appendix.

On the Development of Christian Doctrine. Crown 8vo. Cabinet Edition, 6s.; Popular Edition, 3s. 6d.

On the Idea of a University. Crown 8vo. Cabinet Edition, 7s.; Popular Edition, 3s. 6d.

An Essay in Aid of a Grammar of Assent. Crown 8vo. Cabinet Edition, 7s. 6d.; Popular Edition, 3s. 6d.

Two Essays on Miracles. 1. Of Scripture. 2. Of Ecclesiastical History. Crown 8vo. Cabinet Edition, 6s.; Popular Edition, 3s. 6d.

Discussions and Arguments. Crown 8vo. Cabinet Edition, 6s.; Popular Edition, 3s. 6d.

1. How to accomplish it. 2. The Antichrist of the Fathers. 3. Scripture and the Creed. 4. Tamworth Reading-room. 5. Who's to Blame? 6. An Argument for Christianity.

Essays, Critical and Historical. 2 vols. Crown 8vo. Cabinet Edition, 12s.; Popular Edition, 7s.

1. Poetry. 2. Rationalism. 3. Apostolic Tradition. 4. De la Mennais. 5. Palmer on Faith and Unity. 6. St. Ignatius. 7. Prospects of the Anglican Church. 8. The Anglo-American Church. 9. Countess of Huntingdon. 10. Catholicity of the Anglican Church. 11. The Antichrist of Protestants. 12. Milman's Christianity. 13. Reformation of the XI. Century. 14. Private Judgment. 15. Davison. 16. Keble.

CARDINAL NEWMAN'S WORKS.

Historical Sketches. 3 vols. Crown 8vo. Cabinet Edition, 6s. each; Popular Edition, 3s. 6d.

1. The Turks. 2. Cicero. 3. Apollonius. 4. Primitive Christianity. 5. Church of the Fathers. 6. St. Chrysostom. 7. Theodoret. 8. St. Benedict. 9. Benedictine Schools. 10. Universities. 11. Northmen and Normans. 12. Mediæval Oxford. 13. Convocation of Canterbury.

The Arians of the Fourth Century. Crown 8vo. Cabinet Edition, 6s.; Popular Edition, 3s. 6d.

Select Treatises of St. Athanasius in Controversy with the Arians. Freely translated. 2 vols. Crown 8vo. Cabinet Edition, 15s.; Popular Edition, 7s.

Theological Tracts. Crown 8vo. Cabinet Edition, 8s.; Popular Edition, 3s. 6d.

1. Dissertatiunculæ. 2. On the Text of the Seven Epistles of St. Ignatius. 3. Doctrinal Causes of Arianism. 4. Apollinarianism. 5. St. Cyril's Formula. 6. Ordo de Tempore. 7. Douay Version of Scriptures.

The Via Media of the Anglican Church. 2 Vols. Crown 8vo. Cabinet Edition, 6s. each; Popular Edition, 3s. 6d. each.

Vol. I. Prophetical Office of the Church.
Vol. II. Occasional Letters and Tracts.

Certain Difficulties felt by Anglicans in Catholic Teaching Considered. 2 vols.

Vol. I. Twelve Lectures. Crown 8vo. Cabinet Edition, 7s. 6d.; Popular Edition, 3s. 6d.
Vol. II. Letters to Dr. Pusey concerning the Blessed Virgin, and to the Duke of Norfolk in defence of the Pope and Council. Crown 8vo. Cabinet Edition, 5s. 6d.; Popular Edition. 3s. 6d.

Present Position of Catholics in England. Crown 8vo. Cabinet Edition, 7s. 6d.; Popular Edition, 3s. 6d.

Loss and Gain. The Story of a Convert. Crown 8vo. Cabinet Edition, 6s.; Popular Edition, 3s. 6d.

Callista. A Tale of the Third Century. Crown 8vo. Cabinet Edition, 6s.; Popular Edition, 3s. 6d.

The Dream of Gerontius. 16mo, sewed, 6d.; cloth, 1s.

Meditations and Devotions. Part I. Meditations for the Month of May. Novena of St. Philip. Part II. The Stations of the Cross. Meditations and Intercessions for Good Friday. Litanies, etc. Part III. Meditations on Christian Doctrine. Conclusion. Oblong Crown 8vo. 5s. *net.*

CARDINAL NEWMAN'S WORKS.
COMPLETION OF THE POPULAR EDITION.

Parochial and Plain Sermons. 8 vols. Each	. .	3s. 6d.
Sermons preached on Various Occasions	. .	3s. 6d.
Selection, from the Parochial and Plain Sermons	. .	3s. 6d.
Sermons bearing on Subjects of the Day	. .	3s. 6d.
Sermons preached before the University of Oxford	. .	3s. 6d.
Discourses addressed to Mixed Congregations	. .	3s. 6d.
Lectures on the Doctrine of Justification	. .	3s. 6d.
On the Development of Christian Doctrine	. .	3s. 6d.
On the Idea of a University	. .	3s. 6d.
An Essay in Aid of a Grammar of Assent	. .	3s. 6d.
Biblical and Ecclesiastical Miracles	. .	3s. 6d.
Discussions and Arguments on Various Subjects	. .	3s. 6d.
Essays, Critical and Historical. 2 vols.	. .	7s. 0d.
Historical Sketches. 3 vols. Each	. .	3s. 6d.
The Arians of the Fourth Century	. .	3s. 6d.
The Via Media of the Anglican Church. 2 vols. Each	.	3s. 6d.
Difficulties felt by Anglicans considered. 2 vols. Each	.	3s. 6d.
Present Position of Catholics in England	. .	3s. 6d.
Apologia pro Vita Sua	. .	3s. 6d.
Theological Tracts	. .	3s. 6d.
Select Treatises of St. Athanasius. 2 vols.	. .	7s. 0d.
Verses on Various Occasions	. .	3s. 6d.
Loss and Gain	. .	3s. 6d.
Callista	. .	3s. 6d.

BATIFFOL.—**History of the Roman Breviary.** By PIERRE BATIF-
FOL, Litt.D. Translated by ATWELL M. Y. BAYLAY, M.A., Vicar
of Thurgarton, Notts. With a New Preface by the Author. Crown
8vo. 7s. 6d.

DOBRÉE.—**Stories on the Rosary.** By LOUISA EMILY DOBRÉE, Author
of "Stories of the Seven Sacraments". Part I. Crown 8vo. 1s. 6d.

FOUARD.—**The Christ, The Son of God.** A Life of Our Lord
and Saviour Jesus Christ. By the ABBÉ CONSTANT FOUARD,
Honorary Cathedral Canon, Professor of the Faculty of Theology
at Rouen, etc., etc. Translated from the Fifth Edition with the
Author's sanction. By GEORGE F. X. GRIFFITH. With an
Introduction by CARDINAL MANNING. Third Edition. With
3 Maps. 2 vols. Crown 8vo. 14s.

Saint Peter and the First Years of Christianity. By the
ABBÉ CONSTANT FOUARD. Translated by GEORGE F. X. GRIFFITH.
Crown 8vo. 9s.

St. Paul and His Missions. By the ABBÉ CONSTANT FOUARD.
Translated, with the Author's sanction and co-operation, by GEORGE
F. X. GRIFFITH. With 2 Maps. Crown 8vo. 9s.

CHRISTIAN BIOGRAPHIES:

Henri Dominique Lacordaire. A Biographical Sketch. By H. L. SIDNEY LEAR. With Frontispiece. Crown 8vo. 3s. 6d.

A Christian Painter of the Nineteenth Century; being the Life of Hippolyte Flandrin. By H. L. SIDNEY LEAR. Crown 8vo. 3s. 6d.

Bossuet and his Contemporaries. By H. L. SIDNEY LEAR. Crown 8vo. 3s. 6d.

Fénelon, Archbishop of Cambrai. A Biographical Sketch. By H. L. SIDNEX LEAR. Crown 8vo. 3s. 6d.

A Dominican Artist. A Sketch of the Life of the Rev. Père Besson, of the Order of St. Dominic. By H. L. SIDNEY LEAR. Crown 8vo. 3s. 6d.

The Life of Madame Louise de France, Daughter of Louis XV., also known as the Mother Thérèse de S. Augustin. By H. L. SIDNEY LEAR. Crown 8vo. 3s. 6d.

The Revival of Priestly Life in the Seventeenth Century in France. Charles de Condren—S. Philip Neri and Cardinal de Berulle—S. Vincent de Paul—S. Sulpice and Jean Jacques Olier. By H. L. SIDNEY LEAR. Crown 8vo. 3s. 6d.

Life of S. Francis de Sales, Bishop and Prince of Geneva. By H. L. SIDNEY LEAR. Crown 8vo. 3s. 6d.

Henri Perreyve. By A. GRATRY, PRÊTRE DE L'ORATOIRE, Professeur de Morale Evangélique à la Sorbonne, et Membre de l'Académie Française. Translated, by special permission, by H. L. SIDNEY LEAR. With Portrait. Crown 8vo. 3s. 6d.

DRANE—A Memoir of Mother Francis Raphael O.S.D. (Augusta Theodosia Drane), some time Prioress Provincial of the Congregation of Dominican Sisters of S. Catherine of Siena, Stone. With some of her Spiritual Notes and Letters. Edited by Rev. Father BERTRAND WILBERFORCE, O.P. With Portrait. Crown 8vo. 7s. 6d.

The History of St. Dominic, Founder of the Friar Preachers. By AUGUSTA THEODORA DRANE, author of "The History of St. Catherine of Siena and her Companions." With 32 Illustrations. 8vo. 15s.

FÉNELON.—Spiritual Letters to Men. By ARCHBISHOP FÉNELON. Translated by H. L. SIDNEY LEAR, author of "Life of Fénelon," "Life of S. Francis de Sales," etc. etc. 16mo. 2s. 6d.

Spiritual Letters to Women. By ARCHBISHOP FÉNELON. Translated by H. L. SIDNEY LEAR, author of "Life of Fenelon," "Life of S. Francis de Sales," etc. etc. 16mo. 2s. 6d.

GIBSON.—The Abbé de Lamennais and the Liberal Catholic Movement in France. By the Hon. W. GIBSON. With Portrait. 8vo. 12s. 6d.

JAMESON—Works by MRS. JAMESON:

Sacred and Legendary Art. With 19 Etchings and 197 Woodcuts. 2 vols. Cloth, gilt top. 20s. *net.*

Legends of the Madonna: The Virgin Mary as Represented in Sacred and Legendary Art. With 27 Etchings and 165 Woodcuts. 1 vol. Cloth, gilt top. 10s. *net.*

Legends of the Monastic Orders. With 11 Etchings and 88 Woodcuts. 1 vol. Cloth, gilt top. 10s. *net.*

History of the Saviour, His Types and Precursors. Completed by LADY EASTLAKE. With 13 Etchings and 281 Woodcuts. 2 vols. Cloth, gilt top. 20s. *net.*

LYONS.—**Christianity or Infallibility**—Both or Neither. By the Rev. DANIEL LYONS. Crown 8vo. 5s.

RIVINGTON.—**The Primitive Church and the See of Peter.** By the Rev. LUKE RIVINGTON, D.D. With an Introduction by the CARDINAL ARCHBISHOP OF WESTMINSTER. 8vo. 16s.

SODERINI.—**Socialism and Catholicism.** From the Italian of COUNT EDWARD SODERINI. By RICHARD JENERY-SHEE of the Inner Temple. With a Preface by CARDINAL VAUGHAN. Cr. 8vo. 6s.

TYRRELL.—**Nova et Vetera**: Informal Meditations for Times of Spiritual Dryness. By GEORGE TYRRELL, S.J. Crown 8vo. 6s.

VINDICATION, a, of the Bull "Apostolicæ Curæ"; a Letter on Anglican Orders. By the CARDINAL ARCHBISHOP and BISHOPS OF THE PROVINCE OF WESTMINSTER, in reply to the letter addressed to them by the Anglican Archbishops of Canterbury and York. 8vo. 1s.

WISEMAN.—**The Life and Times of Cardinal Wiseman.** By WILFRID WARD, Author of "William George Ward and the Catholic Revival". With 3 Portraits. 2 vols. Crown 8vo. 24s.

MANUALS OF CATHOLIC PHILOSOPHY.
(Stonyhurst Series.)
EDITED BY RICHARD F. CLARKE, S.J.

Logic. By RICHARD F. CLARKE, S.J., D.D. Crown 8vo. 5s.

First Principles of Knowledge. By JOHN RICKABY, S.J. Crown 8vo. 5s.

Moral Philosophy (Ethics and Natural Law). By JOSEPH RICKABY, S.J. Crown 8vo. 5s.

General Metaphysics. By JOHN RICKABY, S.J. Crown 8vo. 5s.

Psychology. By MICHAEL MAHER, S.J. Crown 8vo. 6s. 6d.

Natural Theology. By BERNARD BOEDDER, S.J. Crown 8vo. 6s. 6d.

Political Economy. By CHARLES S. DEVAS. Crown 8vo. 6s. 6d.

ENGLISH MANUALS OF CATHOLIC THEOLOGY.

Outlines of Dogmatic Theology. By SYLVESTER JOSEPH HUNTER, of the Society of Jesus. Crown 8vo. 3 vols., 6s. 6d. each.

LONDON, NEW YORK, AND BOMBAY:
LONGMANS, GREEN, & CO

5000/3/98.

CPSIA information can be obtained
at www.ICGtesting.com
Printed in the USA
BVHW041415270319
543861BV00013B/128/P

9 781164 042402